Norman Ohler is an award-winning novelist and screenwriter. He is the author of the *New York Times* bestseller *Blitzed*, as well as the novels *Die Quotenmaschine* (the world's first hypertext novel), *Mitte* and *Stadt des Goldes* (translated into English as *Ponte City*). He lives in Berlin.

'*The Infiltrators* is an astonishing story of the anti-Nazi resistance – a story of love, incredible bravery and self-sacrifice, which could end only in death – and it is brilliantly told.' Antony Beevor, bestselling author of *The Second World War*

'Deeply engaging, enticingly written and extremely affecting... Original and fascinating... This is a remarkable story, powerfully told, of love and courage and of the balance in the relationship between a couple... A timely reminder of what some citizens are willing to do in the face of autocracy and oppression that once again haunts our times.' Philippe Sands, *Spectator*

'Gripping... Will appeal to anyone who relishes Ben Macintyre's tales of wartime espionage and cryptic codes, underpinned by terrifying risk, desperate courage, and double dealing... Moving at a cracking pace through a succession of snapshot cross-cut chapters, it is ripe for transformation into a film or television series. But great heroism is properly honoured here: Ohler has done his research diligently and he has an enthralling story to tell.' *Sunday Telegraph*

'Ohler masterfully establishes his trustworthiness as a narrator, which is crucial as we travel with him back to the 1930s and then on through the war. He weaves a detailed and meticulously researched tale about a pair of young German resisters that reads like a thriller.' *New York Times*

'Lively... Ohler has given vim to the historical narrative, restored humanity and a genuine love story to the communist canonisation of Schulze-Boysen.' *The Times*

'*The Infiltrators* describes an idealistic young German couple, Harro Schulze-Boysen and Libertas Haas-Heye who set up an anti-fascist network that burrowed deep into Nazi society and leaked to the Allies. With depressing inevitability, betrayal and merciless punishment intervened – but this is nonetheless an uplifting tale of heroism.' Simon Heffer, 'History Books of the Year', *Daily Telegraph*

'An unforgettable portrait of two young lovers and their circle of friends in the anti-Hitler resistance, *The Infiltrators* offers a fascinating glimpse of life in Nazi Germany, where the simple self-assertion of youth was a political act, and daily life was a minefield where missteps could have fatal consequences.' Joseph Kanon, bestselling author of *Leaving Berlin*

'A thrilling and urgent true story. Inside Nazi Germany, as tyranny spreads, a few friends decide to resist, and a secret circle of anti-fascists starts to grow. They are not mythic heroes but instead flawed humans struggling for meaning in a time of terror: writers, artists, a fashion designer, a dentist. With skill and passion, Norman Ohler brings these remarkable men and women back to life. *The Infiltrators* is a gift of a book – one I feel a little stronger, a little braver, after reading.' Jason Fagone, bestselling author of *The Woman Who Smashed Codes*

'Ohler creates a taut, absorbing tale of anti-Nazi resistance. Told in the present tense, the narrative conveys a sense of immediacy and encroaching terror... Sharply drawn characters enliven a tragic history.' *Kirkus Reviews*

'The fascinating and tragic tale of a ragtag, idealistic crew of nonconformists hiding in plain sight while secretly working to fight the Nazis from within... This unbelievable yet true story is richly detailed thanks to the participation of descendants of these courageous resistance fighters; with their help, Ohler succeeds in vividly thwarting the Nazis' attempts to erase these heroes from history.' *Booklist*

'This deeply researched and stylishly written account unearths an appealing yet overlooked chapter in WWII history. Espionage enthusiasts will be riveted.' *Publishers Weekly*

'Remarkable... Vivid and engaging.' *Times Literary Supplement*

'*The Infiltrators* paints a picture of a marriage of intellectual equals who are driven by a single shared cause: to bring down the Nazis from within. In telling this story the book draws on diaries, letters and Gestapo files, many of which are previously unpublished, bringing much greater detail to an otherwise known but under-reported story... Gripping.' *All About History*

'Norman Ohler has achieved a historically significant work of discovery with great literary skill.' *Augsburger Allgemeine*

'Norman Ohler has told the story in the form of a gripping thriller... although Ohler's book reads like a crime novel, everything in it did actually happen.' *Berliner Zeitung*

'Very well researched... unbelievably gripping... a page turner... A remarkable book about two remarkable resistance Red Orchestra fighters.' *Deutschlandfunk Kultur*

'A powerful and swift read, racing along like an expressionistic railway, but every sentence is also threaded with intelligence and empathy.' *Die Welt*

'Such a subject could not fail to arouse the interest of Norman Ohler. The journalist who demonstrated his mastery of investigative non-fiction in *Blitzed*... finds here historical material which he recounts as a thriller.' *Livres Hebdo*

'With the help of new archives and with the pace of an addictive thriller Norman Ohler rebuilds their resistance ensuring them a posthumous victory which will not be forgotten.' *O.C. Le Nouveau Magazine Litteraire*

ALSO BY NORMAN OHLER

*Blitzed*

# The
# INFILTRATORS

## The Lovers Who Led
## Germany's Resistance
## Against the Nazis

## NORMAN OHLER

Translated from the German
by Tim Mohr and Marshall Yarbrough

Atlantic Books
London

Published by arrangement with Houghton Mifflin Harcourt Publishing Company.

First published in Great Britain in 2020 by Atlantic Books, an imprint of Atlantic Books Ltd.

This paperback edition published in Great Britain in 2021 by Atlantic Books.

Excerpts of unpublished letters accessed through the Red Orchestra Collection at the German Resistance Memorial Center and the archives at the Institute for Contemporary History. Used in English translation by kind permission of E. Schulze-Boysen.

Illustration credits: All images reproduced by permission of the German Resistance Memorial Center, Berlin, with the following exceptions: page 11, "Guillaume: Leurs Silhouette No. 9" by Orens, October 11, 1908; page 42, bpk-Bildagentur; page 131, Gyula Pap/Design and Artists Copyright Society; pages 64, 156, 215, 221, Bundesarchiv.

Book design by Margaret Rosewitz

1 2 3 4 5 6 7 8 9

A CIP catalogue record for this book is available from the British Library.

E-book ISBN: 978-1-83895-212-9
Paperback ISBN: 978-1-83895-213-6

Printed and bound by CPI Group (UK) Ltd, Croydon CR0 4YY

Atlantic Books
An Imprint of Atlantic Books Ltd
Ormond House
26–27 Boswell Street
London
WC1N 3JZ

www.atlantic-books.co.uk

*For the kids*

It would make an amazing story if it weren't so illegal.

— A GESTAPO OFFICER


To articulate what is past does not mean to recognize "how it really was." It means to take control of a memory, as it flashes in a moment of danger.

— WALTER BENJAMIN,
"Theses on the Philosophy of History"

# CONTENTS

# FOREWORD

# 1

When I was about twelve years old, I was sitting in the garden of my grandparents' house, set in a valley on the outskirts of a small city in southwest Germany, near the border with French Lorraine. In March 1945 the town, which was also the place of my birth, was leveled by the British and Canadian Royal Air Force, with more than 90 percent of the baroque buildings destroyed. My grandmother and grandfather fared the same as almost everyone else: nothing of their home survived the hail of bombs. So my grandfather built a new house after the war "out of rubble," with his "own hands." He dubbed it Haus Morgensonne, or the House of the Morning Sun, and the gravel road that led there he named Wiesengrund, or Meadowland, and it was later labeled as such on official maps.

We often played a board game called Mensch Ärgere Dich Nicht (Man, Don't Worry), similar to Sorry, in the garden of the House of the Morning Sun. Before the dice were rolled my grandfather usually said, "Play hard but fair!" This directive scared me a bit, even though I had nothing against fair play and he wasn't particularly serious about playing hard, since, after all, we were only trying to have as much fun as possible while passing the time. But on this particular afternoon, fair or unfair, I refused to roll the dice until he told me a story about the war. We'd seen a documentary that morning at school about the liberation of a concentration camp, the piles of eyeglasses, the emaciated faces, cutting effectively to shots of jubilant Germans hailing Hitler. Not a single pupil was allowed to leave the room before the film was over.

So I wanted to know whether my grandfather had anything to do with all of it. At first he shook his head and wanted to start playing the game. But I took the two ivory-colored dice and looked at him searchingly. Mottled sunlight shone through the leaves of the apple tree and cast a pattern of light and shadow on the yellow game board. He explained he had been working for the Reichsbahn, the German railway. That wasn't news to me, and I pressed him to tell me something interesting, something concrete.

Lost in thought, he stared at the evergreen trees that lined the edge of the meadow. Then he coughed. Finally he slowly and casually said that he'd been a true and avid railroader because he'd always loved the reliability and precision of the railroads. And that he could never have imagined what was going to happen. I immediately asked: What happened? Hesitantly, he told me that he'd been working as an engineer — did I know what an engineer was? Even though I didn't really know exactly, I nodded. During the war, he continued, he'd been transferred to the northern Bohemian town of Brüx, a hole at the junction of the Aussig-Komotau, Pilsen-Priesen, and Prague-Dux lines.

One winter evening, as fresh snow covered the black double lines of the tracks, as well as the meadow, the trees, and the frozen Eger River, an arriving train was shunted onto a siding, my grandfather said with a halting voice, a long freighter with stock cars that had to let a munitions transport pass. Wheels screeched as they crossed the shunting switch, calls rang out, a long whistle. Steam billowed and dissipated. The stock cars were uncoupled. Silence descended on the white-covered valley again.

But something wasn't right. My grandfather felt it; his railroader instincts told him. After a while he left his little station house and approached the siding. The only thing audible was the gurgling water of the Eger flowing beneath its frozen surface. Uneasy, he walked along the entire row of cars. Just as he went to turn away, something moved in one of the narrow ventilation slits on the upper half of a sliding door on one of the cars. A tin cup on a string was lowered from the opening, clanged against the wood of the side of the car, got stuck on the door handle, broke free, and then dangled slowly down and dipped into the snow next to the tracks. A moment later the string tightened and pulled the filled vessel back up. A child's hand — only a child's hand would fit through the slit — appeared above and grabbed hold of the cup.

People, not livestock! People in the stock cars, even though this was contrary to the transportation regulations! What a mess. You just didn't do that sort of thing at the Reichsbahn. He went back to his station house to try to get some information about where the train was heading. Theresienstadt. The name meant nothing to him. A small place a few kilometers north of Bauschowitz, last station at the border of the protectorate. He went back out again to have another look at the cars, but two sentries in black uniforms came hustling toward him, machine pistols at the ready: SS. Grandfather turned around and walked quickly back. A gruff call followed him threateningly.

*It's war,* he thought, peeking out of the steamed windows of the overheated station house a short while later. With trembling fingers, he buttered himself a piece of onion bread. *Must have been prisoners of war, Russians.* But he knew this wasn't true. The train had come from the west. The hand was a child's. He also knew he wasn't going to do anything. "I was scared of the SS."

He told me this in the sun-flooded garden of his yellow house, and even though I loved him, because he was my grandfather, whom I'd only ever called just Pa, I hated him and he could feel it. We began to play the board game.

Then something strange happened. In the middle of the game his hands started to tremble, and he gazed into the distance so as not to have to look me in the eye. His voice sounded frail: "I thought back then that if anyone ever found out what we'd done to the Jews, it would be horrible for us."

I stared at him, unable to speak a word. My grandmother sat at the table and just watched us. At that point I didn't yet know she had Alzheimer's. My grandfather stood up without saying a word and went inside the House of the Morning Sun.

A few minutes later he reemerged and handed me a padded envelope. I opened it and emptied its contents onto the game board. It was his Party membership book, with lots of colorful stamps with the Reich eagle affixed in each month he'd paid his party dues: in mint green, pale red, light blue. There wasn't a single one missing. There was also a Hakenkreuz stickpin lying there — his Party badge. My grandfather made a gesture of surrendering it all to me, a twelve-year-old, and said: "Please. Take it. I can't have it in the house anymore."

My grandfather suddenly seemed to be sitting very far away from me. The distance between us was overwhelming, even though I could have touched him with my hand. Everything was suddenly beyond reach: the garden around us, the apple trees behind our little table; the table itself seemed in another dimension, and I couldn't move the game pieces anymore. My grandmother sat there like a statue, blurry on the left edge of my field of vision, my grandfather somewhere in front of me. I closed my eyes. Everything was silent. A stillness you could hear. At some point I opened my eyes, put everything back in the envelope, and took it.

It is not always cold in Berlin. There are summer days when the city glows and the hot, sandy soil of Brandenburg chafes between your toes. The sky floats so high that you feel its blue belongs to outer space. Then life becomes cosmic in this city where simultaneously so much happens and nothing at all. There were days like this in August 1942, when a handful of people were sailing on Wannsee for the last time in their lives, and there are days like this seventy-five years later, when I meet a man named Hans Coppi.

Hans himself is approaching seventy-five, though he seems younger. He's slim and tall (like his father, who was known as "Stretch"), wears round glasses, and has an alert, ironic gaze. I don't know exactly where this meeting will lead — I'm the author of a nonfiction book about the Nazi era, but I really want to write novels or make movies. But what Hans Coppi has promised is an *authentic* story, one that screams to be told in another nonfiction book.

Hans grew up as a sort of VIP in the eastern part of Berlin during the Cold War. This had to do with his parents, who posthumously came to be regarded as celebrities. They'd been in the resistance, so-called antifascist fighters. His mother had been permitted to give birth to him in a Nazi prison. Then it was off to the guillotine for her. Hans Coppi, a degreed historian, has spent his entire life trying to figure out what happened to his parents and why they, along with a group of friends who went sailing for the last time that summer of 1942, had to die so young.

I'd always thought I knew the most important Nazi resistance fighters: Graf Schenk von Stauffenberg with his bomb of July 20, 1944; Georg Elser, the manic lone wolf with the homemade explosive device that missed Hitler by just a few minutes in 1939; the upstanding and yet truculent Sophie Scholl and her morphine- and Pervitin-consuming brother, Hans. But according to Hans Coppi, there's another story that belongs in this canon, one surrounding a couple with whom his parents were friendly: two people who fought the dictatorship longer than all the others and for whom this fight was also a battle for free love. Their names were Harro and Libertas Schulze-Boysen, and over the course of the years more than a hundred people assembled around them and formed an enigmatic network that consisted of nearly as many women as men, all of whom wanted to do something against a world where injustice had been made law. It's a story of young people who wanted one thing above all others: to live — and to love — even if the era in which they came of age was steeped in death.

It's not easy, what Hans Coppi has undertaken: to find out what really happened back then. Because when Hitler learned of the plot against him hatched right in the center of the capital of the Reich, he was so furious that he ordered all evidence of these remarkable activities erased, to falsify the records beyond recognition. To bury and obscure the truth about Harro and Libertas and all the others. And the dictator nearly succeeded.

I meet Hans Coppi at a café at Engelbecken, the intersection of East and West, where the urban parables of the old capital of East Germany rub up against the former city of West Berlin. Here, socialist high-rise blocks stand opposite ornate nineteenth-century apartment buildings. Here, Saint Michael Church, built by a student of the famous architect Schinkel, roofless since a bombardment in World War II, still projects toward the sky into which Hans Coppi squints skeptically on this hot summer afternoon, because he knows that in the early evening the accumulated heat will dissipate over this strange and sometimes so fraught city.

My young son has come along to the meeting. He's barely a year and a half but is as big as a two-year-old. He finds our conversation less interesting than the ducks on the nearby pond. Every time a duck slips from its nest in the reeds into the water because the boy's gotten too close, I get up and keep him from scurrying to the edge of the pond, bring him back to the table, and offer him a sip of his rhubarb juice. Perhaps it would have been better to have left him at home so I could focus entirely on the meeting. But Hans Coppi seems undisturbed by the interruptions. He watches us attentively.

When, two weeks after the arrest of Harro in September 1942, Hans's parents were also arrested, he may have felt it in his mother's belly. She was initially detained with other women at the police facility on Alexanderplatz and then, in late October — heavily pregnant — was transferred to the women's prison on Barnim Strasse. There, at the end of November, she was allowed to give birth to her child and named him Hans, which was also her husband's name.

Suddenly I cringe: I hear a clink and look over at my son. He's taken a bite out of the juice glass sitting in front of him. It takes me a moment for it to fully register. But the missing half circle of glass is unambiguous. I carefully fish around in his mouth and remove a perfectly formed half moon of glass. Fortunately he isn't hurt. I look at him, bewildered, and he looks back somewhat puzzled as well. I didn't know that a little child could bite through a glass, particularly so cleanly, and he apparently also didn't know it. Hans leans his head to the left: "The boy's got a lot of energy." And suddenly I realize why my son has come with me to this meeting, because now I hope that he, like Hans Coppi, will master life by grappling with history.

It's hot in Berlin that afternoon, and after the conversation I head with my child to Wannsee, to swim and because there are more ducks there. And because the lake is closely associated with the events depicted here. It's August 30, 2017, seventy-five years since Harro's arrest. The wind kicks up and a storm blows in.

# 3

Searching for clues in Berlin's Mitte neighborhood: Where the Reichssicherheitshauptamt, or Reich Main Security Office, once stood, today there is a memorial site called Topography of Terror. Here were the headquarters of the Gestapo, the Nazis' secret police. Here is where Himmler had his office, and did yoga for two hours every morning before setting about his daily murderous business. Eichmann engineered the genocide of the Jews here. And in the concrete basement, which housed a jail, Harro and then Libertas were imprisoned, as well as Hans Coppi's father. Harro's cell, number 2, is, like the others, no longer here. The building had been severely damaged in a Royal Air Force attack, the ruins torn down after the war. In the 1970s a demolition company was based here, while on a ring-shaped racetrack you could zoom around without a driver's license. Today, in what was once the basement, there's an exhibition that also memorializes Harro Schulze-Boysen.

I meet Hans Coppi in front of the information placard in the open-air portion of the museum. He seems fragile on this day. He asks how my son is doing, and then we walk together along a canal-side street formerly known as Tirpitzufer toward Bendlerblock, the current German Defense Ministry on Stauffenberg Strasse. The German Resistance Memorial Center is housed there. In that solid building from the 1930s, a room on the fourth floor stores all that Hans Coppi has found in his decades of research, all he has carried there in order to illuminate the events surrounding Harro and Libertas and all the others. It's a room full of letters, photo albums, files and notes, interviews with witnesses, diaries, interrogation transcripts.

As odd, dramatic, or improbable parts of the following series of events may sound, this is not a fictional account. I find it particularly important in this case, where the truth has been distorted many times, not to add another legend, but to report as accurately as possible, combining my skills as a storyteller with the responsibility of the historian. Everything in quotation marks is documented with a source. Still, this is not a scholarly book, and I have tried to occupy the hearts and minds of these characters in a way that a novelist is better equipped to do than an academic historian.

The location is Berlin, a city that has lived through many metamorphoses, filled with people who shared similar desires: people who liked to eat well, go to the movies or out dancing; who had families, raised children, or just wanted to be loved. People who met up in cafés even when figures in black uniforms were sitting at the next table. Dabs of color in a sea of gray and brown. People who wondered how to react to insupportable political situations: how to conduct themselves during times that demanded conformity. People who clearly distinguished themselves from my grandfather, who just kept his head down and performed his duties as an engineer for the German railroad.

— *Norman Ohler,* Berlin

# PROLOGUE:
# THE THICK OF IT

Der Oberreichskriegsanwalt               Berlin, 18 January, 1943
St. P.L. (RKA) III 495/42
To:
Frigate Captain E. E. Schulze
<u>Field Post Number 30 450</u>

Concerning your request of 9 January, 1943, I hereby inform you that
the aforementioned confiscation of assets does not only mean the
confiscation of any valuables in possession of the convicted but also,
as an additional punishment, that the *remembrance* of the convicted
shall also be destroyed.
By order of
Oberstkriegsgerichtsrat d.Lw.

This letter from Dr. Manfred Roeder reached Erich Edgar Schulze three
weeks after the execution of his son Harro.

# 1

The first of September, 1939, is a Friday. The sky is overcast. During the
afternoon it is seventy-four degrees, though it gets cool toward the evening. It is a day when everyone in Berlin feels that something fundamental
is changing. People hustle along Kurfürstendamm, nicknamed Ku'damm,
the main boulevard of Berlin's well-to-do city center, full of shops, department stores, and restaurants. It is rush hour: the cafés and bars are full, and
excited chatter fills the air.

Sir Neville Henderson, the British ambassador, enters a pharmacy in
the neighborhood of Mitte, and asks for codeine, an opiate, to calm his
nerves. When the pharmacist asks for a prescription, Henderson alludes

to his position with British humor: If the medicine poisons him, the pharmacist will no doubt receive a reward from Goebbels. Henderson is thus able to get the drug prescription-free, and walks back to the embassy more serenely.

At 6:55 p.m., the air raid sirens sound. Traffic grinds to a halt, cars honk and quickly turn in to side streets, pedestrians search for shelter. Word gets around: Polish aircraft are attacking Berlin. In reality, German Stuka dive bombers have entered the capital's air space, accidentally causing the alarm. The all-clear is given at seven p.m., after five fearful minutes of screaming sirens. The war that Hitler has initiated with his invasion of Poland on this day has suddenly become real for Berliners.

Dusk starts around eight-thirty. Because of the blackout directed on this first day of war, night falls more quickly than usual. Kurfürstendamm, radiating brightly the evening before, is dark, the thousands of bulbs in the cinema marquees extinguished, the ads for the brand-new *Wizard of Oz* and the still running Clark Gable vehicle *Too Hot to Handle* invisible, the windows of department stores covered in cardboard.

A crowd has gathered in front of the grand Sarotti neon sign advertising chocolates. For years it has dependably burned bright, but now, ominously, it is out, no longer promising sweets. The giant neon Deinhard champagne bottle, from which artificial pearls of light normally bubbled, juts blackly into the sky as well, as if empty: the party is over. A bus with its headlights darkened shudders to a halt, its interior lights also turned off, making the passengers look like ghosts.

Nobody is shopping along the broad sidewalk. Some pedestrians have glow-in-the-dark patches on their chests the size of a button; others hold glowing cigarettes. Driving has suddenly become adventurous, particularly in the side streets, all the more so in the ones lined with trees.

On this, of all nights, the young German air force officer Harro Schulze-Boysen is celebrating his thirtieth birthday at the home of friends, a married couple named Engelsing. Herbert Engelsing also has a birthday, in his case his thirty-fifth, and they've decided to party together.

Harro's friend Herbert is a producer and legal advisor for Tobis, one of the most important film production companies in Germany. Sponsored by Goebbels, he has excellent political connections, without ever having to renounce his humanistic ethos. His position in the movie business is so influential that despite the Nuremberg Race Laws, after much back-and-forth and with Hitler personally intervening on his behalf, he was even permitted to marry his great love, Ingeborg Kohler, who is deemed "half Jewish."

The Engelsings' villa in Grunewald, in this poshest neighborhood west of Ku'damm, is one of the few places in Berlin where one can speak freely and where the type of socializing cultivated seems to ignore the very existence of the dictatorship. The Engelsings' circle of friends includes famous actors like Heinz Rühmann and Theo Lingen; the writer Adam Kuckhoff and his wife, Greta; as well as the dentist Helmut Himpel, whose skills are so widely renowned that German film stars make pilgrimages to his practice, and who still secretly treats his Jewish patrons — who can no longer be seen entering his office — privately at his home, for free.

Ingeborg Engelsing is a slender, gamine woman who loves to play hostess. She stands in the door of the two-story house at Bettinastrasse 2B in Grunewald, her hair tousled, her smile charming. She is only twenty-two years old, thirteen years younger than her husband. Initially Inge and Enke, as her spouse's nickname goes, had considered canceling the party with Harro because of the start of the war. Then Inge decided: "Now more than ever!"

It's twenty past nine, and in the British embassy, unlike in most of the rest of Berlin, the lights burn brightly, like a flame of reason denying the darkness of ignorance. Sir Neville Henderson, by now likely flush with codeine, sends a message to Joachim von Ribbentrop, the German foreign minister, conveying London's demand that all Wehrmacht forces be immediately withdrawn from Poland. France follows with the same note half an hour later, at 9:50 p.m. No ultimatum is issued, and the word *war* is still avoided. Both of the Western powers have, however, begun to mobilize.

In the villa in Grunewald, Harro's wife, Libertas Schulze-Boysen, reaches for the accordion. She wants to play to express her contradictory feelings: on the one hand, her hope that this momentous shift — to a shooting war — will spell the end of the Nazi menace, and on the other, her fear of what all could happen before then. She boisterously plays "La Marseillaise," the French national anthem, and everyone sings along. Next comes "It's a Long Way to Tipperary," so beloved among the British military — a greeting to friends in England, the global power whose decisive intervention everyone at the party now counts on. Then she belts out the Polish national song. Most of those in the room don't know the words, but Harro sings ardently along:

*Poland is not yet lost*
*As long as we're alive*

The chorus is so loud that Inge Engelsing steps outside the house, worried, to make sure the neighbors can't hear it. But the heavy velvet curtains in front of the windows sufficiently muffle the sound.

At some point in the wee hours of the morning, when the party is starting to fade, a small group gathers around Libertas. The gramophone is playing, and there is a question on everyone's mind: Will the so-called Thousand-Year Reich last only until the end of 1939, or will it manage to hold on into 1940?

Harro joins the circle. His chin trembles with hate when he speaks about the Nazis. Unlike most of the other guests, he doesn't believe the regime will implode so quickly. It's delusional to think the end is just around the corner and that the first air strikes on Berlin could come at any moment. Because of his job at the Luftwaffe, he knows the Royal Air Force is in no condition to strike and that the British need time to build up militarily. "I don't wish to destroy the hope that petty bourgeois Hitler is facing an inescapable catastrophe," he explains, "but it's not that simple." Initially, the dictatorship will in fact get stronger, he argues. Poland has no chance; it will go down quickly — child's play for the German war machine. France, too, represents no problem for the Wehrmacht, in Harro's view: the country has no fighting spirit. Then will come the attempt to capture England. Here, success is questionable — but in any case, the western European powers alone won't be able to defeat Germany.

Russia will get entangled in the war, Harro predicts. But it will take the United States to assure a final victory. It will be a long time before the Western powers are capable of a counterstrike, and in the meantime the dictatorship will become ever more violent and unhinged.

With his lively blue eyes, Harro looks around, from one friend to the next, his lips pressed together tensely. In earlier times Inge Engelsing had considered him "too handsome and inconsequential." She's revised her opinion, however, and now sees in his striking features a luminous quality, something defiant and beautiful when he defends his ideas in such a fiery manner. Everyone gapes at him and his prophetic words, and suddenly Harro realizes what a peculiar figure he cuts, in his military uniform at his own birthday party in the somewhat helpless company of liberal spirits for whom mere lip service is already seen as a risk.

Dawn breaks as he asks Libertas for one last dance. The two of them swing together, and they do it well, as always. Everyone in the room marvels at them. Nobody knows the risks they are willing to take in order to stop the insanity of the Nazi war machine that's been unleashed that very day.

# PART I

# ADVERSARIES

(1932–33)

No one could risk more than his life.

— HANS FALLADA

It was an attempt to join together in overcoming all the old antagonisms. We were known as "adversaries."

— HARRO SCHULZE-BOYSEN

# 1

In the fall of 1932, democracy still rules in Germany. There's unrest at the university — a brownshirt has hung swastika banners from the student memorial wreath and a leftist has cut them down. Now the two enemy camps stand in front of the main building of Berlin's Friedrich Wilhelm University filled with hate, separated only by a narrow gap, "ready at any moment to go at each other if a word of provocation comes from either side," as a college friend of Harro's recalled.

On one side, the red students gather, the socialists and communists and a sprinkling of social democrats. From the right, the Nazis and members of the allied nationalist students' corps scream their battle slogans decrying "Judah" and "the system." The university has been frequently paralyzed by political protests during the insecure Weimar Republic. This time, too, the president of the university wrings his hands helplessly, appealing in vain to both sides.

Harro Schulze-Boysen is a young political science student, and on this day he's slept in at the so-called Red-Gray Garrison. One of the first communal living arrangements in Germany, it is an eight-room apartment on Ritter Strasse in the central Berlin neighborhood of Kreuzberg. There is no furniture, and everything is shared — cleaning, cooking, money.

Alongside Harro is Regine, a slim young fashion designer from a formerly wealthy family. Wearing nothing but lipstick, she swishes the strawberry blond hair out of her face — and suddenly says something so shocking, so in love as she is, that Harro gets up, throws on his trademark blue sweater, and shuffles into the kitchen to look for something edible. He finds nothing but two dry bread rolls, but it doesn't matter — at least there's a nice cup of tea.

*Does he want to have a baby . . . ?* Is Regine harboring bourgeois dreams?

Harro is twenty-three and wants to radically alter society. Along with his best friend, Henry Erlanger, and others in their circle, he is serving the future of not one child, but many — the children of all of Europe, of the whole world. There's enough to do, especially during the current devastating worldwide crisis: soup kitchens all over the place, bank failures, unpayable rents, six million unemployed in Germany alone, depression and helplessness across all classes, the imminent fall into the abyss always looming. An entirely new society is necessary; the situation is polarized. Parties like the Social Democrats or the German Center Party no longer seem to represent the people. But what is supposed to replace them? And just what is *the people,* anyway?

The thoughts in Harro's young mind are far too complex to offer up simple solutions. His goal is still too diffuse, and he's even intrigued by right-wing positions, supporting, for instance, the battle against the Versailles Treaty, which saddled Germany with expensive reparations after the country lost the Great War. Such thoughts, anti-parliamentarian impulses, pervade his thinking, all of it still half baked.

How are you supposed to responsibly raise a child when there are so many fundamental questions to settle? How can Regine not understand this? Harro looks down the hall into the large room where she's lying on a mattress seductively. But he has to go. Off to university.

The streetcar is jammed, kids scurrying around, the smell of sweat and tobacco in the air, ads on the varnished pale wood doors: KAKADU — THE BEST BAR ON KURFÜRSTENDAMM. A drunk leans against a window, dozing; a haggard woman of about fifty stares brazenly at the tall, blond Harro with his athletic build and gleaming blue eyes. Horse carriages, hackneys, freight trucks. VOTE SOCIAL DEMOCRAT! A line in front of the unemployment office, the people surprisingly well dressed, different from the morphinists on a bench, with their deep, dark eye sockets and sickly bodies, still addicted from the war, when opiates were dished out liberally to wounded soldiers.

"Europe was the clock of the world. It's stopped," Harro had written in the most recent *Gegner,* the publication he works for: "The gears of the clock are beginning to rust. One factory gate after the next is closing." Everywhere, economic processes that grant power to cartels are surging. *Capitalism must be banished!* thinks Harro. But communism doesn't lead to anything good either: just a rigid apparatus, slaves to Moscow. COME TO SOVIET RUSSIA! screams another ad: CHEAP EDUCATIONAL TRAVEL FOR DOCTORS, TEACHERS, WORKERS.

"I'll say it again, I'm not a communist." That's what he told his worried mother, Marie Luise, who runs a bourgeois household in Mülheim, a city far west of Berlin, near Germany's Dutch border. "The communist party is a form of expression of the global socialist movement," Harro had written in a letter to her, "the Bolshevik Party being typically Russian. Hence not suitable for Germany."

On the streetcar winding through Berlin, Harro looks out on a tumultuous city — one rife with what he calls "big city disease." The neighborhood of Friedrichshain, for example, is known as the Chicago of Berlin because of its gangsters. It's a confounding, unsettled time — one ripe for experimentation.

Harro steps out of the tram close to Alexanderplatz, where the road is being redone. Workers are ripping up the old cobblestones as if tearing scabs off wounds, then pouring hot asphalt into the hole. The ground shudders as a U-Bahn rumbles underground. The leaves are already brown on the trees, and it's getting cold. Striding easily, with his hands in his pants pockets, he nears the plaza in front of the university, where beggars are sitting at small tables in front of the university's gates. Suddenly he sees the standoff between the groups of students — leftists versus right-wingers — and he realizes immediately that the situation calls for decisive intervention on his part. Harro knows the crowd, and they all know him and his blue sweater. He enjoys the trust of students from across the political spectrum — because he debates things so effectively, but also because he stands out. He has a rare quality that is all the more noticeable at a time of chaos: charisma.

As the desire to fight is rising in those on both sides, he retains his amiable and upbeat equanimity: he greets one brownshirt after the next with a handshake, asking what's going on, listening placidly to the saga of the removed swastika banner. No, he's no friend of the Nazis — he thinks they're dullards and rejects their anti-Semitism outright — but he's still able to talk to them. Next he wanders over to the other side, where they're loudly singing "The Internationale," and shakes hands there, as well. It's the side that appeals to him personally: he reads Karl Marx and he can damn well distinguish between an internationally oriented ambition for a just social order in which everyone has access to education, living space, health care, and the extreme right wing, the anti-Semitic affectations of the Nazis, with their goal of division and discrimination.

After a while, the rallying cries on both sides begin to subside. Everyone looks at him, including the university president, and like any instinctive revolutionary, Harro seizes the moment, continuing to shake hands, going back and forth between the two sides now, managing to defuse the conflict.

Things with Regine are moving along briskly. Together the occupants of the communal apartment are a merry bunch: artists, gays, gay artists, revolutionaries, bohemians. They're all young and attractive and lead erratic lives in this erratic Weimar era. For Harro, the most important thing isn't love, but politics, just as it has always been. He is, as a friend says of him, an "ardent German," with a "very deep German cultural awareness, artistic and philosophical, possibly innate, inherited from his family but also acquired."

Harro's most renowned relative is a brother of his paternal grandmother, the grand admiral Alfred von Tirpitz, who'd built the ocean fleet for Kaiser Wilhelm so Germany could hold its own in a war with Great Britain. Into his old age, Tirpitz sported a two-pronged beard that impressed the grandchildren with its pair of martial-looking wedges protruding downward. Uncle Tirpitz is the battleship of the family and the great model for the adolescent Harro. He wants to do just as much for "the German cause" as Tirpitz, and "champion the country, consciously working toward its improvement," as he says in a letter to the legendary great-uncle.

Harro's father, Erich Edgar, who also served in the navy, is involved, like Tirpitz, with the right-wing German National People's Party. With his intellectual leanings he could have been a scientist, perhaps even an artist, but Erich Edgar, known as E.E. for short, with his strong sense of duty, exemplifies the Prussian work ethic. He's a father who tells his son not only that he *can* cry, but that he *should*, in order to show that he indeed has feelings, but just *one* tear, please, then immediate composure before a second one falls. Harro's mother, Marie Luise, is less disciplined, but spirited: a tenacious, assertive person of small stature and sometimes great excitability, a lively, romantic woman who always has a decisive opinion, sometimes speaks before she thinks, and as a result often leaves dumbstruck her cool-headed husband, who is reserved even in bed, as she later in life complained to her grandchildren.

Harro has a perfect political sparring partner in his father, a professorial figure with a huge collection of books who often sits upright at his mahogany desk, reading by candlelight for hours at a time, almost otherworldly in his rigor. Erich Edgar's goal is to raise a free-thinking conservative. But increasingly over time Harro overtakes his father in his skills at argumentation, because his mother's hot blood also flows in him, and passion is as much a part of politics as rationality.

The vehicle for Harro's engagement, the *Gegner,* has in 1932 developed a new concept under his direction: to change from a static publication to a bona fide movement. Toward this end he set up what were called *Gegner* meetings, where authors and readers enter into dialogue: "public contradictory debate nights," as one of the flyers puts it. Harro writes confidently to his parents about the approach: "There's not a newspaper in Germany that manages to zero in on people who have something to say in such an autonomous way."

Developing visions beyond party boundaries, transcending conventions, and testing novel arguments appeals to many. Young people looking for answers to the burning questions eating at everyone take part in the evening *Gegner* gatherings at Café Adler on Dönhoffplatz. The meetings quickly become so popular that they are taken beyond Berlin and staged in other German cities as well. "There's extraordinary discipline and a strange camaraderie between left and right," reports a participant, indicating how unusual such behavior is among overheated twenty-somethings: "Young people who would immediately start throwing punches at each other on the street instead listened to arguments, united in the collective rejection of the boastful, doctrinaire party bigwigs."

Even if the way forward is still unclear, Harro attributes the *Gegner* movement to a rebellious moment, and speaks of an "invisible alliance that numbers in the thousands, who might still be distributed around in various other camps but who know that the day is approaching when they'll all need to come together." Harro wants to reconcile the society that is threatening to split apart — just as he had at the university. "A people divided by hate ... cannot get up again," he writes in the *Gegner* — a twist on the words of Abraham Lincoln: "A house divided against itself cannot stand." It's no easy task that Harro takes on in this late phase of the Weimar Republic.

# 3

There are manic days and nights that fall of 1932, the last months of freedom, one of the most inspired periods in all of German history, with Berlin possibly the most intellectually vibrant city in the world. One literary circle feeds into the next, and Harro's best friend, the slender, dark-haired Henry Erlanger, drags him around everywhere. "The crust is suddenly broken, as the old powers, those of the Weimar system, are finally beginning to stand down" is how a friend of Harro's describes the equally precarious and exciting situation: "Suddenly heads everywhere were emerging above the fog clouds of jargon and starting to speak in a language that was in a new sense shared . . . It was intoxicating."

This rush-inducing discourse comes to fruition, among other places, in the editorial offices of independent publications such as Carl von Ossietzky's *Weltbühne,* where Kurt Tucholsky, one of the most prominent political authors of the Weimar Republic, writes, or Harro Schulze-Boysen's *Gegner,* housed in a sparsely furnished attic room with a view of Potsdamer Platz. From the hall, visitors enter directly into the first of the two long, narrow rooms, the second filled with books from German philosophers, a typewriter, a seating area, a fold-up cot. Harro often stays overnight here because it's convenient just to sleep at the office, where there's always something to do: editing text, speaking to new writers, preparing contracts — plus in the evening the theater is nearby, putting on things like Brecht's *Rise and Fall of the City of Mahagonny,* a "fairly crazy piece, music definitely good," as Harro describes it to his parents.

It's a fulfilling, exciting existence — despite or perhaps because of the unsure future. "Every person feels inspired by the voice of God at some point," Harro rhapsodizes in a letter from the *Gegner* period: "And you can supplant this arrogant word through *knowledge, need,* or *desire*; but it remains the same." The mission, perhaps seemingly pretentious, but bitterly necessary: saving the world from impending ruin. Because while "the discussions between fish and roast, over tea and whisky continue blithely along, outside the SA is marching steadily forward with firm steps."

There's a photo of Harro from this time over which his mother regularly frets: his facial features are more striking than usual, and his beautiful blue eyes look possessed — and that's what he is as he races from one event to the next in his light coat, colorful shirt, tousled hair, feeling "never more alive." He tirelessly writes and makes connections, and then also becomes the publisher of the *Gegner,* now pouring every penny he gets from his parents into the magazine, on top of all his time. If there aren't enough paperboys he throws a bag over his shoulder and stands in front of the university or technical college selling copies by hand, newsboy cap on his head. "The *Gegner* is gaining genuine renown," he reports home to Mülheim: The print run has risen to over five thousand copies, and with the publication of the October 1932 issue comes a hundred new subscribers. November 1932 begins chaotically. A strike breaks out among public transport workers: no S-Bahns or U-Bahns run, no buses, no streetcars. During the resultant conflicts with the police, three people are killed. Shortly thereafter, in the national elections on November 6, the share of the vote won by the Nazi Party (NSDAP) drops for the first time, 4.6 percent to be exact, while the German Communist Party (KPD) jumps by 2.6 percent. Panic breaks out in the Hitler camp. "The year 1932 was a streak of singularly bad luck," writes Goebbels in his diary: "It must be shattered in pieces. The future is dark and murky; all prospects utterly vanished."

But Harro senses that behind the curtains, capital is working tirelessly for a Nazi power grab. He follows with suspense the government declaration by Kurt von Schleicher of December 15, 1932, in which the Reich chancellor rejects not only socialism but also capitalism. Will industrialists come to regard von Schleicher as an unreliable waffler as a result? Hitler on the other hand has been cultivating the kings of industry for years. In January 1932 he'd made clear in a speech in front of the influential Düsseldorf Industry Club that the "socialist" element in the NSDAP program was merely a way to pick up votes among the working class and lower middle class. In no way did it reflect a desire to reduce the political influence of businessmen. Moreover, it's clear that the Nazi rearmament plan holds out the prospects of massive contracts for German manufacturers. Since the speech, contributions to the party have been flowing generously.

# 4

Industrial leaders aren't the only ones Hitler is cultivating. The Nazi leader from the small Austrian town of Braunau has also become the great hope of major landowners. Fifty kilometers north of Berlin, on the morning of January 30, 1933, the nineteen-year-old Libertas Haas-Heye awakes and looks out the window of her chambers at the forecourt of Schloss Liebenberg, her family's ancestral home. The snow that covers everything — the manor house, the farmhouse, the fieldstone church — glistens in the morning sun. The fountain, a gift from Kaiser Wilhelm, a close friend of her grandfather's, is also coated in gleaming white. Libertas gets up, pulls her nightgown over her head, and throws it into an open wardrobe.

It's a special day. The local Liebenberg branch of the SA is to set off for Berlin, because today it is actually about to happen: Hitler will be appointed chancellor of the Reich. Libertas's uncle, Fürst Friedrich-Wend zu Eulenburg und Hertefeld, the titled head of Schloss Liebenberg, wants to witness this historic moment, and has asked Libertas if she'd like to accompany the group.

But before they're supposed to leave, Libertas first saddles her horse. It's named Scherzo, referring to a type of musical composition, because the horse is always moving in rhythm and is maniacally agile. Just like its owner — at least most of the time.

There's a melancholy note to Libertas as well. Ever since she can remember, her parents have only sporadically looked after her and her older brother, Johannes. Ten years prior they'd divorced: her father, Otto Haas-Heye, is a prominent fashion designer, art professor, and bon vivant, at home in all the metropoles of Europe; her mother, Tora, on the other hand, finds the fashion world "horrible," is weak of nerve, and shields herself from the somewhat too-real world, preferring to hole up at Schloss Liebenberg. For a while a governess had looked after Libertas; later the Jewish artist Valerie Wolffenstein, a co-worker of her father's, had taken over supervision of her. The time with Valerie had been pleasant, but had not lasted. Libertas had lived in a Berlin boarding school, then in Paris, London, and Switzerland, always ready to leave again almost as soon as she settled in someplace, ready to get accustomed to yet another strange city: to make new contacts, win new sympathies, prove herself and orient herself anew. Over time she's developed techniques to appeal to others. Libs comes across as open and fun-loving, and charms people with her cheerful demeanor; she can sing well and plays the accordion captivatingly, with knowledge of thousands of songs.

Her ride through the Liebenberg Forest, with the clopping beat of Scherzo's hooves muted by the snow, is an absolute joy. It's an ice-cold day, this January 30, but beautiful, with a clear blue sky visible through the white-powdered branches of the tall trees that fill the estate. Libertas knows every tree along the way to Lankesee, their private lake. "O, you, my Liebenberg, where the green boughs of the weeping willows toward the heavenly pond bow." She'd come up with that poem at fourteen, inspired by Rilke.

There is an artistic tradition at Liebenberg. Her mother loves to perform, above all else, the "Rosenlieder," the "rose songs" known all over Europe and written by her own father, Fürst Philipp of Eulenburg, Libs's grandpa, whom she loved deeply. He'd also written "Fairytale of Freedom," in which a character named Libertas pops up, the embodiment of individual freedom, after whom Libertas was named. The Fürst died in 1921, more than eleven years prior, but she still remembers him well.

Grandpa Philipp wasn't just another person. Earlier, in a long-before faded and yet still very present era, he'd been the most intimate friend and closest advisor to the Kaiser. But there'd been a scandal surrounding the friendship, the biggest of the Wilhelmine era and the first homosexual scandal of the twentieth century, covered in the press worldwide.

In 1906, a shocked public read in a series of articles by Maximilian Harden in the newspaper *Zukunft*, or Future, that the Kaiser tarried too long at Liebenberg palace, and not because the deer hunting alone was so scintillating. There was talk of a Round Table that secretly determined the policies of the empire, and which indulged in occult sessions — and in gay activities. Fürst Philipp von Eulenburg, it was said, ran proceedings in a negligee.

The sweetheart of Libertas's grandfather:
Kaiser Wilhelm II, depicted here in a French caricature.

One sensation after the next shook the prudish, so-called Iron Age of Prussia. Berlin, where life was supposedly strictly regimented, quickly surpassed Paris, Rome, or London in terms of disreputability. Suddenly the former "Sparta on the Spree" became the new Babylon, and the posited moral superiority of the Prussians evaporated. The entire world now sneered at Berlin's sexually charged subculture — or marveled at it, or even traveled there to mingle in it: a self-fulfilling prophecy. "That's chaste Germany for you!" read a headline in the French newspaper *Figaro*.

The scandal stained not only Berlin's sterling reputation, but also the honor of Libertas's once distinguished family. When in April 1908 a fisherman from Lake Starnberg attested during a subsequent trial that he'd had sex in his barge with Eulenburg, Fürst Philipp was arrested. He denied the charges anew — and was then accused of perjury. Wearing dark sunglasses in order to remain anonymous, he had to take the train into Berlin again and again for doctor's appointments and to appear before judges. Occasionally, whether because he'd really been so affected or for strategic reasons, the once vital man was even carried into court on a stretcher.

In order to save his own neck, Kaiser Wilhelm had distanced himself from Eulenburg, his best friend. He had stopped visiting Schloss Liebenberg and surrounded himself with new advisors who seemed diametrically opposed to the peace-craving of the now discredited Liebenberg Round Table. On a warm day in June 1908, the case against Eulenburg was adjourned due to his lack of fitness to stand trial, and never taken up again. The suspicion of homosexuality could be neither confirmed nor cleared. While this meant the Fürst was not legally convicted, he did suffer personal and societal condemnation — a stain on his reputation that he was unable to erase during his lifetime. Reclusive, with hardly any visitors, he lived at his palace until his death in 1921 and looked after his grandchildren, including Libertas. The aging aristocrat told them stories of summer trips with the Kaiser on the yacht *Hohenzollern* in the fjords of Norway, where they hunted whales. His former best friend, the Kaiser, the only one who could have rehabilitated his reputation, never got in touch again, not even while in exile at Castle Doorn, in Holland, after losing the First World War.

# 5

On Wednesday, January 30, 1933, as Libertas is preparing to depart for Berlin, Harro is in the city phoning a fellow *Gegner* writer, Adrian Turel: "Hitler is chancellor! Take the underground to Potsdamer Platz and have a look at the festivities. Then maybe you can stop by the office. Nothing'll happen to us right away."

Turel covers his typewriter, hops on the train, rides to the center of town, and walks down the median of the grand boulevard Unter den Linden. In the road on both sides of him, massive columns of SA stream past with torches in their hands for the procession later, stepping lively, like gladiators striding into the arena. "I was going against the stream. And then I see: coming toward me were a Jewish industrialist and his wife, people I knew well. I greeted them happily as Jewish comrades, in the middle of the military-style columns of SA people ... and said: 'For goodness sake, trouble's brewing! Get out of here!' At which the woman smiled and said to me with childlike naivete: 'But my dear Turel, don't be hysterical! It's just a Volks festival.'"

6

In the icy cold, several cars drive to the train station in Löwenberg, not far from Liebenberg. In one of them sits Libertas, and next to her, her uncle Wend, who is fifty-one, a man with a grin like a stripe across his face and what little hair he has on his head slicked back. Libs knows how much this day means to him: the Nazis are taking over in Berlin. Wend is smitten with this Hitler fellow. Two years prior he'd had an audience with him, and the man from Braunau was reassuring: "I'll lead the battle against Marxism ... until the total and definitive annihilation and eradication of this plague ... I'll fight to that goal ruthlessly, with no mercy." That suited the estate owner, because in Liebenberg, too, people had demanded the breakup of the manorial land held by the one great local landholder, namely the Fürst.

In order to support the Nazi Party, Wend had sent a Hitler-approved circular to his friends among the landed gentry and large landholders, urgently recommending they all read *Mein Kampf,* which he said contained "an abundance of brilliant ideas." Wend had set aside his initial misgivings about Hitler's possible socialist tendencies: "If we don't want Bolshevism, we have no other choice than to join the party that despite a few socialist ideas is the polar opposite of Marxism and Bolshevism." Not only does he believe that the NSDAP can best solve the country's problems, but he's also convinced that "without Hitler, no form of government is possible in the long run." And weren't the Nazis predestined to rehabilitate his father, Fürst Philipp, since Maximilian Harden, the writer who triggered the Eulenburg scandal, was a Jew?

But what does Libertas think of the powerful new movement? Is she as enthusiastic as her uncle? On that day, after a one-hour train ride, they take part in the torchlight procession, and Libertas enjoys it. On the other hand, she knows little of Hitler's goals, and isn't terribly interested in them, as she lives from the heart and the gut. These are the places from which she hopes to write her poetry. Of course, Nazi propaganda is meant to appeal to exactly these same places, places beyond the level of rationality. When the Liebenberg group disembarks the train at Lehrter Bahnhof and heads toward the Brandenburg Gate along with the excited masses, Libertas is for that reason also moved.

Though politics may not be her cup of tea, Libertas, too, seeks to follow the suddenly powerful movement, and in March 1933 joins the local Liebenberg chapter of the Party with the member number 1 551 344.

# 7

Like so many others, Harro believes Hitler's cabinet will soon fail. Every coalition of the past decade has proven untenable over the long term, so why would it be any different this time? Which is why Harro doesn't think about shutting down the *Gegner*. He's convinced that the moment has now finally arrived when change is possible, and he wants to be part of it. "Completely convinced that the political situation has in no way come to a standstill . . . it would seem crazy to give up the paper now," he writes to his parents.

He trusts that the energy the Nazis have unleashed can be put toward a genuine social revolution, and that the right-wing populist discontent stirred up by the new leader might be put toward progressive ends. Since he believes Hitler to be a mere puppet of capital, he thinks it impossible for the so-called Führer to deliver on his promises to the people. Harro prophesies that the contradiction within the NSDAP between socialist rhetoric and the financial support of industrialists will lead to it falling apart. "The first two weeks in power have in no way convinced us," he writes fearlessly in the *Gegner*'s edition of February 15, 1933.

But the Nazis are more tenacious than initially thought — and above all more brutal. The NSDAP places just two additional ministers alongside Chancellor Hitler, but their portfolios are crucial. With the interior minister Wilhelm Frick as well as Göring, who as Reich commissioner for the Prussian Interior Ministry is master of the entire Prussian state police system, the brownshirts hold control of the security organs. The regime can immediately take efficient action against any opposition — and the Nazis' anti-Semitism is quickly put into practice.

The first boycotts against Jewish businesses, shops, medical practices, and attorney's offices take place within weeks of the NSDAP's rise to power. The racist ideology rapidly expands into the Law for the Restoration of the Professional Civil Service, which forces so-called non-Aryans into retirement. The underclass in Germany may still be having a hard time, but suddenly there is a multitude of people who are worse off because they've had their civil liberties taken away.

"The first two weeks in power have in no way convinced us":
Harro in *Gegner*, February 15, 1933.

This is coupled with massive oppression of *all* dissenters. A pluralism of opinion, as practiced by the *Gegner*, is no longer desired. One single voice shall prevail: "In Berlin there are ten loudspeakers set up on each of the largest public squares around which veritable hordes of people have gathered this evening," boasts Goebbels in mid-February at the Sportpalast, a large Berlin venue, before Hitler steps up to the podium: "In front of these speakers is an audience of around 500 to 600 thousand people who will hear the speech by the Führer and Reich Chancellor."

Propaganda and suppression increasingly dominate daily life. Hermann Göring puts in place the so-called *Schiesserlass*, or Shooting Decree, whereby the police are permitted indiscriminate use of guns against political dissenters. Work in the editorial offices of the *Gegner* changes as a result, too. The wheat is separated from the chaff, "because those who had previously just gone along must now make an active personal commitment based on the question: fight or capitulate," as one editorial participant puts it.

Two of Harro's colleagues receive a very practical demonstration of which way the wind is blowing. They're sitting in *Tary Bary*, a hip restaurant in Wilmersdorf, where Russian food is served alongside American cocktails, when they are arrested, taken to the police headquarters at Alexanderplatz, and "interrogated by subordinate criminal detectives" and cursed as "Asian subhumans." Still, Harro proves unperturbed: "If I end up in prison as a result of this objective, I have no problem with it, because in that case I am in the right."

When the *Gegner* team arranges to stage another evening of political discussion at the hotel Nordischer Hof on Invalidenstrasse in Mitte, the police begin their targeted surveillance of Harro and his friends. The goal of the operation is a "deliberate appraisal of the political position of the *Gegner* circle."

The planned *Gegner* evening takes place at eight o'clock on February 16, 1933. The room is filled with two hundred people of all political stripes. Even some Hitler Youth members take part, in a "friendly, well-informed, engaged" manner. The police observe but rarely intervene. "An officer stood up one time and suggested that something said in the discussion was going too far," reports one participant. "The amazing thing about the event was the absolute unanimity and brotherly solidarity expressed in the comments by speakers . . . Despite their various political priorities, everyone was united in 'nevertheless' and 'not wanting to give up.'"

Harro shows his true colors in his talk, not reacting obsequiously to the new rulers like the majority of the general public. Rather than ducking and weaving, he goes on the offensive, encouraging everyone in the room to disregard personal interests and advocate for freedom, to live for revolution, with all the dangers and consequences it might entail. It is a speech full of civic courage in the face of suppression that's gaining ground daily.

On February 19, 1933 — Hitler's chancellorship is just three weeks old — Harro takes part in the last major demonstration against the right-wing regime. Despite icy temperatures, ten thousand people from all parts of the city stream into the central Lustgarten square. Several times members of the SA shoot bullets into the air from their taverns as the masses pour forth. Meanwhile, about a thousand artists, writers, and scientists gather in the Kroll Opera House, protesting the censorship of art, research, and the press. As Harro is making his way there, a policeman fires off a few shots that whizz by close, "but he missed," he writes to his younger brother, Hartmut, laconically — as if nothing bad could ever happen to him.

On February 24, 1933, Göring orders the state criminal police, or Landeskriminalpolizei, to henceforth report all surveillance and assessment of a political nature. Systematic spying ramps up.

Three days later, on February 27, it's still bracingly cold in the city. Several more centimeters of snow have fallen. That evening the sky over Berlin is lit up by the glow of fire, a velvety red that saturates the air. It's the Reichstag burning.

Without evidence, the regime claims that an unemployed Dutchman, Marinus van der Lubbe, arrested at the scene of the crime, set the fire on the orders of the German Communist Party, the KPD. Before dawn, 1,500 people in Berlin and 8,000 nationwide are arrested, among them the writers Erich Mühsam, Carl von Ossietzky, and Egon Erwin Kisch. Harro is spared for the moment. The following day the Nazis suspend civil liberties with the Decree of the Reich President for the Protection of People and State, also referred to as the Reichstag Fire Decree. "Now the clampdown will be ruthless!" reads a headline in the *Völkische Beobachter*, the NSDAP's party paper.

Personal freedom, freedom of opinion, the rights of association and assembly, privacy of correspondence: all of it is gone with the stroke of a pen while smoke is still rising from the wreckage of the Reichstag. So-called wild concentration camps — early, largely unregulated models of the bigger concentration camps that would operate a few years later — spring up: in the water tower in Prenzlauer Berg, for instance, and in many other places in Germany. The lists the Nazis have prepared now come into play, filled with the names of social democrats, communists, dissenters. It doesn't take long before a police inspector turns up at the editorial offices of the *Gegner* to interrogate Harro. In the police report, it states:

> The association isn't composed of a set number of members, and is in no way governed by any sort of charter. The group of people who are drawn to this association is composed for the most part of young individuals of all ranks and political affiliations. The approximate number of possible participants cannot be ascertained. The leader for all intents and purposes is the student Harro Schulze-Boysen, Lutheran, Prussian citizen. The offices are located in Berlin on

Schellingstrasse 1, on the fourth floor, and consist of two rooms. The leader of the association resides here, using it as his official address. There is nothing known to this department about Schulze-Boysen politically, and he's never had any previous interactions with the department. The impression following the investigation confirms the supposition that the association has radical communist leanings.

"Radical communist"? This will not be the last time it's insinuated about Harro.

# 8

On one of the last days of February 1933, Henry Erlanger is strolling along the central section of Lützowstrasse. As he passes the neoromantic red-brick synagogue, which has room for more than two thousand congregants, he sees a *Gegner* colleague by the name of Schreiber coming out of a corner bar known as a meeting place for the SA. Schreiber is dressed in a brown shirt.

The *Gegner* circle convenes a discussion; Schreiber denies everything. Werner Dissel, one of Harro's closest friends, starts to keep tabs on the spy thereafter. His report reads: "One night Schreiber came to my door at 11 PM and said that he needed to speak to me. But he didn't want to come into the apartment, and asked me to go for a walk with him. We went through the woods toward Krumme Lanke lake. In the middle of the conversation I suddenly had two gorillas at my sides who worked me over with their fists and beat me up."

On March 3, two days before the new national election in which Hitler wants to see his power confirmed, Harro, too, feels the heat. He's arrested for the first time and taken to a cellar, probably in the basement of the jail at Alexanderplatz. "Horrible chicanery," he writes his parents on a post-card when he makes it out. "Just released." But he has good things to say about his fellow prisoners: "I met terrific people during those hours. For that reason: now more than ever!"

The Reichstag election of March 5, 1933, does in fact give Harro grounds for hope that political empowerment is still possible. In Berlin, for instance, Hitler's party earns just 31.3 percent of the vote, while the Social Democrats (SPD) receive 22.5 and the Communists (KPD) 30.1, meaning the two workers' parties together represent significantly more votes than the right. But the mandate is of little use to the Communist Party: the regime has all the Communist representatives arrested. As a result, the NSDAP has an absolute majority.

The Nazis move swiftly to prepare the Enabling Act, which renders parliament meaningless. When, with the exception of the Social Democrats, the civil parties approve this self-disempowerment on March 23 and the needed two-thirds majority is reached, the path is smoothed for the next step, the banning of all parties other than the NSDAP. The totalitarian noose is getting tighter and tighter, with the consolidation of power accompanied by a rapid buildup of the machinery of persecution. The kidnapping of critical voices speeds up, as well: ever more people are removed from the street, locked up, and abused in order to "reeducate" them. Something as inconsequential as a joke at Hitler's expense can lead to serious consequences. There are suddenly informants everywhere. It becomes increasingly difficult to trust others.

Not all of the regime's measures find support among the populace. A boycott of Jewish businesses, warehouses, banks, and medical practices imposed on April 1, for instance, is lifted after just twenty-four hours because so few citizens keep to it.

Harro tries during this time to organize a meeting in the Brown House, the Party headquarters in Munich. He hopes to reconcile his social-revolutionary ideas with the leadership of the Hitler Youth there. He still continues to entertain the illusion that, in principle, everyone can pull together for the good of the country. When he does indeed receive an invitation, he shows it triumphantly to his *Gegner* friends. It takes them hours to make him understand that there can be no common ground with the fascists and that he must not travel to the Bavarian capital.

Harro realizes they're right a few weeks later, when the National Socialist authorities knock at the door on Schellingstrasse again.

# 9

On Wednesday, April 26, 1933, it's a cloudless sixty degrees in the German capital, a wonderful spring day. Hitler has been chancellor for three months. Harro Schulze-Boysen is twenty-three years old.

On this date, Hermann Göring, number two in the new Reich, orders the creation of a secret police agency. On the same day, the free spirits of the *Gegner* gather for their weekly editorial meeting to discuss the role of the church in the frighteningly fast development of the Nazi state when there's a loud knock on the door of Schellingstrasse 1, near Potsdamer Platz.

Harro opens to men in black uniforms. What do they want? If there's a new police power, it's the SA, with their brown shirts. This is the SS-District III from nearby Potsdamer Strasse 29, known as the Henze Commando of the Hilfspolizei.

The men shove their way in, end the editorial meeting, and confiscate some of Harro's books, including his photos and letters, some records, notebooks, and writings. They stuff everything into a leather suitcase, then force Harro and Henry Erlanger, along with the other *Gegner* authors, down the stairs while beating them.

Henry's real name is Karl Heinrich, his father is a Berlin banker and Jew, his mother a Catholic from the Rhineland. In the past the reserved Henry had complemented the swashbuckling Harro perfectly. As a mutual friend describes him, he is "the eternal assistant director type: diligent and jovial, the sort of good spirit you need … always in keen support of all things *Gegner*." Unlike Harro, the introverted Henry has no direct political ambitions; he doesn't understand how to curry favor with others by using diplomatic niceties. Literary expertise is more important to him. He particularly likes to read contemporary philosophy. As a trained librarian, Henry is interested in anything on the printed page.

They're herded into a small van, which takes them to SS-District III headquarters. Harro defends himself verbally during the interrogation. He is not aware of anything he has done wrong and insists that he simply publishes a paper that discusses the future of Germany and Europe openly and without blinders. But precisely this is a serious offense. At dawn he finds himself back in the van, huddled close to Henry. They're driven all over the city, kicked and punched by their minders. Fear creeps into Harro. Even if it's not the first time he's had trouble with the authorities, up to now he hadn't thought he was really in any danger. This time something feels different. Suddenly his unshakeable belief that everything will come out all right no longer seems sufficient. What are they planning to do to him and Henry?

At some point the van stops. The door flies open. Isn't that Reichsstrasse — and over there the Spandauer Bock, the famous garden restaurant where the streetcar stops? *Get out!* Harro blinks in the light of the streetlamp. The scent of spring hangs in the air. Henry stumbles next to him.

Well-worn steps lead downward: another cellar. A wooden door stands open. They are forced to enter. Straw on the floor, an improvised sleeping area with black-red-gold flags as sheets, mocking the fallen Weimar Republic. There's already someone lying there, another *Gegner* writer, Adrien Turel. They'd grabbed him from his apartment hours before. Harro and Henry must lie on their backs next to him and "shut up."

Bright lights stay on all night. There's no way to sleep. A uniformed giant keeps watch at the door, sitting on a stool, toying with his pistol: removes the magazine, shoves it back in with a click, takes it out again, shoves it in again, all while the three friends lie next to each other in the floodlights. Their persecution is completely unjustifiable in their eyes, and as a result they're still harboring hope that it'll all turn out to be a big misunderstanding. It's possible to bridge any differences through reasonable debate, right? That's the concept behind the *Gegner.* But what if one party doesn't stick to it? Just a short time ago, before the Nazi takeover, it was fine to write critical texts. How is it possible that it's being so severely punished all of a sudden? What right do these brutes think they have? And what will they do to Henry, the "half Jew"?

At about one o'clock in the morning, someone throws open the door and yells: "Is there a Turel here?"

Adrien sits up.

"Look alive! What's your name?"

"Adrien Turel."

"What?" asks the SS man, holding his hands over his ears. "All I hear is *Jew!*"

But Turel isn't a Jew; he's a Protestant from Switzerland. Once the error is cleared up, he's ordered released — his nationality saves him. But Turel refuses to go and insists on staying with his friends. A guard takes him outside against his will.

Harro and Henry now have their hair cut off with garden shears, and Henry is taken into an interior courtyard. There the *real* Jew has to run in a square along the walls while the SS men stand in the center, striking him with bullwhips.

"You, too," somebody yells at Harro. "Undress!" He strips off his favorite blue sweater, which has accompanied him everywhere.

The second time Harro, his torso bare, has to make his way around the courtyard, the whips rip open his skin. He wipes his face, his chest. Where his hands find blood, his skin feels swollen. He's shoved against the brick wall. Two men hold his arms, four others grab his legs. One of them pulls his pants down to his knees, another produces a knife, leans down, and stabs the blade into Harro's thigh, cutting a line and a hook at a right angle, then another line and hook, and then repeats the two right-angle hooks in

21

mirror image, making a swastika, and with every line and every hook, the hatred in Harro grows.

# 10

Two days later, on April 29, 1933, the slender twenty-year-old Regine Schütt is walking in an elegant gray flannel suit from her father's birthday party to the office of the *Gegner*. She's looking forward to an evening with Harro: She'll sketch her fashion designs, he'll work on articles for the paper, they'll make love even though they're not married. When the front door is locked and nobody answers the doorbell, she walks to a nearby bar to call Harro from there. But she doesn't get that far. "They took him away," says the barkeeper. "We saw it."

Regine immediately sets off to search for Harro. She hits one pub after the next because she's heard that every SA division maintains an unofficial headquarters in some dive or other. There are a lot in the center of town, and it's like looking for a needle in a haystack, but she can't think of any better way to go about it. Good-looking, well dressed, and showing no fear, she asks respectfully and politely in each locale: "Have you or your detachment arrested a Harro Schulze-Boysen?" To a man, those asked, some of them drunk, answer her straightforwardly. The strawberry-blond Regine is the type of person who is generally well received, and as a result the men try to make an upstanding impression.

Finally, on the evening of April 30, four days after Harro's arrest, she meets a young guy from SS-District III who confirms: Yes, we have him. He also gives her the location where Harro's being held. She sets off immediately, though not to the Spandauer Bock, but to the Botanical Garden, because she knows that's where the federal court councilor Dr. Werner Schulze lives, Harro's uncle. She doesn't have his exact address, but with the help of the phone book she can whittle down the possibilities, and, at three in the morning finds the correct location. She shares everything she's learned with the family, who, she believes, will have a better chance than she does at securing Harro's release.

When Harro's parents, who live hundreds of miles west of Berlin, learn of their son's disappearance, his mother, Marie Luise (maiden name Boysen, a "strong woman, though quite short") as Regine later describes her, sets out for an office of the NSDAP and registers herself as well as her husband. She's convinced that having a Nazi pin will improve her chances of seeing her son alive again. She learns to her dismay that the pin will only be sent by post a few weeks later. But she doesn't give up, explaining excitedly that she's the longtime chairperson of the local section of the Women's League of the German Colonial Society ("Which was true!") and, as such, is attending a Colonial Society event that very evening at which she must speak ("Which wasn't true!"), and she wouldn't want to do so without a pin. Her moxie bears fruit: They make an exception and she gets a pin on the spot, sticks it to the breast of her understated two-piece dress, puts on a subdued hat, and makes her way to the train station. She boards the next train and rides through the night, arriving early in the morning in Berlin, where she is collected at the station by her brother-in-law.

Once he has told her about Regine Schütt and the information she's provided about which unit has Harro, Marie Luise hurries to Potsdamer Strasse, "between Potsdamer Platz and Potsdamer Bridge on the lefthand side if you're coming from Potsdamer Platz." There her gaze falls on a sign that identifies the Naval Officers Union. Quickly she goes in, since she knows a few naval officers through her husband, Erich Edgar, who'd served as a lieutenant commander in the navy — she hopes to be able to enlist additional help through these channels. And indeed there are two officers there, also wearing pins on their lapels. When they hear of Harro's arrest, they agree that if it's the SS then she needn't worry, because there won't be a hair out of place. The SS aren't the SA, they naively claim; there's not much known about them, but they're considered rather "correct."

With one lead satisfied, she goes to the office of the SS-District. Two men are sitting at a table. "Where's my son, Harro Schulze-Boysen?" She notices how the two exchange a glance. "We have no way of knowing," one of them says. Just then one of the naval officers from before enters the office and says he was sorry not to have been able to help her better, given that she's come all the way from western Germany. He's just knocked at the door of Henze, the head of the Hilfspolizei commando, a floor above. Henze is willing to see her, but she should make it quick, as he has little time.

Harro's mother excitedly mounts the steps. She knows she has to pull herself together: you have to appear confident in this new system that is so difficult to gauge. That's why it's important not to give in, not to be intimidated. She finds the correct door and is admitted.

"Your son hasn't been writing in the manner of the Party," says Henze, who has a shadow beneath his nose.

"My son is an idealist," she counters, "who's only twenty-three years old, obviously still immature. I promise to keep him out of politics." She says these words with conviction, because she really believes that Harro occasionally goes too far with his notions of revolution. "If he took a bit of a beating," she continues, since she can imagine that the Nazis aren't too squeamish in dealing with their opposition, "it wouldn't be so bad. A young man can quickly get over that sort of thing."

"Yes, they won't have treated him lightly," mumbles Henze into his shadow.

Marie Luise senses that there's something keeping him from releasing Harro despite his desire to be helpful to her as a fellow Party member. "I'll make you another promise," she says: "I'll take him away from Berlin."

Once Henze has agreed to allow Harro to be released that evening to the apartment of Marie Luise's brother-in-law, she goes there and waits. But her son doesn't arrive, not that evening or during the night. In the morning she rings up Potsdamer Strasse, but Henze pretends not to be there. When she finally gets his deputy on the line, he says that it's utterly impossible to release Harro: A serious crime now has occurred, and Harro is a suspect.

"But he couldn't have done anything that awful while detained," says his mother into the phone, distraught.

# 11

No, Harro hasn't done anything awful in the converted basement. Yet what Henze's deputy says is nonetheless accurate: There has been a crime in the meantime, and a serious one. Henry is no longer able to get up from the dust. He'd continued to run round and round, and the men had continued to whip him. It went on for days, and at some point his heart gave out.

Henry's corpse sits on the ground like garbage that's been swept into a pile. He'd been the good spirit of the *Gegner,* and Harro had spent many nights out on the town with him. They'd evolved together. But Harro has been unable to protect Henry from the SS, unable to do anything for him, anything at all.

Now Harro, despite his feelings of guilt, needs to get tougher, much tougher — or he'll die, too. No, these brutal idiots won't break him, that he promises himself. They'll find him a tough nut to crack! He's superior to them, both intellectually and physically. Suddenly he's convinced that they aren't capable of killing him, and determines that he will stand up to them. He wrenches himself off the brick wall and runs another round of the courtyard as if possessed. The whipping starts again. His left ear is half detached from his head, his lips are cracked, his face cut, his nose like putty. He's bleeding, inside and out, and he does it for Henry now. If he's able to keep going and survive — if he can take more pain than they dish out — he will have defeated them.

"This is my lap of honor!" he yells to his torturers as he manages to complete a last round of the courtyard.

"Man, you're one of us!" answers one of the SS men, impressed by Harro's show of courage. "We should sign you up!"

But Harro is *not* one of them. He is truly their *Gegner* now — their adversary.

# 12

It is the night before the first of May, 1933, and Marie Luise hasn't given up on her son. She has even managed to mobilize the president of Berlin's police, Admiral von Levetzow, an old navy comrade of her husband's. Which is why a green police van is racing northwest beneath a clear, starry sky, why officers jump out and pound on a cellar door of the Spandauer Bock and demand on the orders of their president the immediate release of the prisoners. But there's just one prisoner left, and the SS men seem unsettled by the visit from the regular police. They don't have any authority to commit political murder yet. Grumbling in protest, they release Harro.

Marie Luise is standing in her robe in the doorway of the house near the Botanical Garden when the vehicle comes to a halt. White as a sheet, with dark rings beneath his eyes, not a button left on his frock coat, and with his head shorn like a convict, Harro gets out and faces his mother. He had always beamed, had always been so full of hope and lust for life and open to everyone. Now the swastika on his thigh burns and he winces in pain, contorting his face, which no longer looks like that of a twenty-three-year-old. He's had an experience that lets him know something his mother can't yet know — something that at this particular moment in time not enough people understand clearly: The Nazis are brutal, unscrupulous murderers who shy away from nothing.

His mother takes him to a hotel, where she registers him under a false name out of fear of being tracked down again. She arranges for two private security guards and gets a doctor. Then Regine comes to visit. She carefully lies down next to Harro and they make love. His kidneys have always been sensitive, but now he doubles over whenever she touches him in the wrong place.

It's strange, but he doesn't feel weaker, just different. He has a new, bitter taste in his mouth. He's young, but he's already tasted death. There's now a distance between him and this world that can be so hostile.

Regine tries to caress his wounds, but they are too fresh. The swastika burns like fire, but far worse is a hemorrhage that's much deeper inside. It's certainly not the same in bed with her as it had been before.

# 13

Harro's mother, Marie Luise, is so appalled by Henry's murder that she makes it her duty to "report this crime to the police." She can't categorize the motivation for the violence against Henry Erlanger and her son, doesn't understand how arbitrarily the Nazis are already throwing around their power. Harro, who has lost any naivete during the days and nights in the subterranean torture chamber, tries to persuade her not to file a complaint, since the consequence will be his rearrest. In order to carry out resistance, he now knows, techniques and tactics other than those available to Marie Luise will need to be employed. The rule of law is as dead as Henry Erlanger. But his mother won't allow herself to be swayed.

As a result of Marie Luise's complaint, Harro is once again taken into custody, just as he had predicted. But this time, he is arrested by the newly created Gestapo (short for Geheime Staatspolizei, or secret police), whose officers wish to question him about the episode.

On May 1, 1933, Labor Day, Marie Luise bursts into the police presidium at Alexanderplatz. Agitated, she insists on being permitted to see von Levetzow, and waits for him, wearing her Nazi pin prominently on her chest. She is shuffled into a room with large windows from which she can witness the SS, SA, and Hitler Youth march past with flags and music on their way to the central Labor Day rally at Tempelhof Airport. At some stage, an official enters and lets her know: "We've heard about the misfortune you've had with your son. But it wasn't SS personnel, they were communists in disguise."

Marie Luise knows better than that, and when it becomes evident the police president will not see her because he is himself leaving for the rally, she's only able to speak to one of his deputies, a man named Bredow, a former district administrator, "who was happy to have landed another post and didn't want to risk doing anything that could imperil his position," as Marie Luise remembers it. "I reported everything, first and foremost the murder of the young half-Jew Erlanger."

But Bredow doesn't know how to react to this matter, which seems to him unpleasant and complicated. The regime has been agitating against the Jews for months. Are the police even allowed to look after their interests anymore? In other German cities, too, where Jews, communists, social democrats, and intellectuals are being harassed by the hordes of SA this spring of 1933, the same question arises — and is answered in differing ways. In Leipzig, for instance, the conservative mayor Carl Friedrich Goerdeler insists his police stand by Jews in the face of Nazi attacks. But Bredow lacks the civic courage of Goerdeler. "I can hardly arrest and punish an entire company of the SS," says the Berlin police official, irritated.

"Why not, if they're criminals!" responds Marie Luise, housewife and mother, who still believes in the rule of law.

Finally, as workers from all over the city stream toward the Tempelhof rally in ten massive columns of fifty thousand people each, Harro is paraded in front of her. "Mama, you brought me in here with your complaint about Erlanger's murder," he calls, shaking his head. "Now get me out again!"

But it's not that easy — Harro spends another night in detainment, on a rough straw mattress that hurts his fresh wounds.

The next day, around ten a.m., Marie Luise Schulze meets with Bredow again in the police headquarters and demands "he write a note — as Levetzow's representative — ordering the release of my son." When she leaves Bredow's office holding this written confirmation, a man rips it from her hand and disappears behind a door with the freshly painted inscription GEHEIME STAATSPOLIZEI — the Gestapo. Agitated, Marie Luise goes back to see Bredow, who no longer wishes to help her. His secretary, who is braver than her boss, approaches the furious mother: "Come on, I'll take you to the prison gatekeeper. I know him, he'll let you in." Marie Luise follows her through a labyrinth of hallways until they reach a heavy iron door, and later that day, Harro is indeed set free again.

His mother subsequently meets with Levetzow, the police president, who makes it clear that her concession for Harro's release will be for her to drop her complaint and spare the police from "bringing the SS to justice." She thinks for a moment about just how to react to this circumspect suggestion that she not pursue her murder complaint any further. "If testimony is needed of me, I am always ready to give it," she says.

But as expected, her testimony is no longer needed. It is a time of upheaval, fear, and disputed competence in the prosecutorial apparatus of the consolidating Nazi regime. Nobody's going to stick their neck out for a dead "half Jew." As Marie Luise summarizes her devastating experience with the Berlin police, "Erlanger's barbarous murderers get off without so much as a slap on the wrist."

# 14

Libertas moves to Berlin at this time. Her life is now set in the city so influenced by the scandal surrounding her grandfather Philipp. Here it will be decided whether, with all her independence and restlessness, she will transform herself into a goddess of freedom, or instead, like the Fürst, she will come to ruin by acting out her desires.

It begins well: She's just nineteen, and, with no professional experience or technical training, she's landed a promising position that brings her close to her second-biggest passion, after poetry: film. Metro-Goldwyn-Mayer, the largest Hollywood studio, lures her to their Berlin branch on Friedrichstrasse. But perhaps her auspicious start in the world of work isn't as astonishing as it initially appears. MGM fired the bulk of its Jewish employees during the spring of 1933: more than half of their total staff, including practically all the managers. The German head of the studio, Frits Strengholt, even divorces his Jewish wife at the behest of the propaganda ministry; she later ends up in a concentration camp.

The studio must plug the resultant holes, and offers a job in the publicity department to Libertas, who comes from an exalted household, has well-cultivated communications skills, and even the correct party affiliation. She gets her own desk with typewriter and telephone, and from now on she informs the media about upcoming cinematic releases and organizes press screenings in the best cinemas on Kurfürstendamm.

Her work quickly bears fruit: The film *Sons of the Desert,* with Stan Laurel and Oliver Hardy, is a sensation, as is the musical *Dancing Lady,* with Joan Crawford, Clark Gable, and Fred Astaire. MGM, which also has Greta Garbo under contract, prospers in the Nazi empire, which is the second-largest film market in the world. Photos of Hollywood stars grace the popular newspapers and magazines. Cinema posters hang all over the capital of the Reich, and thanks to Libertas's activities, all the important productions are reviewed extensively in glossy publications. "We have terrific income in Germany," the studio boss Louis B. Mayer succinctly puts it.

But the American studios must pay a steep price. Goebbels has even dispatched a censor to Los Angeles: German consul Georg Gyssling. He's not shy about suggesting edits, and Hollywood listens to him because

Gyssling has genuine leverage. It stems from Article 15 of the German film regulations: any company that produces films critical of the Nazis, regardless of where in the world, will have all future films banned from German cinemas — a nightmare scenario for American producers. As a result, they acquiesce without much grumbling when their films are shortened or a plotline is eliminated in order to suit the Nazi leadership in distant Berlin. Profit over principle, that's the way the studio bosses do business, and they collaborate to the point of self-denial with the anti-Semites in Berlin — a scandal that's swept silently under the rug.

The obsequiousness toward Hitler is far-reaching. At the behest of Nazi leadership, a well-funded film project intended to bring international attention to the inhuman treatment of Jews in Germany is dropped. Herman Mankiewicz, who together with Orson Welles would go on to write one of the greatest movies of all time, *Citizen Kane,* is working in May 1933 on a screenplay called *The Mad Dog of Europe.* Three kilometers of newsreel footage from the *Deutsche Wochenschau,* the German Weekly Review, have already been assembled in order to be woven into the film and authentically show what is happening to Jews in Germany. An actor has been chosen who is the spitting image of Hitler: the Führer is to be portrayed in film long before Charlie Chaplin's *Great Dictator.* The rest of the cast will be the crème de la crème of Hollywood. "This picture is produced in the interests of DEMOCRACY," Mankiewicz's screenplay begins confidently, "an ideal which has inspired the noblest deeds of man." The story follows a Jewish family, the Mendelsohns, and their relationship with their neighbors and best friends, the Schmidts — until Hitler's racist policies turn them against each other. When Consul Gyssling gets wind of the project, he pulls out all stops, indicating that not only will all American productions be banned in Germany in the future, but that the property of all U.S. film studios will be confiscated if the film is made. Again Louis B. Mayer backs down: "We have interests in Germany . . . we have terrific income in Germany and, as far as I am concerned, this picture will never be made." At this critical moment, when Hollywood could have warned the world, the final cut falls not to the filmmakers but to Goebbels.

No wonder Libertas's work for MGM fails to alter her immature, Nazi-oriented worldview. To her, the career is what's important, and what could possibly afford her more fun than the glamorous world of film?

But is it really an unadulterated joy?

There's a photo of her from this time, taken at Friedrichstrasse 225, the MGM office, where she's sitting at her desk with a typewriter in front of her. Next to her are several stacks of paper, and in the background a handful of binders. She's wearing what to her tastes is conservative: a black knitted dress with a housewife-like white lace collar. Crucial is the date of the photo: May 10, 1933, the day of the infamous book burning. Just a few minutes' walk away, trucks are standing in the streets for everyone to see, stocked with more than twenty-five thousand books, literary works that will perish within the course of the night. The large pyre on the opera house plaza has already been built, again just a short walk from the MGM office.

In the first row with crossed legs is Libertas, listening to Hitler's
"Peace Address" on May 17, 1933, at the Berlin office
of the Hollywood studio MGM.

What does Libertas, who comes from an artistic family, make of the the fact that the writings of the journalist and satirist Kurt Tucholsky are supposed to be burned, along with the novels of the great authors Heinrich and Thomas Mann, the texts of Sigmund Freud, and Bertolt Brecht, whose song lyrics she so likes to sing?

Libertas had always wanted to be a poet; she grew up with books. Now seventy thousand people are streaming past her window so as not to miss out on the spectacle. Students from the city's universities have organized the book burning, "cleansing" the university libraries. Bookstores are taking part voluntarily, without any complaint about the financial losses. Culture is being destroyed. Does Libs not care at all? Can she sit there in good conscience — or more to the point, in a good mood — and gather with the staff in a room decorated with a wall-sized swastika flag to listen to Hitler's speech, as another photo taken at the office around that time shows?

In the picture Libertas can be seen in the front row with crossed legs, only a few seats from Frits Strengholt, the head of the office. Hollywood under the swastika — and Libertas with a reserved, skeptical look on her face, looking toward the front of the room, where the radio is situated, waiting for the words of "the Führer."

# 15

After his release from SS and police detainment, Harro walks like a ghost through the streets of Berlin, which no longer belong to him. He feels watched, threatened: marked. He no longer goes to the university; the idea of continuing his studies seems absurd. On Kurfürstendamm he runs into the writer Ernst von Salomon, someone he knows from before. "I didn't recognize him" is how von Salomon describes the meeting: "He stopped me. His face had greatly changed. He was missing half an ear, his face was stamped with red, barely healed wounds. He said: My revenge will be served ice-cold."

Not long afterward, Harro invites his former *Gegner* friends to a café on Potsdamer Strasse. Downstairs is a pastry shop, upstairs a gallery with tables. They set the chairs in a circle, which in itself is bold at this moment in time, because it indicates discussion, and keep watch below to see who comes in and who goes out. Harro informs everyone about Henry Erlanger's fate and what happened to Harro himself in the basement of the Spandauer Bock. He tells his friends about the conditions imposed on him: He is no longer to be politically active and must leave Berlin for at least one year. But he's not going into exile from Germany. He sees himself as an "explosive aimed at the fascist power grab," and must stay for that reason. The friction of the situation in Germany is his lifeblood. His goal is to go legit for the purpose of the "infiltration of existing organizations." The operating principle: "Trojan horse" — to fade into oblivion, to pretend one has learned a lesson, and reintegrate full of remorse. The strategy is to appear outwardly unsuspicious in order to change the system from within — an approach that will be described thirty years later, during the student movement of the 1960s, as "the long march through the institutions."

But where will Harro go? Which institution can and will he infiltrate? He says goodbye to all his friends, shakes hands one last time, and hugs everyone. He leaves the city that same night.

# PART II

# WORK AND MARRIAGE

## (*1933–39*)

This sort of existence can only be a dream, one thinks — and one awaits what will happen next.

— LIBERTAS SCHULZE-BOYSEN

# 1

**H**arro applies to an institution that couldn't be more inconspicuous, the Deutsche Verkehrsfliegerschule, or the German Air Traffic School, in Warnemünde, a port town on the Baltic Sea. A "Curriculum for Sea Reconnaissance" is offered there. The civilian designation is misleading, as in actuality the facility is part of Göring's secret buildup of the air force — *secret* because the Treaty of Versailles doesn't allow it, aiming to keep Germany without a strong military.

It's a move that is surprising only at first glance. Military connections run in the family, so in signing up for training, Harro is following in the footsteps of his father and great-uncle, Admiral von Tirpitz. Only instead of joining the navy, he wants to become a pilot — true to character, he wants to aim high. It's a move that he also hopes will keep him out of the Gestapo's line of fire, as well as offering him new career possibilities after his aborted effort as publisher of the *Gegner*.

He is twenty-three years young. While he may have put his revenge on ice, he's still hot for action and self-realization. It may seem like a mixed bag of motives that leads Harro to enlist, namely security from persecution as well as the hope that military life will suit him and allow him to *serve* his country instead of struggling against it. But first and foremost, what is driving him is his wish to establish a stable position that will enable him to continue his fight against the Nazis. His decision reflects a faith that Great-Uncle Tirpitz would have shared: that while Germany's military and political parties may work together in the nation's government, they occupy distinct zones of power. A belief that the air force — like the army and navy — represents a source of stability in German affairs, and a bulwark against the sort of chaos the Nazis represent.

# 2

Suddenly, sleeping in as long as he wants with Regine on the attic floor of the flat on Potsdamer Platz is no longer in the cards. Now it's all about getting up at five in the morning when the door to his new dorm room, filled with warm mustiness and loud snoring, is thrown open and a raw voice shouts an old Prussian command: *Up and at 'em!*

Together with Harro, several dozen sleep-drunk men with backs bent from their cardboard mattresses stuffed with sawdust jump up and sullenly but with feverish haste throw on their uniforms. It's a word that has an enormous, imperious ring that Harro now learns: *Dienst,* or duty, and the voice that issues orders all the livelong day belongs to the *Unteroffizier vom Dienst,* UvD for short, meaning duty officer, a guy with a steel helmet. The young men he bosses around are a bunch of aspiring German pilots born from 1900 to 1910, among them a couple of unusual and adventurous figures, like Harro, for instance, with his recurring nightmares about Henry Erlanger being beaten to death.

Every free Sunday, Regine Schütt takes the train to the Baltic coast and tries to cheer up her boyfriend. She knows Harro's frustrated at having to follow mindless orders when he so badly wants to lead. How awful it is for him to be penned in with people he can't engage with, in a place where "cowardice rules," as he puts it in a letter home — and where a broken propeller hangs symbolically from the dorm wall.

During the visits, he and Regine sit on a field cot fancied up with quilts and pillows, and she tells him about Berlin, bringing him up to speed on the developments within their circle of friends in order to connect him in spirit to the capital. Harro, however, wants to make a clean break with the old life he so loved. Since the days and nights in the torture cellar, he knows what kind of adversaries he's dealing with. He believes he needs to function like a machine now, totally organized against the nearly overpowering enemy: the Nazi regime that is tightening its grip on Germany by the day. Every muscle in his body must be taut: no distractions anymore, no mistakes or weaknesses. Or as he puts it in a letter to his sister, Helga, who is a year younger: "You can do all sorts of things, but you can never give up your independence! Best to live in a way that allows you to pack up your tent at a moment's notice, with just a small suitcase."

He explains to Regine on the beach at Warnemünde that to keep up his old contacts seems risky to him, since he must operate under the assumption that he's being watched.

Harro is also more guarded with Regine. Ever since the torture he's had problems tolerating intimacy, since it causes him pain. He increasingly distances himself physically, emotionally, and mentally not only from Berlin but also from his girlfriend. The very fact that he still feels the threads of his old life pulling at him makes him want to cut them, one after the next, in order to swim freely toward something new.

# 3

Every day at the crack of dawn Harro stands in front of the mirror that's stuck inside the door of his locker. He feels alone, even when his comrades are fussing about around him. His insides grate and claw; it's his kidneys. But he won't let himself show it. His gaze is that of an officer — exactly like his father's gaze: neck muscles taut, jaw set, body straight as a candle, hair neatly parted, a touch of severity in his eyes. It's a dashing look that he likes, in the trainee uniform that he's proud of — just like his father and uncle were proud of their uniforms. Harro is still a patriot, perhaps more so than ever; he won't let his love of country be usurped by the Nazi regime. But it's not a calm pose he captures in the locker mirror, not one that's a given. It feels as if something has permeated him, something that doesn't belong there. Something that the body wants to dislodge, making him twitchy. It's the deposits in his kidneys, the result of the beatings at the hands of the SS. The uniform may sit perfectly, but it's draped on an entity that's damaged. The pain comes in waves, from deep within his side, always unexpected, like a surprise attack. Cramp-like muscle contractions — colic. His urine is red. Duty calls regardless.

They head over to the airstrip at six in the morning in sweatpants and sweaters for early morning exercise. They work out for hours. The field exercises are tough, and some of his classmates break down and give up after a few weeks. "There's horribly strong competition here," he writes to his parents: "Already 50% of our group has quit. Someone's always being kicked out and sent home." Harro continues despite the internal injuries. He steels himself for the task ahead, which nobody knows about — and which isn't yet clear even to him. He marches in lockstep: *Keep that flag high, tighten up those rows.* He sings the Nazi propaganda songs, and heartily, even if it pains him, because anything less would stand out. He notices the burning fervor of some of his classmates and looks down on them for it.

His camouflage works. The uniform sits well, "not top-class perhaps, but it looks quite nice," as he himself describes it. His military performance level is flawless, and his superiors even laud him as "the best horse in the stall." Nobody has any inkling of the revenge he's plotting for Henry's murder. Nobody understands why he avoids the showers: because he doesn't want anyone to see the scars that remind him daily of the death of his friend and his own failure to save him. It's his striking chin they should notice, his penetrating gaze and svelte torso. The racist Nazi obsession with breeding perfect human beings seems to have been realized in him. He becomes the group leader and is appointed liaison officer — which is a bit embarrassing to him. "Yes, the last few months have been tough, but I wouldn't want to have missed out on them," he reports to his father, who becomes the most important family member to him during this thoroughly masculine period of duty to the so-called *Vaterland*: "To survive in the face of all the violence — it also makes one strong. And I feel times are coming in which one cannot be strong enough, in every sense."

Protect oneself, prepare, and ready for battle: Harro runs across the grounds in Warnemünde with sunglasses on, slinks into the classroom, sits in the back row: meteorology, air rights, radio, Morse code. He studies horse riding, shooting, driving vehicles — skills that one day might prove useful. Political discussions, however, are ignored, which is unusual for him: "I'm appalled anew every day at the hubris and flippancy with which one handles the toughest questions of the era," he writes to his father during this time. It's no longer the great, interconnected world that he had until recently been attempting to engage with, but rather a narrow sliver: "intellectual matters are given a wide berth."

Harro personally is going down a path that all of Germany is taking. It's a creeping depletion, a functionalization of the private, a hardening of the entire personality. But for him this contortion makes sense; he sees it as a tool for survival, for making him battle-ready against the regime. The haircut done with garden shears in the torture chamber is starting to look presentable again: "The hair on top of my head, which is precious, no longer looks odd; it's supposed to be short here anyway. Everything here is more military. Next we get gray-blue uniforms; that's why I'm not buying a blue one first."

This transformation isn't easy. It necessitates a permanent disguise. Instead of wearing his favorite blue sweater and communicating openly, which is his nature, he plays along with the game that's been forced upon him. The dictatorship has gotten inside his body. At the mess hall he seeks shelter below the larger-than-life portrait of Alfred von Tirpitz that decorates the back wall of the room. He tries to be normal — meaning, like the others. But he senses that a few of them suspect something's not right about him. When he lets his gaze fall over the rows of faces, he doesn't see like-minded people. No Henry Erlanger anywhere. "I sit here — from my standpoint — as if I'm in prison," he writes to his father: "So far removed from all the things that genuinely animate me mentally, and my nerves get ever more sluggish by the day. I'm curious how much longer I can muster the will. There is nothing that can sustain it over time. Basically I'm an honest and upstanding person, and dissembling exceeds my powers." It's not like it used to be, when he was marveled at for his way of doing things, for his energy, his crazy ideas, his spirit: "All in all it's just incredibly difficult to live in a world that is completely foreign to me — intellectually speaking — and with a different awareness than everyone else. And that will never change for me, and I just have to take on the consequences of this fact."

There's just one place where he can exhale, and that is in the sky. Harro loves flying, whether in a glider or in what they call heavy barges, the seaplanes. He's in the air as much as possible. When he soars on an updraft in a glider, or makes a controlled dive and matter feels so light, all his burdens fall away. Up there the metallic gray Baltic glitters in all shades of the rainbow even on overcast days. Then he feels no pain; rather he follows the edge of the wind, follows it with a sixth sense, a flier's sense, one that can't be localized but electrifies all his nerves. "To fly is a pure thing," he writes to his sister, Helga: "Up in the air it is the best of times." His eyes hidden behind aviator glasses and his blond hair beneath a flier's cap, he can calmly think things through. His view reaches all the way to Denmark, where Prince Hamlet dealt with similar problems. Like Hamlet, Harro must avenge a murdered father: Germany, poisoned by the Nazis. In no case can he adjust to the new power relationships or get in bed with the perpetrators, as so many are doing. He's wide awake up there in the sky, and that much more perceptive about what's playing out below. From a distance he registers the tremors of the continent like a seismograph: "I have the vague but certain feeling that in the end we are approaching a European catastrophe of massive proportions," he notes during these weeks — more than six years before the war actually does break out.

Once, in a heavy flying boat, he soars over the brick gothic Lübeck, home of the Nobel Prize–winning writer Thomas Mann, who had long since fled the Nazi terror for Switzerland. Would it not also be better for Harro to leave and live as a journalist and writer somewhere else, in a free country? Does he really have to fight against the regime? When he glides over the toy-size buildings of the flight school, over Warnemünde and Rostock and above all over the sea, he thinks of Henry Erlanger and knows that he cannot flee, but must instead be active. It's essential to operate sensitively, like in a glider: carefully discern the wind and use it for lift — not to nosedive, not to smash down. For everything, there is a right time, calm preparation, and if it's necessary to land, then land, and get out, step onto the terra firma of one's own convictions, so as not to sink in the "sea of hypocrisy and mediocrity," as he calls it, this world that "hails an empty hat on a stick."

This world certainly doesn't make it easy for him. The newly created Gestapo is now handling the Erlanger case and won't leave Harro alone at the German Air Transport School. Fritz Zietlow, a Nazi of the first hour who had signed up to be a Party member as early as 1923 and works in security services for SS Standartenführer Henze, contacts Regine Schütt and visits her several times at her apartment, aiming to convince her that Henry Erlanger killed himself. Zietlow continues to apply more and more pressure from afar, and the conflict with the authorities is coming to a head. Henry Erlanger's mother hasn't heard anything from the regime about the whereabouts of her son's remains. Then the police tell her a body has been fished out of the Hohenzollern Canal near Plötzensee with distinguishing marks that match her description in the missing person report. The mother is presented a mutilated corpse: It is indeed her son. Suicide is given as the cause of death — though from Harro she knows that isn't true. The body is cremated, the ashes handed over, and she has Henry interred at the family gravesite on the shores of the Rhein.

Still, despite repeated demands, for Harro it's out of the question to sign a false Gestapo report. In response to his refusal, Zietlow tells Regine point blank that it would be easy to cause a plane crash over the Baltic Sea.

Harro takes the threat seriously and stops his beloved flying. It is not the only thing he leaves behind. He now makes a clean break with Regine in order to be fully independent, standing before her and explaining his reasoning in rational terms, despite the fact that it tears him up inside, because he loves her and she loves him, too. But he's no longer able to show her the same level of emotion as he had before — and he doesn't know how to explain that to her. He no longer feels that he can satisfy her, that he can protect her and give her as much as she needs. "I will probably die for my beliefs," he tells her, and adds that he needs to be free to make that decision — and without feeling responsible for another. As a result he can no longer maintain a romantic relationship and suggests instead that she fight with him side by side, purely politically, without any romantic element.

Tears fill Regine's eyes. In place of the young, desirable fellow she'd wanted to spend her life with, she now sees a lost soul. Is it not more important to love than to be consumed by a futile battle?

If he wants to end their relationship, she tells him, he shouldn't hope to see her in the future under the guise of political solidarity.

Harro nods. He hadn't wanted it any other way. He is now alone.

## 4

On Harro's twenty-fourth birthday, September 2, 1933, the "grandest and largest fireworks show in the world" is set off — not for him, but at the first Nuremberg Party Rally. Leni Riefenstahl films it; Albert Speer lights it. Three hundred and forty chartered trains carry participants to Nuremberg, where victory over political opponents is celebrated triumphantly. "Power and its brutal exercise can achieve a lot," proclaims Hitler, while Goebbels tells the jubilant masses that the "settlement of the Jewish question by legal means" is just one part of much bigger plans, and he threatens "exceedingly unpleasant consequences for the entire Jewish race."

The message is clear as far as Harro is concerned: Henry Erlanger was one of the first Jews murdered by the Nazis but far from the last. The brownshirt regime is coming together terrifyingly, and nobody can hope any longer for its quick demise. Still, Harro doesn't let himself be intimidated. He sees political developments with clear eyes, and still views the ruling party's refusal to engage in discussion as its essence: "I see a mass of minions . . . , clueless citizens, gullible youths, but no great, clear statesmanlike spirit," he tells his father. When it comes to his emotional state, he reflects on his time at the flight school in a letter to his old *Gegner* colleague Adrien Turel:

> I'm convinced that you of all people will have understood why I've so thoroughly withdrawn into myself during these months. You must know that Warnemünde has meant primarily and above all a pupation, to use the language of insects . . . One just keeps one's mouth shut. At first I was still quite angry about all the events in Berlin. But I restrained myself and then came to see that I took a bite out of the political pie too early. As a result I had to take one on the chin.
> — Then I also began to see that this misstep made me stronger and more mature . . . Bit by bit my desire for action is growing again. I've cast off all resentments and fought to make myself fully accept the

new situation mentally. Without this self-transformation I might as well have thrown myself on the scrap heap. But I tell you, I've pulled it off.

It doesn't take long before his words are put to the test.

# 5

As autumn draws to a close, Harro takes the train back to Berlin. It's five below, but the thick gray coat of his uniform protects him, and protection he needs: He's been summoned by the Gestapo.

On a chilly November day, Harro enters for the first time the gloomy headquarters at Prinz-Albrecht-Strasse 8. Armed SS men stand on either side of the entrance. There's no sign identifying which agency is housed within, but Harro knows that unbound evil waits behind these walls.

Men in ill-fitting suits:
Gestapo headquarters at Prinz-Albrecht-Strasse 8 in Berlin.

As Harro enters the foyer, the doors — which have no handles on the inside — clang shut and lock behind him. Inside, a guard in a black uniform looks him over through a gatekeeper's window, asking for identification and the name of the official he's supposed to see. Harro holds out a summons. Another button is pushed, another buzzer, and he finds himself in a grand staircase. Leaded-glass windows give an almost churchlike effect, light falling on the parquet floors and arched ceilings. There's not a soul in sight, but Harro assumes he's being watched. Now he must prove he has himself under control.

He's greeted and escorted through a door into an office, where he takes a seat. Two officials are sitting there, one of whom is Zietlow. He asks Harro to finally confirm that Karl Heinrich Erlanger killed himself. That he'd been depressed for a long time, suicidal even, and due to the extreme nature of his condition, his treatment at the hands of the SS had caused him to take his own life. Zietlow has written out a statement and pushes it across the table.

Harro reads through it. There it is, the made-up story. It would be so easy just to sign it and take the pressure off himself. Should Harro stall? Should he ask for time to think it over, or smoke a cigarette? Would the police be willing to use violence to make him comply?

Harro doesn't sign the statement. Instead, he refuses to be subjected to further requests to falsify the truth. He walks out the door with his head held high, and as the lattice doors clang shut behind him, it sounds to him like the sweetest music.

"The relevant Commissar was very nice and conscientious," Harro notes after the interview. But he doesn't fool himself. When the Gestapo is "nice," it most likely means he'll have to be doubly wary going forward.

# 6

Warnemünde demonstrated to Harro that he could exist inside the system, that he could get by and not stand out: that is the first step. He has transformed himself from a bohemian who hoped to turn the world upside down by the sheer force of his charisma, with his boundless energy and passion for debate, into a disciplined soldier. Into someone whose interior life is opaque to outsiders. When his training ends on April 1, 1934, and the Imperial Air Ministry — Reichsluftfahrtministerium, or RLM for short — in Berlin is simultaneously restructured and starts to hire new personnel as part of Germany's ongoing attempt at rearmament, Harro applies for a position as a simple office clerk.

He has two reasons for doing so: First, Göring's ministry is one of the most powerful in the capital, and full of career opportunities; second, he can feel secure there in the knowledge that according to law the Luftwaffe is subject only to its own jurisdiction — meaning he'll be shielded from the Gestapo. "I could have found far better things to do in financial terms, but at the moment I don't think of that as the main concern, but rather my personal security," Harro tells his parents when he's hired.

The decision has been made: Harro moves back to Berlin, the city where he had spent so much time, where he had been tortured and seen his friend murdered. He returns to a place full of memories both fond and traumatic, renting a small apartment on his own in a new neighborhood in a western part of town.

It is not an easy restart. The Air Ministry has some rigid rules. On his first day of work in Behrenstrasse in Berlin's Mitte neighborhood, he must sign a paper handed to him by Flight Captain Hilmer Freiherr von Bülow, the head of the department where Harro is starting, Abteilung IV Fremde Luftmächte, or Foreign Air Forces. According to the paper, Harro must pledge to always lift his right arm and simultaneously say "Heil Hitler" by way of greeting.

To his relief, Harro quickly learns that neither von Bülow nor Major Karl Bartz, for whom Harro will be working as adjutant, are fanatical Nazis. They are aviators through and through, who put a "downright touching effort" into their new hire, as Harro writes to his parents.

And his job is also not too demanding. Every day he must read foreign papers, magazines, and journals for information on the capabilities of rival countries' air forces. The latest editions of Moscow's *Pravda* as well as the *New York Times* are delivered to his desk each morning by intelligence services. It is something that interests him anyway: to stay informed outside of the Nazi propaganda organs, which for the majority of Germans have become the lone source of news. Finally he can make use of his talent for languages, his good English, French, and Swedish. In addition, he decides to join the student circle around his old friend Werner Dissel and a few others who work on their Russian in their free time.

But there is something that bothers him about the new position: the poor wages of just 120 marks per month. The low pay is partly due to Harro's lack of academic credentials. Even though "earthly goods" have become even more trivial to him since the attack on the *Gegner* offices, when the SS stole everything from him, he's still bitter about the exploitation he experiences at the giant bureaucracy, which leads to his having virtually no life outside of work. This parsimoniousness reinforces his anti-capitalist leanings. If there is good money being earned in the imperial capital, then surely it is at the Air Ministry, where the aircraft and arms industries are engineering lucrative deals with the regime, lining the pockets of managers and high-level officials. Göring, whose substantial belly no longer fits in a cockpit and mandates a custom-made uniform, creates a slipstream of corruption. But for the ordinary employees, who work their tails off from morning to night, there's nothing left; their paltry wages aren't even paid on time.

Harro's initial hope to quickly build a career evaporates as a result. The march through such an institution — in order to change things from within — is arduous and paved with obstacles. Regardless of how friendly Bartz and von Bülow are, Harro isn't happy spending this valuable time in his life without even being fairly compensated. "One is hired," he reports home, "and must, according to popular opinion, be 'happy if you receive your contract by Christmas'! ... It's spectacularly antisocial to let someone work like a dog all day but to drag things out on the bureaucratic front."

To the outside world, the Air Ministry presents an aura of professionalism and efficiency and inspires an impression of a modern, highly technical approach to the art of war, but in fact the Behrenstrasse-based ministry is hobbled by sloppiness and sluggishness, Harro realizes. There's a prevailing mood of fear and conformity that creeps into every office. If the ministry had once had a code of honor as a civilian institution, it becomes apparent to Harro that it is now a rather dishonorable mixture: hard-core Nazism paired with naked greed in the face of the fabulous profits flowing to the aircraft industry as a result of the arms buildup.

The conditions at his office seem to Harro to mirror the streets of Berlin and the entire country, as economic challenges abound. The ranks of the unemployed begin to rise again in 1934; the economic surge of the first months after Hitler's ascent to power has receded. Just as Harro prophesied, the Nazi regime cannot make good on the "socialist" promises of its program and fights internal contradictions.

The way the Nazis deal with social problems is revealed to Harro on May 1, formerly a day to celebrate workers, now renamed in 1934 the National Holiday of the German People. Harro is on duty and must report to the Tempelhof airfield at 10:00 a.m. sharp. There, an endless mass has gathered, "shoved together in horrible cattle market-like pens," as he describes it in a letter to his sister, Helga. "The women sweated, took off their shoes and sat around in their stockings. The men ate sausages and drank beer, as much as they could get hold of. The sun beat down mercilessly." Maypoles stand around festooned with swastikas; signs for the

German Labor Front, which has replaced the unions, hang here and there. To Harro it all seems forced. Then the Reich chancellor speaks. Harro manages to slip out a gap in the fence at one o'clock: "Hitler's speech was nothing but hot air," he writes Helga: "Not a single original thought. Anyway, it doesn't matter . . . Deeds are stronger than any words. And since he spoke so despairingly about the grousers, I don't want to needlessly increase their number."

In the following days, Harro catches wind at the ministry: Everywhere there are rumblings behind the scenes. Demands for a second, real national *socialist* revolution are getting louder. It's the crack in the Nazi system that Harro had predicted: the friction between the conservative camp, which feels a sense of obligation toward industry, and the radical socialist-oriented wing orbiting SA commander Röhm, who is tied to the masses and the youth. Will the Hitler regime fracture along this fault line? The Reichsmark is already weakening on the currency markets in London. "The political atmosphere here in Berlin," Harro writes to his father, "is charged as if with electricity."

The air temperature is also heating up during these weeks. According to the calendar it's still spring, but it feels as if summer has long since arrived. The sky above the capital is cobalt blue, the air humid, summer storms breaking out.

# 7

June 20, 1934, is the hottest June 20 on record. Harro's boss, Hermann Göring, tarries north of Berlin that day in Brandenburg's Schorfheide, where all the villages are decorated because the body of his first wife, Carin, who died in 1931 of tuberculosis, is to be interred at the hunting retreat named after her, Carinhall, not far from Schloss Liebenberg. Hitler, Himmler, and Goebbels are all on Göring's guest list.

An incident on the drive north demonstrates how tense the situation is. While on the Autobahn from Berlin, the windshield of Himmler's Mercedes shatters — an attack, or just a harmless pebble? The column comes to a screeching halt, and SS men jump out and scour the nearby woods, finding nothing.

Later on this oppressively hot day Göring proudly shows his companions his new country manor, complete with firing range, tennis court, boat houses, subterranean bunkers, antiaircraft installation, a swan house, and — for his favorite pets — a lion enclosure. Afterward, the henchmen gather in the great hall, fuss about the apparent attack on the Autobahn, speculate as to who might have been behind it . . . and discuss an upcoming covert action: a planned strike against SA commander Röhm.

It is the final meeting of the Nazi triumvirate before the so-called Night of the Long Knives, their planned attempt to curb the influence of the powerful SA — the very organization that is Harro's last hope that the national-socialist takeover may yet trigger social reforms that benefit the common people.

For his war plans, Hitler needs to maintain a good relationship with the high command of the Wehrmacht, as well as business leaders. Even though Röhm is an old friend of Hitler's, and a Nazi of the first hour, the head of the SA has become a double threat: Röhm wishes to outshine the Wehrmacht's standing with his paramilitary SA — and his socialist tendencies are anathema to the industry bosses. In addition, Röhm's privately well-known homosexuality is a thorn in the side of the former chicken breeder and self-appointed keeper of public morality, Himmler. Through the displacement of Röhm, Himmler also wants his SS, long in the shadow of the SA, to evolve into the leading organization — and, most important, into an economic empire. The concentration camps, run in his eyes in a financially inefficient way by the SA, will be reorganized and form the foundation of a corporate SS, with Himmler serving as the black-uniformed CEO.

The decisive internal reckoning to take care of all social revolutionary aspirations within the Nazi movement once and for all takes place on June 30, 1934. Just prior, the rumor is spread that Röhm is planning a putsch to seize power for himself. At two in the morning, Hitler's plane takes off from near Bonn, landing at about four a.m. in Munich, the "capital of the movement," where he immediately heads to the Bavarian Interior Ministry. The Munich police commissioner and local commander of the SA are ordered there. In a feigned fit of rage, Hitler rips off their epaulets, accuses them of treason, and has them arrested.

At five in the morning, when the heat is still lingering enough to make everyone sweat, the dictator — who had wanted to wait for reinforcements in the form of his personal guard regiment — can no longer stand it. He's worried that Röhm, who is at a lakeside retreat with the entire SA leadership, has gotten wind of the planned assault and is organizing a counterattack.

Impetuously Hitler presses a few SS men into service as escorts. After an hour-and-a-half drive through the Bavarian countryside, they reach the lake, Tegernsee. CLOSED TO THE PUBLIC, it says on a sign outside Hotel Hanselbauer in Bad Wiessee, where the SA leaders are still in bed.

At six-thirty a.m., Hitler storms into room number seven with a whip in his hand, as his chauffeur later testifies, and screams at his close friend, who looks up from his mattress equally bleary and scared: "Röhm, you're under arrest!" Röhm's brown silk shirt and immaculately tailored pants are neatly folded over a chair. "Heil, my Führer!" stammers the SA chief, wiping the sleep from his eyes. Hitler screams a second time: "You are under arrest!" Meanwhile black uniforms enter the other rooms of the hotel and drag the hungover SA leaders, who had caroused wildly that night, into the hallways. The massacre begins. Over a hundred people are shot, including Röhm.

Along with the murders come character assassinations. Goebbels uses the fact that a few of the men were sharing beds at the hotel to discredit the fatally stricken SA. Once again, as was the case with Libertas's grandfather, Fürst Philipp, and Kaiser Wilhelm II, homophobia is being politically weaponized in Germany.

# 8

Harro's parents are worried about their son. The wave of murders that summer of 1934 isn't limited to just members of the SA. Kurt von Schleicher, for instance, the last chancellor of the Weimar Republic, as well as Ferdinand von Bredow, the former deputy army minister, Georg Strasser, a social revolutionary member of the Nazi Party, and others disliked by the regime are also killed. Harro is spared during the purge — not a given, considering his history as a troublemaker — but it is clear to him: There is no longer any hope of evolution within the regime. The "socialist" branch of the Party has been chopped off — a more apt description going forward would be national-capitalist rather than national-socialist.

Ambivalent in his thinking on how to proceed, Harro spends the summer nights walking through the Charlottenburg neighborhood, nervous, uneasy, "dressed slovenly and dingy," as a friend attests — all out of character for him. His only diversion is a new batch of guys he meets while using a friend's paddleboat, which he occasionally borrows from its spot at a small marina on the Havel called Blau-Rot. The leader of this new clique is named Richard von Raffay, known as Ricci, an advertising illustrator from Hamburg, "calm and always funny," as Harro describes him in a letter.

They gladly take Harro along when they go out at night, to the Lunte, for instance, "a third rate Bohemian bar," to the artists' café Josty on Leipziger Strasse near Potsdamer Platz, or to swing at Rio-Rita-Club.

But it's not the same as before, when he bar-hopped with Henry. Harro no longer comes home at dawn feeling like a hero, as he had in the days of the *Gegner*. He no longer writes articles supposed to change the world while Regine cradles him in her arms; now he crawls under the covers alone for a bit of sleep before it's back to "Heil Hitler" at the ministry.

# 9

Metro-Goldwyn-Mayer manages to have four of the top ten most successful films in Germany in 1934. Libertas does her job well. But will she get a chance to further develop professionally? It's not easy for a woman to carve out a career in Nazi Germany, and the Hollywood studio is no exception. Her idea of using her work at MGM as a steppingstone toward her true goal of one day making her own films turns out to have been naïve. She can't get beyond tasks related to publicity, and considers quitting.

Libertas at work for MGM.

But what else can she do? The possibility of getting a degree — especially as a young woman — has been greatly reduced since the 1933 introduction of a law designed to lower the number of students in German colleges and universities by 10 percent. Working in publicity for MGM has introduced her to a slew of journalists, and she ponders whether that might be a way forward professionally: to become a film critic at a newspaper or magazine.

She has made new connections in her private life, too, and these prove fateful. Libertas has also gotten to know Richard von Raffay, and on July 14, 1934, she goes sailing on his boat, christened the *Haizuru,* in lovely seventy-five-degree weather. She's lying on deck in a bikini — officially known as a *Zweiteiler,* or two-piece, something forbidden in public since the passage of the 1932 Zwickererlass, a law regulating bathing clothes — when a paddleboat pulls alongside.

There's only one source that describes the initial encounter. It's a poem Libertas writes about first meeting Harro, describing the golden afternoon light and the arrival of a young man with windblown hair. Ricci von Raffay doesn't miss the mutual attraction between the two, and tactfully asks to be dropped off at the marina, taking his leave and urging Harro and Libertas to continue sailing alone on his boat.

Libertas enjoying the freedom of being on the water.

As Libertas's poem details, "the warm July night" is filled with "caresses" and "bliss" because "their souls had found each other."

When Harro removes his shirt, she is startled to see the welts, which are still visible on his body, the wounds that in places have turned to scars, and as he talks to her, quietly and hesitantly and at points passionately, with an intense look on his face, she runs her fingers over his lesions. A long-desired understanding starts to well up in Libertas, and in Harro, as he senses her tenderness, much-needed healing begins.

# 10

Both have unbelievable energy. There's never a dull moment. They race breathlessly through a beautiful summer. They're young and good-looking, and both come from interesting family backgrounds. Her family name is grander, though unlike hers, his family's reputation is impeccable, with the keyword being Tirpitz. What Harro has — familial security, parents who are approachable — is exactly what's missing for Libertas, who can instead brag of a palace up north.

On August first, Harro moves in to Ricci von Raffay's apartment on Hohenzollerndamm. His isolation is over: now there are large collective dinners to which Libertas also comes. They hold hands, cuddle, go to the cinema, see *Queen Christina* starring Greta Garbo, a new Western with John Wayne, a Johnny Weissmuller Tarzan movie. They also go to clubs and dance through the night at the Jockey Bar, where the pianist, a man named Engel who later joins the Comedian Harmonists, combines a repertoire of jazz and pop standards with bits of Bach and Mozart. Or they go to restaurants, particularly trendy new Asian locales. On Kantstrasse, for instance, one can "eat real Chinese food, with lots of rice, bamboo, spicy sauces, and strange fish."

It is the beginning of a period in Harro's life — he will turn twenty-five on September 2, 1934 — that resembles normality, if not for the swastikas hanging from building façades everywhere. Even if he hadn't wanted a girlfriend since splitting with Regine, he and Libertas are well suited to each other, and the chemistry in bed is good. Harro presupposes knowledge of the Liebenberg scandal when he writes to his parents about Libertas: "She can't do anything about the fact that she's the granddaughter of old Eulenburg. She certainly has none of the qualities ascribed to him."

Harro couldn't make himself seem more innocuous and solid in the eyes of the Gestapo. Being with Libertas from Schloss Liebenberg — she's even a Nazi Party member — seems anything but communist. "I have to hang around with perfectly harmless, good people; they are the ideal associates," he writes to his parents.

For Libertas, as well, the new relationship works. Harro quenches her thirst for knowledge and has an earnestness and depth that speaks to her and dovetails with her own aspirations for intellectual and poetic profundity. Not to mention that he's darn good-looking — and thank goodness he doesn't want to have kids at the moment, and, like her, also rejects the traditional gender roles espoused by the Nazis.

They like to go sailing together, spending as much time as possible on Ricci's jolly boat, which he generously lets them have — they need only pay a small maintenance fee, and the mooring cost at the marina, which they get at a discounted rate anyway. With the sun shining above them, the land quiet and smelling of summer, with just the sound of the breeze in the leaves along the shore, they spend August and September of 1934 floating on the Havel and Wannsee. When the wind picks up they have to be able to count on each other, one of them shouting orders and the other following them without question. When the clouds turn red in the evening they spend the night on the water, making love on the boat while swinging at anchor in some cove.

Passion-fueled *Gegner*, or "adversaries":
Harro and Libertas sailing on Wannsee.

Then it's fall, and Richard von Raffay and his two buddies move out of the apartment on Hohenzollerndamm. Libertas moves in on the first of

October. The couple sublets the other two newly free rooms and maintains a communal style of living. Soon Libs buys a used Opel convertible for a thousand marks. She dubs it Spengler, after Oswald Spengler, the author of the cultural philosophical book *The Decline of the West*. One can only speculate as to whether Libs is showing intellectual pessimism or whether the reference to the populist Spengler is an indication of her still right-wing political views. Either way, Spengler, the car, takes them to all the nice parts of Berlin and even out to relax at Liebenberg, where Libs rides her horse Scherzo while Harro lies on the banks of Lankesee, the family's private lake.

This amorous existence still has little to do with resistance. On the surface, they hew to the rules. They take part in the reception of a British air force attaché — a friend of Libertas's — where there's nothing but high-ranking officers and foreign diplomats and where they make a good impression as a couple; they go on work outings with colleagues from the Air Ministry, and it helps Harro's reputation, because Libertas charms everyone.

Harro's strategy has worked. Everything looks unsuspicious and promising, and the attractive pair, apparently "Aryan" through and through, become a model couple in the Reich capital.

# 11

In this year, 1935, the previously active underground network of illegal publications and flyers of the Social Democrats and Communists barely exists anymore. The Gestapo has infiltrated nearly everywhere with their informants and has largely smashed the illegal work of the Communist Party, which was aimed at preserving its organizational structures. Many people have been taken in, too, including individuals who aren't even leftists.

Harro, observing this, may come to the conclusion that such rigid connections, not based on personal relationships, aren't well suited to oppositional activity in a totalitarian system. Smaller circles, on the other hand, driven not by ideology but by friendship, are tougher to penetrate.

The necessity of action becomes clear in the summer of 1935, when openly anti-Semitic riots break out in the heart of the capital. The flashpoint is a comedic movie enjoying a successful run in the cinemas of Ku'damm: *Pettersson & Bendel,* a Swedish production, and the first foreign film deemed to have "national-political value" by Goebbels. During the film's run, a rumor starts that Jewish viewers keep disrupting the screenings. The daily *Berliner Tageszeitung* picks up the story, and this leads to anti-Semitic attacks in Charlottenburg, the preferred residential quarter of doctors, bankers, lawyers, and artists and of the Jewish upper class and cultural avant-garde. The quarter, by the way, where the dead Henry Erlanger's parents also still live.

On July 15, 1935, a brown-shirted mob assembles in front of a cinema on Kurfürstendamm and assaults passersby they take for Jews. Others protest in front of Jewish-owned businesses and cafés, and attack "Jewish race defilers." For four days, until July 19, 1935, police are unable or unwilling to get the situation under control. "The same people who took part in the riots yesterday are here today at least in part in uniform, on duty, in order to prevent a repeat of events," Harro reports bitterly to his parents.

The Nazi leadership instrumentalizes the events on Kurfürstendamm to fan the flames of public outrage, a supposedly authentic phenomenon that is in actuality artificially induced by Goebbels's propaganda. Also, the regime uses the protests in Berlin's center as justification for the Nuremburg Race Laws that will be agreed to at the party conference of 1935 and which lay out the legal framework for the discrimination, persecution, and later extermination of Jews in Germany.

Even though Harro has no way of knowing how bad things are about to get, he surely can see the storm clouds gathering on the horizon.

# 12

For Christmas of 1935, the couple, now together for a year and a half, travels to Harro's parents' house in Mülheim in western Germany. Libertas is introduced to the family and has the expected impact. Father Erich Edgar, usually so reserved, is enthused. Harro's little brother, Hartmut, falls on the spot for the charming young lady from the castle. Libertas announces to the family that things are "getting ever more grand and beautiful" between herself and Harro. Then she inspects their place. If it was exotic for Harro to go to her family stead and see for the first time the empty suits of armor in the Nordic Hall and the whale's teeth brought from Norway by Fürst Philipp, it is no less fun for her to enter his family's bourgeois abode. Since Erich Edgar spent years as a ship's captain, he has not only antique furniture from all over the world but also drums, a giant gong from China, kilims and carpets from Africa and the Middle East, and tons of books, including tomes and original folios.

Excited and thankful to finally have been given a "family home," she unpacks her accordion and over the course of the evening plays and sings Christmas songs, scout songs, and various folk songs, in German, English, and French. Even Harro's mother, Marie Luise, who is skeptical of the pairing because she had pictured Harro with a solid daughter of the bourgeoisie instead of a difficult-to-read, scandal-tinged blue blood, must admit that Libertas has her amusing qualities, as well as an emotional depth and intensity that she knows all too well herself, qualities she alone in the family has displayed up to now.

For dinner they have roast pork ribs and sauerkraut. Christmas Eve is traditionally a night of simple home-style cooking so as not to necessitate too much work for the housewife. Marie Luise is a miserable chef anyway, who barely does well with anything beyond a fruit compote. It has never bothered Erich Edgar; he's used to it and praises even the most botched dishes. For his part, Harro wolfs down anything edible. Libertas, too, is not troubled by Marie Luise's imperfect cooking. She's eaten royally often enough, and enjoys the hearty food in Mülheim. Everything seems very down-home to her, and she is touched to be the newly discovered daughter of the house. Libertas is even taken with Marie Luise's sometimes overbearing mothering of Harro, because such caring parenting is something she missed out on. The girl from the castle has never experienced such intimacy.

As for the invasiveness that sometimes comes to light in Harro's mother, Libertas takes it for loving — which it is — while overlooking the gulf between his parents, looking past how divided the couple is on many things, how much is swept under the carpet, how they've replaced love with a sort of grudging tolerance. Harro's parents have long slept in separate quarters, the decorations of which reveal much about their respective characters: Erich Edgar's room is ascetic, minimal, like a monk's cell, with a single bed, dresser, and a wash basin with nothing but a toothbrush and razor, while Marie Luise's chamber is far larger, stuffed with her effects, perfume bottles, and knickknacks, and even has its own foyer, featuring a lush greenhouse.

Christmas: emotional, fragile hours. The central heating creates a comforting warmth, the decorated tree is lit up, and then there's the gift-giving: a large breadbox, glass measuring cups, a meat grinder, robes. Nothing luxurious, just more or less utilitarian household items. But this doesn't bother Libertas either. She enjoys it, lounging in a comfy chair, a glass of Mosel wine in her hand, listening to Erich Edgar's funny stories as he sits up as straight as if he'd swallowed a broomstick. He tells a story about Harro, how as a boy he'd seen a man leaving the building with a sack over his shoulder, a full sack; and then he'd noticed the carpets missing from the hallway — and he chased after the man. *Thief!* Harro called, and the man dropped his sack. The carpets were returned to the staircase and everyone was grateful to the kid.

Like the others, Harro enjoys the old stories. The praise does him good, including when the talk turns to his high school diploma, which read in part that it was hoped the nation would benefit from his intellectual gifts. But Harro knows it's about more than stolen carpets these days, and when he looks around at his family — and in particular, at his mother — and then extrapolates from them to the general populace, he finds himself worrying. He gets into a dispute with her on this Christmas Eve, because she makes an offhand comment that Libertas has a "Jewish mouth." As Marie Luise puts it: "I can't get past her Jewish mouth." Harro had already had a similar argument with her the previous summer, when she used an X-ray of his head as an excuse to praise his supposedly "round skull," which would mark him as Aryan. "As long as you say such things," he had written her at the time, "you can't be surprised that I consider a debate with you hopeless. In fact, what you said about a 'round skull' isn't even correct, by the way, but your fundamental attitude toward the whole problem tells me the extent to which you've become a tool of certain very base opinions." In just two and a half years, an intelligent woman who'd had the guts to take on the SS over Henry Erlanger's murder has been so thoroughly distorted that she now thinks in terms of "racial hygiene."

Harro and his mother also diverge when it comes to their respective views on women. In a letter written a few weeks after Christmas, he returns to the theme, which he also considers political:

> If Libs spends her day helping me with work, that is far more sensible and beneficial than if she were to set up in the kitchen and cook, or go to the market, or dust. I do not under any circumstances wish to institute in our home the general middle-European punishment of damning the woman to the kitchen. And not because I maintain some sort of revolutionary or pie in the sky ideas, but exclusively because any marriage between me and Libs not built on a common life's work would be one built on sand, specifically on the degrading condition of women in bourgeois society.

On Christmas Eve, Harro's father had pulled him aside, letting him know that however his son likes to lead his partnership, it shouldn't remain an open, unconventional arrangement.

Marriage — Harro doesn't like it, but the word hangs in the air, and just like Libertas, he understands: Erich Edgar has a point. Without a legal bond, their life together sticks out, and Harro doesn't want that for reasons of personal safety. There is also the more practical matter related to his still paltry wages at the Air Ministry: Marriage would have financial advantages, because a newly married Libs would receive 10,000 marks from her family.

On Easter of 1936, they travel to Liebenberg in order to discuss the details with Libertas's mother, Tora, and on July 26 of that same year, the deed is done. The way Harro writes the invitation to his parents shows the inner distance he feels toward the event:

> On Sunday morning, both civil and church ceremonies. Arrival of a few more close family guests (final total: 18). I've struck the hymn "Jesu geh voran" ("Jesus, Still Lead On") from the program and suggested instead "Eine feste Burg" ("A Mighty Fortress is Our God") which Hartmut must learn by heart, since one person at least must sing. The minister will keep it short. He knows this. Afterwards a big lunch. Libs and I will then depart. You can spend the rest of the afternoon taking walks and sipping tea.

The Schulzes travel from Mülheim a day ahead, and Harro's sister, Helga, comes from Venice with her Italian husband, Carlo. All get their own rooms in the castle, even young brother Hartmut. Making an exception, Harro sports neither his Luftwaffe uniform nor his blue sweater but puts on a tuxedo instead. Libs wears a white dress her father, the fashion designer, back at the castle for the first time in ages, has created for the occasion.

The marriage takes place in the castle's little chapel. It's a "nice and atmospheric wedding, even if not very grand," as Libs's mother, Tora, describes it. She sings "Monatsrose," the first of the five rose songs by her father, Philipp. The married couple receives the obligatory copy of Hitler's *Mein Kampf* from the civil authorities, then they all sit on the terrace, decorated with paper lanterns. Erich Edgar gives an impeccable speech, for which he has done impossibly lengthy preparations. They eat and, particularly pleasing to Harro's father, drink good wine from the Liebenberg cellar. There's pike in mayonnaise, venison with greens and homemade lingonberry preserves, and also a spinach dish with delicate pastry pieces in the form of an imaginary goddess of freedom called Libertas Fleurons. The dessert is dedicated to Harro: Fliegerbombe, or "Aerial Bomb," a creation made with ice cream, cake, candied and fresh fruit, nuts, whipped cream, and chocolate sauce.

Could they be any less conspicuous? Harro, Libertas, and her mother, Gräfin Tora zu Eulenburg, at Schloss Liebenberg during Easter, 1936.

After the meal, cognac and other spirits are served in the Nordic Hall. Erich Edgar smokes one of the three cigarettes he allows himself per day, and there are gifts: Libs gets five hundred marks and a porcelain set from Uncle Wend, silverware from her mother. New towels and sheets come from Marie Luise and Erich Edgar. Marie Luise has had every piece of linen embroidered with the initial SB. The double name Schulze-Boysen, earlier used by Harro only unofficially because he likes the debonair sound better than Schulze on its own, is, with the marriage, now official and entered into the civil registries for Libertas as well. She's in a terrific mood, because with this day she starts a new act, a leap into freedom, she hopes, reflecting her first name — a freedom, however, that can be dangerous under a dictatorship when your spouse is Harro.

# 13

After the honeymoon, which they spend in Sweden visiting relatives of Libertas's and friends of Harro's, the newlyweds return to Berlin, which is festively decked out: the Olympics have been taking place there since the first of August, 1936. "The women wear pretty summer clothes, pleasant young Fräuleins in breezy white dresses hand the laurel crowns to the winners, and the proud new German flag is hoisted for German gold medal winners by sailors in shiny uniforms," Harro's earlier acquaintance Ernst von Salomon writes of the spectacle. "The streets are teeming with foreigners."

But the visitors don't see the true face of the Reich capital; they experience a sanitized, masked version. The display cases for the weekly Nazi propaganda paper *Stürmer*, with its anti-Semitic headlines, have disappeared, just like the signs barring Jews from using public benches; the beach at Wannsee, where it has become customary to wear party insignias on bathing suits, is once again open to Jewish bathers during the Olympic Games. Germany presents itself as a nation of rules, morals, and rights. But it must be clear to the international guests who wander the city center that this peaceful air is only a façade as soon as they walk past the newly dedicated Imperial Air Ministry facility, the menacing new office where Harro works.

In this largest of the administrative buildings of the Third Reich, consisting of several four- to six-story wings and a total of seven kilometers of hallways connecting more than two thousand offices, a large-scale war is being planned. Apparently built in fast motion, though actually erected by six thousand construction workers laboring around the clock in three shifts, this giant vessel, determined to conquer the world, is directly next to the old War Ministry, which will be decommissioned because it is too small, and torn down. Göring's team will take up residence within the new steel-reinforced concrete skeleton: three thousand men strong, including a sizable engineering department to develop new aircraft and construct air bases around the world. Scores of stenographers will type up the military-industrial concepts of tomorrow.

This enormous new Air Ministry is a nerve center of the Nazi brain — but also a tumor. Poison will be produced here, poured into metal, and carried across the sky in order to kill people down on the ground. Here,

59

Nazism takes flight into the upper atmosphere, reaches for the stars, and tries to extend steel arms over all the mountains and oceans of the globe. It's an architectural bridge between the old governmental quarter surrounding the Reich chancellery and the new center of power on Prinz-Albrecht-Strasse, where the Gestapo has its headquarters on the border of Kreuzberg — and where Himmler lives. A giant building that is to make Berlin a global capital: hard-lined and straight, coolly minimalist with modernist functionality, yet ideologically charged. The façade is decorated with shell limestone from Franconia. Not only is this material heavy, it also looks grave and hard. In good weather, the edifice where today Germany's Finance Ministry is housed seems to gleam white from within. It is an ephemeral white, however, that turns noir when it rains.

On his first day of work in August 1936, Harro enters from Wilhelmstrasse, passes between the five-meter-high bronze eagles in the so-called Court of Honor, and enters a cast-iron gate into the receiving hall, which is anything but welcoming with its low stone ceiling lit by blazing cressets formed of upturned lances, which are placed behind screens in stone niches. Harro's shadow dances on the granite floor in the flickering light of the flames; granite covers all the surfaces, including the columns, some of which are not load-bearing but instead meant to create a feeling of being trapped. Shadows skitter across the "Blood Flag" from Hitler's Beer Hall Putsch in Munich of November 9, 1923, during which Göring sustained a gunshot wound in his lower body, making him a morphine addict.

Harro climbs the set of stairs beyond the stone reception hall, not seeing where they lead because the light gleams so brightly on them. All he can make out are the grandiloquent words posted below the relief of the Air Ministry eagle with its twenty-foot wingspan:

*Newly formed again*
*The German Wehrmacht*
*The German cities and beautiful villages*
*They are protected*
*Over them watches the strength of the nation*
*Watches the Luftwaffe*

Harro's fingers glide along the railing made of aircraft aluminum, the signature metal of the air force. He nods to colleagues, passes innumerable doors, crosses evermore hallways and more doors, and hops onto an oak-clad paternoster that, at more than a half meter per second, takes him upstairs much faster than the elevators in other Berlin buildings.

What's strange is the feeling in the long hallway on the fifth floor that leads toward the door with the number 5148 on it — his office. It is so eerily quiet all of a sudden that he hears the clicking heels of approaching patrol guards still several corners away. Long before they come into view he has reached the door to his new workspace, turns the handle, and enters.

One hundred and sixty square feet, standard size for individual offices at the ministry, with a wall of cabinets, an integrated sink, and a safe to store sensitive documents. Left and right as one enters are two doors, which stand open. They connect Harro's room to what is known as the officials' corridor, through which all internal visits and activity take place. It's the reason the external hallways are so empty and quiet, enabling the patrol to march up and down unimpeded and make the place seem so "stately," just as Göring wanted it.

Harro loosens his belt and hangs up his peaked cap, then looks out the window, its frame also made of aircraft-grade aluminum. Outside is the bustle of Leipziger Strasse and the temple-like façade of Wertheim, Europe's largest department store.

Even before Hitler had become Germany's chancellor, it had always been the Führer's goal to one day conquer Berlin's Wilhelmstrasse. With the new Air Ministry, which takes over an entire block on this axis of power, he's finally managed to do so. But just as the Nazis have arrived here, so too has the resistance against them — in the slender figure of Harro, standing at the window, looking out.

# 14

The first military secret that Harro learns behind the limestone façade is a major one. Werner Dissel, his friend from the *Gegner* days, is by now a soldier stationed at the town of Neuruppin in northern Brandenburg, the birthplace of the writer Theodor Fontane. Dissel meets Harro at the casino of the Aviator's Club, which belongs to the Air Ministry. They sit there among all sorts of Luftwaffe officers, and Harro urges his friend not to lower his voice. Only those who speak very quietly seem suspicious. Dissel finds this difficult, however, because what he wishes to report is not for anybody's ears: Two tank regiments stationed outside of Neuruppin have marching orders for Spain.

The disclosure dovetails with information Harro himself has heard at the ministry. Under top secrecy, though easily picked up at his desk through the always open officials' corridor, the Luftwaffe is planning what's known as Operation Condor. It's being run by Sonderstab W, or Special Staff W, under the leadership of the Luftwaffe general Helmuth Wilberg. Participating soldiers receive bonus pay and an expedited discharge. They travel to Spain in civilian clothes, disguised as vacationers, to take part in a "Strength Through Joy" trip organized by the large state-run tourism operator of Nazi Germany. But instead of receiving a hotel room on the beach upon arrival, they are handed an olive-brown uniform without any stripes of rank. Dressed this way, they support the troops of the fascist general Franco in his putsch against the democratically elected leftist government in Madrid. Apart from General von Goltz's activities in the Baltics and Finland during the Russian Civil War, it's the first time since 1918 that German soldiers are active abroad, even if undercover.

When, a few nights after the conversation with Dissel, Harro learns that right-wing saboteurs are to be planted in Barcelona, a republican bastion, to foment a counterrevolutionary movement with the support of Germans, he wishes to warn the authorities there. It's a big moment for him — a turning point. Before, he merely contemplated resistance from within. Now he aims to actively engage in it, putting his life on the line — and those of his friends and potential collaborators.

It's handy that right at this time the London journalist Evan James is staying with him on Hohenzollerndamm. He's a distant acquaintance of Libertas, and is reporting on the Olympics and the atmosphere in Berlin. Harro asks him to pass the list of fascist saboteurs to the BBC. But the young Englishman refuses. It's too risky, he claims, and he wouldn't want to jeopardize his career. Reporting on the Spanish civil war isn't his job.

This response seems to Harro both disappointing and symptomatic of Britain's hands-off approach to Hitler, leaving the dictator alone in the hope that he will be a bulwark against communism while ignoring that his aggression is aimed in *all* directions. Evan James is mimicking in a minute way the appeasement policy pursued by Prime Minister Chamberlain. Harro, with the experience of the torture cellar, knows that appeasement won't work with the Nazis. Still, he's not discouraged by this failed attempt. He decides from now on to conscientiously gather material that will demonstrate Germany's involvement in the Spanish civil war. He's not sure yet how he intends to use this information, but collecting it is a necessary first step.

He gradually realizes that with his decision to work at the Air Ministry he has placed himself in a strategically significant starting point; he's in close proximity to a treasure trove of data. In order to increase his access to it, though, he needs to rise through the bureaucratic ranks, and therefore becomes zealous in his job, executing all his work at the highest level, even writing fawning pieces for the Luftwaffe's house newsletter.

His efforts bear fruit. In an internal staff review, his supervisor, Bartz, attests:

> As the son of a navy officer, S.B. has undoubtedly had a particularly good upbringing, and above and beyond that has with great diligence continued to work to improve himself, so that despite his youth he can be addressed as a fully-fledged personality in intellectual and social terms. He has a fundamentally reputable attitude and view of life, and a characteristic noble-mindedness . . . His always friendly, helpful manner and the straightforwardness of his entire demeanor have made him chummy and very well-liked. Socially he's a good conversationalist, but doesn't overstep the boundaries of his youth during hotly debated discussions and avoids any brusqueness.

A somewhat naïve but at the same time accurate characterization of Harro — though so far they've passed him over for promotions because, it is whispered, of his questionable political views. His lack of a university degree doesn't help things, either. So how is he to ascend in the RLM?

# 15

Enter Libertas. It's her first mission, and she's probably not thinking of any planned illegal activities but that her help is simply beneficial to Harro's career. Toward that end, she deploys her most effective weapon: her charm.

The target is Hermann Göring, her husband's boss, whose country home, Carinhall, is not far from her family castle, and whose forester is the son of the Liebenberg forester. The forester has gushed to the corpulent Nazi huntsman about the rich supply of fallow deer at Liebenberg, legendary record-setting bucks that had enchanted Kaiser Wilhelm thirty years prior. Libertas knows that her uncle Wend received an official call announcing Göring's desire to come in order to fell a prime specimen. On the day of the visit, September 6, 1936, Libertas, too, arrives at Liebenberg.

From her room she watches as three black Mercedes limousines roll onto the palace grounds and park next to the spiked helmet fountain the

Kaiser had given her grandfather when they were still friendly. Göring gets out and repairs with his retinue to the rutting ground, a clearing created for the animals.

Göring during a fallow buck hunt.

After the Reich Minister has blown away two fallow bucks, there's a high tea inside the palace. The honored guest changes attire, putting on a silk shirt with puff sleeves, a leather doublet, and a broad belt that has a platinum buckle and diamonds in the shape of a stag. A forty-centimeter cutlass hangs at his side. It too is decorated with diamonds, as well as laces and pendants. Göring's thick calves are stuck into tall boots. Decked out this way he sits there, and is spirited away by the melodies of the late Fürst Philipp and the voice of Tora zu Eulenburg, dreaming of a world of a heroic Nordic master race, a mythic German past that never actually existed but that under the so-called Third Reich shall be resurrected with great fanfare.

Finally he rises from the tea tray to stroll to his chambers. That's when Libertas intercepts him, waiting in front of his guest room. Always receptive to feminine charms, Göring invites the youngest daughter of the palace in. He happily chats with her, listens to the story of her gifted husband who works at the Air Ministry and wishes to become an officer — but whose applications for promotion have been denied for two and a half years. Despite his capabilities, claims Libertas, Harro must suffer through his monthly wage of only two hundred marks, and no longer sees himself progressing at the ministry. Shouldn't this be changed? Göring nods and promises the charming woman, who speaks so persuasively, to look into the matter. It's a move the second most powerful man in Nazi Germany will one day bitterly regret.

# 16

On October 1, 1936, Harro and Libertas move into a light-filled four-and-a-half-room atelier on the top floor at Waitzstrasse 2, just around the corner from Kurfürstendamm. "Wonderful, even enchanting rooms that seem almost magical," Libertas writes to her mother-in-law, Marie Luise. Especially promising is the second room, which seems ready-made for a salon: more than thirty feet long and nearly twenty-three feet wide, with large lights on the walls and ceiling. Its charm is enhanced by a dark wooden staircase that divides it and leads up to a tiny guest room, where a gallery affords views over the roofs of Berlin.

It's a bohemian abode that they furnish with light modern touches — a sleep sofa rather than a bed, a mirror with no frame — turning down Marie Luise's offer of the old dark ebony dining table and cabinets from Mülheim. Libertas is downright "scared of the style of the furniture." Instead they opt for an office typing table, a roll-front cabinet, and, at the heart of the place, a four-tube radio: "Now in winter, a powerful receiver is very entertaining, beneficial, and technically advantageous. We really can pick up broadcasts from all over the globe with no interference." It's a helpful tool in media-controlled Nazi Germany, if one likes to stay informed.

In order to maintain a free communal living style and not appear too much like an established old married couple — as well as to save money — they sublet two of the four rooms. Of the one hundred marks in rent they pay just the "laughable sum of 50 marks per month," as Libertas reports. She immediately feels comfortable in the new digs: "We are both . . . pleased and enjoy our life. In the evenings we often read together and discuss this or that."

But at the same time the young marriage is troubled, due to the consequences of the torture Harro had endured. Ever since running the gauntlet in the yard of the converted bowling alley, he's been unable to shake the pain in his kidneys. The stones inside "hinder the metabolism of the urinary system, leading to a build-up of 'toxins' in the body, particularly in the joints," as he writes to his brother, Hartmut. Since swearing his loyalty to Hitler at the Air Ministry, it's gotten worse — lately it's a colic that feels like a saw being jabbed into his abdomen. "The little crystals irritate the kidney tissue," he continues to Hartmut: "No wonder one tends to be impatient and on edge. The stones cause a double sensitivity. It does have its advantages, one certainly has a more finely tuned 'antenna' than other people. One senses things more closely, as if the stones were radio crystals."

First and foremost, however, the kidney stones have an effect on his sex life. Ever since the bullwhips had struck his skin and the swastika had been carved into his thigh, Harro has found lovemaking difficult. He confirms this in the letter to Hartmut, where he compares his relationship with Libs in this area to that between a rapier and a sword, though Libs is the sword since he's "not as fiery . . . as she is." Having sex "makes the stones slosh around, causing physical and mental agitation. The result is often bleeding kidneys (red urine), exsanguination in the brain, poor appearance (eyes!)." It sounds as disturbing as it is painful for daily exertion: "With kidney stones, one isn't much good at one's marital duties. One pays more dearly than others for the pleasures of love, so it must be 'worth it,' the stimulus must be stronger than for normal people." The consequence for Harro is abstinence. "A bit of asceticism is good for the soul."

But for Libertas, whose charms seem to make everyone fall for her, it is less good. She's twenty-two and cannot imagine an abstinent lifestyle. Some things that she struggles to say with words, she can articulate through touches.

Libertas senses that she must fight for their marriage, go to great lengths, especially now after the wedding. In order to impress Harro, to show him how serious she has become in her rejection of the Nazi regime, she returns her NSDAP membership book during the winter of 1936–37. It's a risky move, because it draws unwanted attention to her, but the way she manages her withdrawal is clever: "The prerequisites for my political efforts as a woman are no longer applicable since my marriage," she writes in her pointedly formulated explanatory statement. The joke of repurposing the Nazis' own language is as effective as it is inconspicuous. "It goes without saying that like all other Germans, I, too, am always ready to make sacrifices, and I will continue to put my full efforts into the movement. It's just that this commitment must — this is how I understand the Führer — always be kept within a framework that allows for the upkeep of the household and other duties of a wife." On the surface she plays the apolitical housewife, merely at the service of her husband — a duty so sacred that even her Party membership could detract from it. She also signals to Harro with this move that he can depend on her — she will be at his side through this fight.

# 17

On January 21, 1937, a get-together takes place at Waitzstrasse 2 that is "bohemian in a truly Berlin manner." In a letter to his father the planned event sounds rather innocuous: "A nice picnic evening at our place . . . It's a splendid thing to see one's friends from time to time and to take care of all obligations in a sensible way. We provide tea, others bring cookies, wine, etc. For the first hour we read some good things, afterwards there's music and dancing until midnight. Then we kick everyone out."

Twenty-five to thirty people are there that cold winter night, and the stove, for which coal is stored beneath the stairs, manages to "overcome the negative sub-freezing temperatures in the atelier but also in the side rooms." Who is in attendance? Mostly friends, but also friends of friends, people Harro doesn't know that well yet but intends to become more familiar with over the course of the evening. Some of the guests wear berets, others sport dark shirts with open collars: the way one dresses when one's attitude digresses from Nazism. It is not just a simple house party but a gathering that Harro uses as a proving ground: Whom can he trust? With whom can he exchange information in the future?

Music flows from the record player, and then Libertas pulls out her accordion to get people singing and dancing. This type of resistance appeals to her — this is how it should always be! An easygoing get-together, and unlike the earlier *Gegner* events, women are well represented, which is itself a political statement. The Nazis are trying everything to displace women from social life, to corral them in the kitchen. Therefore the parity in a room like the attic of Waitzstrasse 2 on this Thursday night creates a special atmosphere all its own.

But here, too, one must decide who is trustworthy — the Treachery Act, in place since December 1934, makes it a crime punishable by prison to make derogatory statements — even in private — that might damage the reputation of the Reich or the Nazi regime. Thousands are already in concentration camps for rash utterances, perhaps just a Freudian slip. This gives the "picnic evening" a particular intimacy and sharpens awareness. Reading people correctly can be a lifesaving skill.

The spirit of this and subsequent parties is Gisela von Poellnitz, a slim twenty-six-year-old blonde who suffers from a lung condition. Through Libertas, who is a distant cousin of hers, Gisela works as a stenographer for United Press. She's one of Harro and Libertas's subletters, which is how she met Richard von Raffay, with whom she is now together. Ricci shows up to the party dressed all in leather; outside is parked a Harley-Davidson, which has replaced his sailboat. Gisela lets in the guests, introduces people, makes sure everyone has a drink. "Her clever hospitality made things pleasant," one visitor remembers: "At the same time one notices the joy she takes from all the contacts made. She has a sixth sense for people who belong together."

Like Harro, Gisela von Poellnitz has already experienced violence at the hands of the state. In November 1933 she was arrested for the first time without being told why. During the interrogation, she was hit by one of the officials; she struck back and as a result received two months in jail. The following year she was once again detained. A note was seized that contained "gothic verse with communist sensibilities," as it said in the Gestapo report. A subsequent search found in her underwear a membership booklet for the Rote Hilfe, the German branch of the International Red Aid that supported political prisoners; the organization, banned since 1933, was affiliated with the German Communist Party and had earlier been led by Rosa Luxemburg's friend Clara Zetkin. Gisela ripped the booklet out of the official's hand, tore it apart with lightning speed, and swallowed the scraps of paper. This led to another two months in jail. In addition, she'd been denied a driver's permit: "Granting her a license would also facilitate her possible anti-government agitation."

Gisela von Poellnitz, however, is anything but a dogmatic leftist — in fact, she'd not been taken seriously by the communists because of her aristocratic background. She's a rebel and adventurer, and she likes to travel and usually does so alone. She's been to Scotland to pick raspberries, for example, and also toured the Balkans and Greece. To be sure, such solo adventures are suspect given the gender politics of the Nazi regime.

Werner Dissel, the man with the information about the tanks near Neuruppin, is also in attendance at this first picnic evening. Walter Küchenmeister, one of Harro's old intellectual working-class friends, has come with his girlfriend, the doctor Elfriede Paul, who has traveled frequently to London and Paris to help Jewish friends emigrate.

There are all sorts of people present — with differing views on politics and also on personal freedom. What unites them — and it may be the essence of this emerging movement — is an understanding most likely based on the words of Rosa Luxemburg: Freedom is always the freedom of those who think differently. That's the crux of it: whether one can leave the private lives of others in peace or not. What's perfidious and aggravating about the Nazi dictatorship is that it pushes into the most intimate spheres — it wishes to control thought and intimacy, sends homosexuals to concentration camps, bans intercourse between Aryans and Jews.

Tolerating a free approach to love is perhaps the entrance ticket to this party in the atelier, though it is not a requirement. For instance, Dr. Elfriede Paul doesn't think much of open flirtation, finds it gratuitous because of the potential for conflict. And yet she accepts it when others opt for this lifestyle. Her best friend is Oda Schottmüller, who is another party guest. Schottmüller is a thirty-one-year-old sculptor and modern dancer who attended high school with the writer Klaus Mann. She's a mysterious, astute woman with a lusty sense of humor who maintains an affair with the wheat-blond Kurt Schumacher.

Schumacher is one of Harro's oldest friends, a sculptor with a penchant for Albrecht Dürer, a master scholar of the Academy of Art who won the Grand State Prize while still a student. He had received a commission for the door carvings at Göring's country manor, Carinhall, which, as a dutiful Swabian, he completed despite his rejection of the system. Kurt is a lively, sturdy guy with pointy deerlike ears, spontaneous in his cranky pronouncements and uninhibited in his judgments. His wife, Elisabeth, accompanies him to the party. She knows about the affair with Oda and doesn't worry too much about it. Generosity is part of her personality, and besides, she sometimes fancies other men, as well. Not to mention that she is convinced that Kurt will return to her anyway because at some point the self-sufficient, willful Oda won't need him anymore. Elisabeth Schumacher is the daughter of a Jewish engineer who died on the battlefield in the First World War. She is, as a result of her father, considered a "half Jew." Therefore, she isn't allowed to work as a self-employed artist, and labors instead as a mere graphic designer. Because of this, she herself has turned against the Nazi state, offering Harro her help in reproducing some of the covert material he gathers at his job.

It's Harro and Libertas's first party, and because it goes so well, it isn't the last. Every other week they have people over, always on Thursdays. The second get-together takes place on February 4, 1937, a holiday known as Weiberfastnacht that precedes Karneval celebrations, the German version of Mardi Gras. Harro gives a Karneval speech, making fun of the regime, which seems a bit too bold to some in the room. Isn't the circle too large and too complex, thus making such open statements too dangerous? Harro sees it differently. In his view, these parties give the appearance of normal social contact.

But the gatherings are also a way for him to gauge things: With whom can he speak openly — and with whom can he not? Some of those he gets to know better on these evenings are invited to a private rendezvous. In that case, it's off to the roll-front cabinet, where the sensitive materials from the Air Ministry are stashed. The wooden slats are lowered and he pulls out a file folder: his collection of material on the German involvement in the Spanish Civil War, collated on blue and pink sheets of paper; pictures and maps from military journals, some of which Elisabeth Schumacher has managed to reduce photographically to the size of a postage stamp. But most of the guests at the picnic evening don't catch wind of any of that.

So at first the Gestapo officials in Prinz-Albrecht-Strasse 8 take no interest in the colorful crowd at Waitzstrasse 2, even after Harro is reported on in the spring of 1937. A party guest by the name of Dr. Karl von Meran, who is a count and had earlier worked as a Nazi informant both in Germany and abroad, talks at a dinner with a member of Himmler's personal staff about his experiences at a Schulze-Boysen party and pillories Harro as a "cleverly disguised communist," indicating that he has an array of "collaborators" who are equally suspicious. Even that is not enough for the Gestapo to barge in, and the dancing in the loft apartment continues. Apparently they don't put much stock in the word of a known homosexual such as the Count von Meran.

This changes two months later.

# 18

In August of 1937, Harro's friend Werner Dissel is arrested for, according to the Gestapo report, "cultural Bolshevist activities," "communist subversion of the Wehrmacht," and "negligent betrayal of military secrets." These are serious allegations, the result of Dissel's "reconnaissance about military activity for Franco-Spain" coming to light. It concerns the two tank regiments near Neuruppin, the ones he had also told Harro about at the Air Ministry casino. In Dissel's notebook, the Gestapo finds Harro's name and contact details.

Will Harro be dragged into the affair as well? Things are suddenly precarious when he receives a summons to the Gestapo office for the purpose of clearing up some questions. He can assume that Dissel has kept quiet about the conversation at the casino. But it's imperative that Harro does not compromise himself, given the possibility that the two of them could be interrogated jointly.

Just as four years prior, when he was supposed to attest to the ostensible suicide of Henry Erlanger, he ascends the stairs of the dark sandstone building opposite the limestone RLM headquarters, though this time he's a well-groomed member of the Luftwaffe in full battle regalia — a rapier and a 6.35-millimeter Haenel-Schmeisser pistol in his belt.

Harro enters the room where the questioning is to take place. He knows how thin the ice is he's walking on, but he's able to appear relaxed, friendly, and open. As Harro suspected, Werner Dissel is also there. He greets his friend warmly, smiling and acting at ease. He asks the officer whether he is permitted to smoke and whether he may offer the arrestee a cigarette. The Gestapo cop won't be outdone by Harro's congeniality: "Yes, by all means," he answers, as if it goes without saying.

Harro holds out his full pack of cigarettes to Dissel. "Would you object if I gave him the whole lot?" he now asks the policeman with a sideways glance.

"Of course not."

"Would you like to examine them first?"

"Certainly not — we wouldn't even think of it."

In a consoling tone, Harro says to Dissel: "Things won't be so bad. You're not the only one this ever happened to."

Dissel understands the intimation, and while he tries to pull a cigarette out, he discreetly examines the pack and finds some hidden writing. In tiny block letters beneath the silver paper it says: EXTRA FONTANA TERRA INCOGNITA.

Harro offers him a light. Dissel inhales the first puff and thinks intently about the words Harro put there. *Fontana* — that probably means Neuruppin, the birthplace of the writer Fontane. And *extra* could mean extraterritorial, as in outside Neuruppin — where the tank regiment is. *Terra incognita* can only mean that the Gestapo hasn't discovered Harro's part in the whole thing. Now Dissel knows that he can confidently continue to remain silent about the meeting at the Air Ministry casino. Rarely has a cigarette tasted better.

After Harro leaves the room, Dissel is asked: "Why, you muddlehead, didn't you confide about this to your friend, an exemplary German officer?"

"Yeah, I should have," Dissel answers. "But I didn't want to burden him."

Harro heads back to his limestone castle in a good mood. This time he's outsmarted the Gestapo. They're not as clever as they think they are, he concludes, as he closes the door to office number 5148 behind him.

# 19

In the meantime, the Luftwaffe boss Göring has made a telephone call about Harro to Oberstleutnant Stumpff, head of the personnel division and later the leader of the Luftwaffe's general staff. When Stumpff objects to a promotion based on Harro's *Gegner* past and asserts that there's no guarantee he has a positive attitude toward Nazism, Göring brushes aside these concerns. For Göring this is all water under the bridge, old news, and he clears the career path for the son-in-law of his neighborly acquaintance Tora zu Eulenburg.

It is "the personal wish of the Minister . . . that I now pass my training as quickly as possible and become a reserve officer," Harro writes to his parents with satisfaction. Libertas's intervention via Göring is a success: even without a university degree, Harro will follow in the footsteps of his father and great-uncle on an officer's career path. This means more money and more prestige.

It also puts him in a better position to collect secret information.

# 20

The civil war in Spain is escalating. The Basque city of Guernica, where countless refugees have sought protection from Franco's troops, is leveled by the German Condor Legion. It's the first large-scale air bombardment of civilians since the First World War, with hundreds killed. The responsible parties sit in the Luftwaffe Ministry in Berlin, just a few doors down from office 5148.

By this point Harro receives detailed reports about the situation on the Iberian Peninsula on a daily basis. His department, Foreign Air Forces, is combined with the Operations department, where the target planning for the bombings takes place. Guernica isn't the only city the Germans destroy from the air. The snow-white Air Ministry has transformed into a site where mass murder is planned, where desk-bound perpetrators sit along the open officials' corridor. While everyone around him cooperates, Harro sees the situation clearly: "The Spanish atrocities and horrors on both sides offer a small taste of what lies ahead," he writes to his parents: "Medieval cultural treasures, entire cities, etc. are going up in flames and the most modern technical means serve to kill and destroy in ever more refined ways."

Harro collects more and more proof of Germany's responsibility for these atrocities; it's all locked away in his roll-front cabinet at home. But how can he get his information about the saboteurs trying to infiltrate Barcelona into the right hands? After the fiasco with the British journalist who refused to pass it on to the BBC, he needs to find a dependable contact this time.

There is only one power actively opposing the spread of fascism in Spain, and that is the Soviet Union. It goes without saying that the Kremlin has its own agenda, supporting the democratic forces with soldiers, weapons, and materiel while also using this aid to influence the variegated, enigmatic Popular Front government. Harro is aware that "in Moscow, as in Madrid, the Trotskyist-anarchist elements are put up against the wall." Yet the fact remains that the Soviets are the only ones who can halt the advance of the fascist putsch.

Before the war, hungry for action:
twenty-eight-year-old Harro Schulze-Boysen.

Harro puts all his information about the secret mission, including a list of German agents who have infiltrated the International Brigades as agents provocateurs, into an envelope. Now he just needs to pass it off to the Soviets. But how? He assumes that the Gestapo is watching the USSR embassy in Berlin, so he must figure out another way.

He and his friends discuss the problem, and a possibility pops up: Gisela von Poellnitz is planning to visit the World Exposition in Paris. There she could discreetly take it to the Soviet embassy without danger.

The plan is put into action: Gisela, an employee of United Press, doesn't raise suspicion when she takes the train to the international expo. She strolls across les Champs de Mars and the Trocadéro and visits the German pavilion, designed by Albert Speer. She also takes in the Spanish pavilion, where a sensational painting is on display: *Guernica* by Pablo Picasso, which demonstrates to the global public the horror of the German bombing. Motivated in this way, Gisela fulfills her mission and puts the envelope with Harro's information into the postbox of the Soviet embassy in the Bois de Boulogne.

Back in Berlin, Harro and Libertas wait nervously for a sign of life from Gisela. It's a period when the rate of prosecutions is sharply rising, as is the number of death sentences issued to opponents of the regime. In fact, the state is executing so many people that in 1936 Hitler had decided not to use the ax for beheadings anymore but to switch instead to the more efficient guillotine. In Tegel prison, which includes facilities for metalwork, twenty of the killing machines are manufactured.

Harro wonders if this wouldn't be a good moment to disappear for a few weeks to a distant sanitarium to let his kidneys heal and get his body back in shape. It's an opportune moment for Libs, too, to get out of town while her cousin Gisela is in action. Through Richard von Raffay, she knows the Hamburg-based shipping magnate Hans Siemers, whose coal transport ship, the *Ilona,* is about to set off for the Black Sea. Libs has always wanted to go to sea — there's such romance to it, she imagines, and anyway, Gisela has rhapsodized to her plenty about the joys of solo travel. On September 27, 1937, Harro and Libertas drive to Hamburg, where they head to the gangplanks of St. Pauli, the city's port. There, Libs, equipped with an accordion, a Leica camera, art supplies, books, and an empty notebook she hopes to fill with travel reportage, boards the ship.

"The young lad suffers from kidney stones, and his kitty steams around the world," she dryly writes to her husband from her first port of call, the Algerian city of Oran. But Harro isn't the slightest bit bothered by her adventure. He's lying in a sanatorium in Bad Wildungen, in Hesse, drinking radish and celery juice until the first stone passes, happy to have it out: "Later it might have become larger and thus more dangerous and difficult to pass." And while he's left impotent and with battered kidneys, why shouldn't Libertas have some new experiences?

If there's one person who doesn't see it this way, it's Harro's mother, Marie Luise. She's put off by the fact that a newly married couple wouldn't go together on tour, the way it's supposed to be. Instead, one half, and the female half at that, is off alone on a freighter full of brutes, while the other half, in this case her beloved son, lies in a sickbed. Despite being active in the Women's League of the German Colonial Society, which sees its mission as sending young women out into the world to spread German culture, she finds Libertas's adventure on the frothy sea intolerable. That it could be about self-discovery isn't something Marie Luise understands. When, on top of it all, she finds out that back at Waitzstrasse, Gisela von Poellnitz, Libertas's cousin, safely returned from Paris, is serving as Harro's nurse, it's further proof of the rotten morals of the scandal-enveloped zu Eulenburg family.

Harro must explain to his mother that she's part of a generation with a completely different outlook when it comes to relationships. "The fact is that I *wanted* Libs to take the trip, because I like my wife to be her own person even in my absence. If earlier in our relationship she had said she 'couldn't live a day without me,' it would have been a sign of dependence that is unbearable over the long term, at least given our life goals." For him, leading an open relationship is the basis of fighting against Nazism, against staleness and the smugness of the petty bourgeois brownshirts. What Harro means by *life goals* is clear only to himself, however, and his mother can't grasp what he's alluding to: "Precisely when destiny suddenly decides to part us with violence (and we have no guarantee it won't), precisely then, Libertas must if necessary be able to work and function at one hundred percent."

When Marie Luise still laments her daughter-in-law's Black Sea voyage and continues to question the entire relationship, Harro strikes back: "What do you know about the finer points, the impossibly finer points, of the rules that make for a happy marriage? I'm still man enough even today that I feel the desire to fight for the woman and to maintain love despite obstacles. And since I'm no sexual buccaneer and love my wife infinitely, I won't exclude this adventure and the pushbacks from my marriage, but rather bring them into it."

Harro is convinced that their love won't be destroyed by the geographic separation, as his mother prophecies. On the contrary, "the current just brings fresh water and is also conducive to fighting the danger of everyday banality, which threatens every marriage."

And so it is: Libs has nothing in common with the seamen she must be in such close quarters with for several weeks. She's unable to learn anything from them, and instead uses her time to fill her notebook with travel stories. Often she thinks of Harro, and sends long letters to him that become increasingly yearning. She also seems to be cured of any lingering feelings for nameless past lovers. "When it comes to being true, my boy, you need no longer worry," she writes on October 21, 1937. With every additional day the trip lasts, she misses Harro more and realizes from afar what she has in him: a soul, an intellect, with whom interaction will always be interesting. A man she can trust, with whom she feels secure. Harro understands her, unlike the people far afield or the seamen with whom she rolls so many cigarettes and "without batting an eyelash throws back four beers in a row and is still misunderstood in the end ... *Ach*, you," she writes to him on November 1, 1937, with the Crimean on the horizon: "How I sense with every further hour that we two belong together, indivisible! You'll get your kitty back just as you kissed her in that horrible parting hour, only a bit stronger and shrewder. Indeed!"

# 21

During this period as a grass widower, Harro runs into Günther Weisenborn, a friend from the *Gegner* days, at a bus stop on Ku'damm. Weisenborn is an old acquaintance of Bertolt Brecht and a former dramaturg at the Volksbühne theater. He's published successful novels and theater pieces, some under pseudonyms, the harmless ones under his own name — and is always dangerously close to trouble with the Nazi censors, who had burned his novel *Barbaren* as part of the book burning on May 10, 1933. Would Weisenborn be suitable for the resistance, Harro wonders? They meet up a few times more before the writer is extended an invitation to Waitzstrasse 2.

"Here sat a small, dark-haired man with glasses named Walter, with one of those intelligent worker's faces from the Ruhrgebiet region," writes Weisenborn about his first visit to the illegal gathering, which is attended by Walter Küchenmeister and Harro. Kurt Schumacher is also there — "a young, bright artist's face, with short blond hair and a certain fanatical gleam in his eyes," as Weisenborn describes him. The four of them sit together, drink tea, and talk of this and that, before the conversation turns to the regime. "If you're opposed to it, don't you have to do something about it?" Kurt asks him.

"Of course . . ." answers Weisenborn, unsettled. "But does it make any sense to do something? It's almost surely futile, and the risk is incredibly high."

"But what if," Harro responds, looking at him kindly, "many people — hundreds of thousands — undertake something? Wouldn't that make it different?"

The four young men sit at the table and continue talking, their cups of tea now cold. They are defying the Nazi dictatorship by giving voice to these dangerous thoughts, but then again it is dangerous even to *have* such thoughts at all.

In the end, they all shake hands. Speaking openly creates an atmosphere in which deep friendships can develop, a bubble of truth in a city full of lies. "These are people with courage — and they've *given* me courage," is Weisenborn's conclusion, and he'll be back.

What he doesn't yet know: he will fall hopelessly in love with Harro's wife.

# 22

By Christmas Eve, 1937, Libertas has safely returned from her sea voyage — and with a full notebook. Accompanied by her mother on piano, she sings Christmas songs in the Nordic Hall, where a huge Christmas tree has been erected, around which the gift tables are arranged. Libs and Harro have decorated the tree with tinsel. Unfortunately there's no snow, and it's a walk through the mud to the Liebenberg church, where the celebration takes place, this year without the pastor. Instead the ideologically suitable schoolmaster officiates.

In the past, the former had always rehearsed traditional Christmas songs with the village children, but to everyone's disappointment, this year the practice has been replaced with Führer-accented propaganda, true to Himmler's efforts to replace the Christian holiday with a pagan "solstice celebration." But Libertas's aunt Marie, wife of Fürst Wend zu Eulenburg and as such the head of Liebenberg, demands "Silent Night" in a loud voice, and everyone joins in. "The decrees of the Secretary of Culture or Propaganda . . . are in this case easily outweighed by the true power relationships of the agrarian sector," Harro comments dryly.

At seven-thirty they open presents. Harro and Libertas unwrap a silver, four-color mechanical pencil, an ashtray from China, twelve silver tea-spoons (Swedish) from Grandma Augusta, a pair of black leather slippers Tora has picked out for Harro, and, as the main gift for him, custom-tai-lored riding pants, which, at fifty marks, are expensive — but Marie Luise and Erich Edgar contributed toward them as well.

The pants are an investment in Harro's health, because the motion of riding is supposed to help break up the stones in his abdomen. Despite his stay at the sanatorium in Wildungen, they still plague him so much that Libertas takes him during the holidays to a local doctor who specializes in the condition. The physician believes that his spleen and pancreas are also damaged, about which Harro reports to his parents: "It's very difficult for a doctor to do anything. The entire body is 'sclerotic' . . . it must be relaxed through a birth (not to worry, a male birth, meaning an accomplishment, a work, which will get the blood pumping anew)."

What Harro means by the word "work" is clear and imprecise at the same time. The fact that he'll do everything in his power to thwart the Na-zis is decided by now, and Libertas knows this as well.

On the day after Christmas it's cold, and the following night it snows. The couple drives back to Berlin along icy streets in their car, Spengler. The festivities are over, and things will get serious again straightaway. "You know, of course," Harro writes to his parents on December 27, 1937, as if they could read between the lines, "that there is but one thing I will devote myself to, as long as I live. Libertas and I are completely in agree-ment in this regard."

# 23

It snows and snows. The Reich capital disappears beneath a blanket of white, which suits the city, as it dampens its noises, smooths its edges, and drapes its urbanity in a soft shroud. During the day the sun shines, which is rare for Berlin at this time of year, and it makes winter beautiful. Libertas enjoys taking "a little run" through the Tiergarten park.

On January 12, 1938, Libertas and Günther Weisenborn meet for the first time, in Harro's presence. Since Libs never hides anything, and in-stead openly flirts, Harro cannot miss the attraction between the two. A week later they see each other again: "I read in front of about 30 listeners at the Schulze-Boysens, followed by criticism and discussion, came across well," the writer notes in his unpublished diary. The next day he goes with

Libs for a meal at the Chinese restaurant Tientsien; three days later the two of them have wine and go see a movie.

Libertas finds much to like about Weisenborn: he's a born entertainer who constantly makes her laugh, whether it's about his adventures in South America, where he lived with indigenous people, or his life as a street reporter in New York. The mirthful gleam behind his horn-rimmed glasses is his most deadly weapon, and gives him the necessary intellectual touch: a party animal in buckskin shoes with crepe soles — but first and foremost a terrific writer. The chemistry between the two doesn't seem to bother Harro. They all have fun going out together, on January 27, 1938, for instance, to a huge costume party attended by seven thousand (!) people, where Weisenborn dances with Libs "for a very long and wonderful time." Afterward they attend an "atelier party that's really cooking."

Günther and Libs also draw closer together artistically. He wants to help her develop her writing talent; he thinks her ship-bound diaries have potential and wants to show them to the publisher Ernst Rowohlt. In return she is able to help him with a new theater piece he's working on. It is to be called *Die guten Feinde,* or The Good Enemies, and will tell the tale of Robert Koch, the famous doctor and supposed inventor of a vaccine for tuberculosis that turned out not to work. In order to advance things — the project as well as their friendship — the two of them drive to Dresden on February 10, 1938, where Weisenborn wants to discuss the Robert Koch idea: "Rented two rooms in Hotel Bellevue, magnificent! We wash up, stroll through Dresden in the rain, eat lunch at the Ratskeller. Lips [*sic*] dog tired, afternoon at Heyne-publishing house with her. Then back to the hotel, we are in her room, nice. Then to the opera. Lips and I sit in the loge, a grand evening, Lips is magnificent! Later a festive dinner, that night in her room: wonderful, close one."

At ten-thirty in the morning on February 17, 1938, something unforeseen happens. It's a cold, sunny day, and while Hitler prepares for the occupation of Austria, the country where he was born, Gestapo officers knock on the wooden door of the boathouse Blau-Rot, where Harro once borrowed the rowboat of a friend, and first met Libertas. Gisela von Poellnitz, who has taken up a romantic residence there with Ricci von Raffay, is arrested for the third time in her young life.

It's not about the envelope she dropped at the Soviet embassy in Paris, as she initially fears. It concerns an unrelated incident five years prior. Harro and Libertas, however, don't know this. All they hear from Gisela's brother, who is questioned the following day, is that she's in the claws of the Gestapo and that they've secured documents: translation work Gisela was supposed to do for Harro at the Luftwaffe.

The result is a Gestapo inquiry among Harro's superiors at the Air Ministry: Did this constitute a chargeable offense of the betrayal of state secrets on the part of Harro Schulze-Boysen? Flight Captain von Bülow is asked to provide a statement about the evidence, and Harro is worried. He himself deems the papers harmless, but will von Bülow see it the same way? And what if Gisela has talked about her trip to Paris while in detainment, or the Gestapo already knows about it? Will he land in a Nazi torture chamber again?

Harro and Libertas quickly get rid of all potentially compromising materials in their apartment and plan an escape to Amsterdam together with Günther Weisenborn. Libs's brother, Johannes, lives there, working as a journalist. "There was feverish activity," writes Weisenborn about that dramatic February day of cruising through Berlin hiding potentially dangerous papers: "I followed Harro's car in my own, as he had more experience than me and knew how to keep a lookout. If he tapped his brake lights three times in a row, I was to stop immediately. If he kept flashing them more often I was to turn off or go back the other way." A love triangle on the run from the Gestapo: Weisenborn couldn't have thought up a better plot for a novel.

Back at his apartment, Harro gets the all-clear from the Air Ministry. There's been a meeting in his department to discuss the case: "The translation materials found with Frau von Poellnitz have been reviewed; none of it contains any secrets in the sense alleged. Schulze-Boysen has not opened himself up to any charges." Harro, Libertas, and Günther call off the getaway. "I can't cross the border now that it's been decided," Harro states. Instead the three of them go to a masquerade ball on a houseboat on Wannsee: it is, after all, the season of Karneval.

# 24

Harro's friendship with Günther Weisenborn doesn't suffer from the affair — and neither does his marriage with Libertas, initially. Gradually, however, he does start to marvel that it just keeps going between the two. Very openly, as if it were the most normal thing in the world, they test Harro's penchant for liberality; they go without him to a lake, stay overnight in a hotel, and on the way back to Berlin she introduces her lover to her mother over tea at Liebenberg. Harro might have reckoned with a short, insignificant dalliance, but instead it is developing into a deeper relationship. Still, he consoles himself, at least with Weisenborn, Libs is in good hands. Whatever it is she tells Günther, Harro does not need to worry, because Günther, too, belongs to the network and won't rat on them.

Harro just hopes that Libs is picking up some writing skills along the way. That his friend is having such fun with her in bed does get to him, though; after all, *he* is her husband, and it's apparent to all that Libs isn't satisfied by him. Or does it just go with the territory in a circle of friends determined to ignore societal norms that an emancipated woman sleeps with whomever she wishes rather than restricting herself to her husband? He even tells his parents about the situation, getting it out of his system: "Lately I've seen ever more of Günther Weisenborn, the writer of several decent books . . . Now he's at our place often, and Libs finds him nice, as well. Actually more than just 'nice.' He knows a lot, and we can learn from him. Libs needs a mentor for her writing."

Still, it must be embittering for him to have to share his wife, whom he loves, with another at a time when he himself has problems with impotence. But Harro doesn't interfere even as the pair enter into a more intimate intellectual relationship as well, meeting regularly at the library to work together on the Robert Koch piece and afterward eat at Café Kranzler, have a drink at the Romanische Café, "dance and laugh happily" at Dschungel Bar, or drive "at two in the morning to Potsdam," where they sleep with each other in a hotel.

For her part, Libertas enjoys the affair. This is what it's like to live the life of a writer! It's a form of existence she could get used to. She loves to express herself artistically, and make love, and what could be wrong with that? She's never been closer to self-fulfillment than in the spring of 1938. Perhaps Günther Weisenborn is indeed helping her to expand her freedom into new dimensions and to become less emotionally dependent on Harro, all the better to survive on her own in the case of an emergency. Isn't that what they've been striving for the whole time?

# 25

On July 5, 1938, Gisela von Poellnitz is released after nearly five months in Gestapo custody. She's emaciated, her skin as white as paper, but she's kept mum about the real purpose of her trip to Paris or Harro's information about the German intervention in the Spanish Civil War. But something has happened in prison that everyone feared and suspected might occur: Already weak in the lungs, she has contracted tuberculosis, a life-threatening infection.

From now on the young adventurer can no longer live in the boathouse with Ricci von Raffay, can no longer cruise with him on his Harley, can no longer go to wild parties or on adventurous solo voyages; instead she needs constant medical care. Dr. Elfriede Paul, the girlfriend of Walter Küchenmeister, secures her a spot first in a respiratory sanitarium in Brandenburg and later one in Switzerland, but Gisela is in bad shape from the start. She becomes increasingly thin and diaphanous, regardless of how many care packages of food her friends send her — regardless of how often Libs visits her, always shaken by her cousin's appearance, lying pale and Madonna-like in the pillows.

Libertas is also not doing well this summer. Gisela's life-threatening condition upsets her, and now there are also problems in her affair with Weisenborn. Torn between the two men in her life, she suffers from pain in her abdomen and worries she's pregnant; additionally she has a circulatory disorder and even passes out at one point.

In order to recuperate, to distance herself from everyone, and to gain clarity, she travels at the end of July 1938 to Bavaria and into Switzerland, a place she's loved since attending school in Zurich from 1928 to 1932. In the Swiss metropolis she meets Ignazio Silone, an Italian émigré author and former Italian communist and anti-fascist — and an acquaintance of Harro's. Silone is well connected, including to Thomas Mann, who lives in exile in Küsnacht on the shores of Lake Zurich.

Upon learning of Silone's connection to the famous writer, Libs comes up with a plan to tell Thomas Mann about her husband. She's worried about Harro, who — unbeknownst to her — at that same time has been added to the *A-Kartei*, the blacklist initiated by the much-feared leader of the Reich Main Security Office, Reinhard Heydrich. The list compiles names of those suspected to oppose the regime based on their previous activities, all of whom are to be "immediately arrested" in any political crisis and detained at concentration camps — in Harro's case, in Sachsenhausen.

"She was scared that something could happen to Harro, and hoped that in such a case the public will be informed about him and his moral rectitude," Silone writes about Libertas's visit. He promises to introduce her to Thomas Mann, despite the fact that the writer's busy because he's in the process of giving up his residence in Switzerland and preparing to move his family.

Before long, Libs gets her chance. In the middle of August, the Mann family wants to drive into the high mountains of the Engadin one last time to stay at the famous Waldhaus-Hotel in Sils-Maria and bid goodbye to Europe; after that they're off to the United States, to Princeton. For now, though, the *Magic Mountain* author is still in Zurich, and on August 6, 1938, he visits the publisher Emil Oprecht, accompanied by his son Golo. Silone is also invited and turns up with Libertas. "Ate and drank, chatty — then thunderstorm," writes Thomas Mann in his diary of the soiree. Libertas is introduced to him and talks about Harro and his activities. It isn't clear from the sources whether more contact followed from this initial meeting. But a Gestapo memo from 1942 claiming Harro Schulze-Boysen undertook "overtures to Thomas Mann" suggests it did.

Libertas returns by train to Berlin, where soon overtures of a totally different sort are made. Harro's brother, Hartmut, now sixteen years old, visits Waitzstrasse. It's not clear who comes up with the idea, but there is evidence that Libertas introduces Hartmut to sex and that Harro is aware of it, and may even have encouraged it. He has certainly been open with his family about his love life before, but never like this. Are he and Libs thumbing their nose at the Nazis, with their increasingly restrictive notions of propriety and family values? Or is Libertas following her passions and Harro struggling to keep pace?

Whether the parting of ways is linked to this initiation rite or not, Libertas's affair with Günther Weisenborn draws to a close. Already she had sent him a pained letter from afar while in Switzerland. But they still meet and work on the Robert Koch play together. There are talks about possibly mounting the piece in the capital: "The Staatstheater Berlin has an option, but Gründgens isn't sure just yet," Libertas writes to her mother-in-law, Marie Luise. "He needs to ask Göring, as with all problematic things. But I think something will come of it." Together with Weisenborn, she travels to Bremen to prepare for the premiere there. They stay in a hotel on September, 26, 1938, where they hear on the radio Hitler giving his speech announcing the annexation of the so-called Sudetenland, a large area of Czechoslovakia inhabited by a mix of Germans and Czechs: "It's the last territorial claim I have to make in Europe," the voice clangs on the radio. "But it is a claim I will not relinquish and which, God willing, I shall fulfill."

For Harro, this political development means overtime at the Air Ministry. Even if he is not actively engaged in supporting Hitler's aggressive behavior, the territorial claims to Czechoslovakia require every man to be at his desk: The proposed annexation develops into an international crisis that threatens to lead to armed conflict. In the army's high command, some generals are convinced that a war at this particular moment would mean the demise of Germany. As a result, a plan for a putsch against Hitler is finalized, the implementation of which is imminent.

But then a foreign head of state gets in the way of the anti-Hitler Wehrmacht generals: Neville Chamberlain. In order to preserve peace at any price, the British prime minister visits Germany several times in quick succession, coming to the Rhine, then to Hitler's Alpine hideaway at Berghof, and finally to the Munich conference, where the fate of Czechoslovakia, whose president isn't invited, is sealed. Hitler emerges as the great victor of the affair. The Wehrmacht marches into the Sudetenland without resistance. The generals who'd been preparing the putsch call it off.

Even if he isn't privy to these developments among the military command, Harro, from his desk, can still see the "materiel and psychological 'machinery' of world politics" as if through a microscope, as he writes to his father. As far as he's concerned, British interest in the destruction of the Soviet Union is obvious and as a result the German Reich will be given a free hand in the east. This corresponds to Hitler's polemic comment that Czechoslovakia is a Bolshevik aircraft carrier in the middle of Europe. A statement like this certainly has its desired effect in London.

The days are exciting that fall of 1938 — only the nights are lonely. Sometimes, at the end of the workday, when Harro walks toward Waitzstrasse along Ku'damm, with its lavish neon lights, and rounds the final turn, the empty apartment stares at him like an abandoned film set. Sometimes there's a note at the door where Libertas has written that it'll be a late one. The affair with Weisenborn is apparently not over after all.

On the evening of September 30, Harro goes for a beer with Günther to clear the air for good. The next day Weisenborn writes in his diary: "Not seeing her. Don't want to anymore."

It's a private victory for Harro — but he doesn't lose sight of the geopolitical situation: "Peace has now suddenly 'broken out,' as I quite distinctly realized on Wednesday evening when the news first arrived," he writes to his father on October 1, 1938, continuing with prophetic foreboding:

> Whether it breaks out permanently in Europe, as Herr Chamberlain believes, will dictate how posterity judges these days. If, however, we are once again on the verge of war in one or two years, then there will be ten times as many victims as there would have been if things had come to a head now . . . and then history's verdict will be severe. Let's hope for the best.

In October, to address the Czechoslovakian crisis, which for Harro brought world conflicts into sharp focus, he and Walter Küchenmeister write their first illegal pamphlet: *Der Stosstrupp,* or The Raiding Party. In it, the annexation of the Sudetenland is depicted as the precursor to a violent human catastrophe.

To produce the leaflet, Kurt Schumacher acquires the necessary paper from a wholesaler. As an artist he can do so without attracting attention. As for the postage stamps, the sculptor buys batches of them here and there, never in suspiciously large amounts. Kurt's wife, Elisabeth, undertakes the task of making fifty copies of the pamphlet. Using the telephone book, Libertas tracks down addresses of people she regards as intelligent: teachers, doctors, lawyers, and others who might effectively spread opinions. Anyone typing addresses onto the envelopes, stuffing them, and affixing the stamps wears cotton gloves.

Then Dr. Elfriede Paul sets off in her car, a Ford. As a doctor, she can always justify any trip in case she is stopped. Even wearing ladies' gloves while tossing the letters in the mailbox won't raise suspicion given the cool October weather. She mails only a couple of envelopes per postbox, then she drives on. It's the first coordinated action taken by the circle of friends, and successful, as everything goes off without a hitch: a test run — and proof that they can count on each other.

# 26

At the Air Ministry that October, Harro speaks with his superior, Bartz, asking for compensation for the many hours of overtime, a raise of at least four hundred marks, as well as a onetime bonus to cover a vacation, which he desperately needs in order to stay fit for duty and put his marriage back on track. If his demands are not met, he insists, he will resign in the new year.

Whether or not he really would have carried out this threat — which might have worked against his own intentions to infiltrate the system — the pressure works. Bartz wants to retain him, as he sees in Harro a "man of truly superior character and ability." The demands are met, and Harro and Libertas take their first lengthy holiday abroad together. With their new car, a light-blue Fiat convertible they dub Caesar, they drive on the Autobahn to Bayreuth, and the next day through Munich and across the Alps into Italy. They reach Venice at dusk, "at the most beautiful time as the palazzos look even better than in daylight because you can't see the crumbling facades and dirt," as Harro writes to his parents. They park Caesar in a garage and meet Harro's sister, Helga, who lives with her husband and first child in a big, beautiful apartment in an ancient Venetian building on a canal.

Resistance and love: Harro and Libs with "Caesar,"
their light blue twenty-four-horsepower Fiat convertible.

The next afternoon Libertas and Harro cruise across the Adriatic in first class, with sun and excellent meals, to Dubrovnik, once known as Ragusa when it was still an independent maritime republic. In the shops of the old city, they take pleasure in buying clothes and accessories: leather belts, a knit vest, a silver brooch. The largest purchase is a kilim, two meters by three, in blue and red wool, for thirteen hundred dinars, or about eighty-five marks. "Before we started haggling he wanted 2000 dinars!" Harro writes proudly to his father, who he knows will appreciate his bargaining skills. In the same antiques shop Libertas finds a historical Ragusan crest — and can barely believe it when she sees the inscription. It's made of silver, with red stripes and black letters spelling the word LIBERTAS.

It's a sign! For the very least that Harro has chosen the right vacation spot. It will be their motto for the next fourteen days: freedom — trying to find out what that actually is. Because it could also mean never returning to cold Germany. There is much to recommend that, and they quickly become fond of the Yugoslavians. They like them and find they have "far more composure than the Italians," as Harro writes. They are told of a place they mustn't miss: the beautiful island of Korcula. There one could begin a new life, if one only took the chance. There one could have children, let them grow up in paradise.

They decide to take a shot. They climb aboard a steamer and arrive in the old harbor of Korcula at sunset on November 1, 1938, as people sit in front of their houses drinking freshly produced wine. Boats are moored in calm, pellucid water in front of the Hôtel de Ville. There's grappa and fish, and in the morning coffee and cigarettes along a quiet quay. Then he only has to strip off his blue shirt and hop into the equally blue water. Korcula has a calming effect on Harro. The bags under his eyes disappear and his body is no longer so hunched, not as calcified as usual. And Libertas finally gains a bit of weight eating Bosnian dumplings for lunch. Should they stay? Turn their backs on the insanity and drop out? As they talk about it, they see a framed photo hanging in the Hôtel de Ville. It's an all too familiar figure, in white pants, black sportcoat, and a white cap with a visor. It's Eulenburg's neighbor and Harro's boss during a visit to Korcula in the spring of 1935: Hermann Göring, with a lavish yacht in the background.

One thing is clear to Harro: Just as Korcula was once part of Venice's sphere of influence, there is now another shadow darkening the Dalmatian coast from the north. Fascism, international industry in cooperation with authoritarian government, will continue to extend its tentacles into the farthest corners of the earth. It's a development that must be impeded, and Harro can best do that in Berlin and nowhere else. The idea of remaining on the island and living as a writer is a charming one. But who would print their texts? How would they earn money? And even more important: If everyone who is opposed to the system fled, there would be nobody left to fight the Nazis from within.

They finish their vacation with heavy hearts, ferry back to Venice on the steamer, and retrieve Caesar. Wearing leather caps against the wind, they drive with the roof of the convertible down, Harro in a light coat, Libs in a jacket and long skirt. In Zurich, the last stop before they return to the Reich, they meet once again with Ignazio Silone, and are shown one last time how it feels to live as an exile. Silone, previously the Italian representative of the Comintern, tells of witnessing, up close while in Moscow, Stalin's murderous purges, and how he has broken with the communists as a result. Silone describes himself as "a Christian without a church, and a socialist without a party" — and somehow also as a person without a country, since he doesn't want to live in Mussolini's Italy. Harro's view of communism is similar. He knows a few communists and is open to working with them, but he himself is too freedom-loving and undogmatic to follow a party line.

"What a person!" Silone later says of his encounter with Harro: "I don't know if I've ever met such courage and integrity anywhere else. Libertas loved him without reservations, and she was unable to entirely suppress her worries about what might happen to him."

Harro and Libertas take their leave and hop into the light blue Fiat. After they've "victoriously conquered all the customs problems," on November 8 they take the Reich Autobahn to the capital, arriving on November 9, 1938. Just as horses take it up a notch in the home stretch, Harro makes use of the 1934 introduction of no speed limit to race homeward. They arrive just in time to drive along Kurfürstendamm and the surrounding streets before millions of glass shards imperil the tires.

It's an evening that will go down in history, this ninth of November, 1938. While Harro and Libs turn in to Waitzstrasse and park their car, Günther Weisenborn is walking down Kantstrasse just a few blocks away. As he nears Fasanenstrasse, it looks to him as if there is a huge festival taking place at the synagogue. All the windows are lit up brightly. But suddenly the light turns a dark red that seems to glow directly from the depths of hell — and black smoke bursts from the roof. A crowd stands on the sidewalk as if nailed in place, faces illuminated by the flames. Nobody does a thing; there is only silence. A fire truck belonging to the Berlin fire department is parked close by, not on duty. The firemen sit around a table playing cards and smoking cigarettes, jovially chattering away.

All over Charlottenburg, Jewish businesses will be destroyed in these hours of so-called Kristallnacht — Crystal Night; the nice-sounding name is meant to downplay the viciousness of it — and their owners will despairingly try to undo what's been done, sweeping away the shards of glass and placing their goods back on the shelves with trembling hands. Greta Kuckhoff, one of Harro and Libs's future collaborators, records vivid details of the terrible scene that night. "On Kurfürstendamm eighty percent of the shops are Jewish owned," says a passerby, falsely, and baits a shopowner: "They shouldn't have pushed their way into everything. Anywhere there's money to made on the quick, they set up shop and won't let anyone else have a piece." Elsewhere, in front of a clothing store, a jeering mob gathers. Behind the smashed window people are looting — young people, but also older folk, otherwise demure people — grabbing whatever they can get their hands on: coats, pants, shirts. The Jewish owner stands in the doorway, tears running down the stubble on his face. In his hands he holds a tailcoat that has been spat on again and again. He tries to clean it with his sleeve as the mob taunts him. Once upstanding citizens shout curses and racists slurs — once normal people after five years of Hitler.

There it is, the shadow that Harro sensed even in Korcula and that "blankets us all, not allowing for any more innocent merrymaking," as Libs writes shortly afterward to Erich Edgar and Marie Luise. It's a difficult return: "This is the new daily reality. A hailstorm of strange worries crackles down on all of us."

Still, they've recharged their batteries in the south, and their love is perhaps stronger than ever before. "What can I write about these things at length. As long as Harro is with me (and that will hopefully still be a long time), there is nothing, absolutely nothing, that seems bad."

They've returned to Nazi Germany, with which, after Kristallnacht, conciliation is no longer possible. Harro pledges his eternal love to her with a kiss of Libertas's silver ring, which she always wears. One single kiss. With it they are now together until liberation from the dictatorship — or until death.

# PART III

# RESISTANCE AND LOVE

## (1939–42)

Here in Berlin I just don't get around to writing. There is so much stuff to do.

— HARRO SCHULZE-BOYSEN

On the other hand, times like these have the advantage that one learns a lot, often more in a few days than in a year otherwise, and that is certainly an advantage.

— LIBERTAS SCHULZE-BOYSEN

# 1

She wears a military blue coat, tall Cossack boots — *the fashionably tall boot of the elegant woman!* — and a beret and has a cigarette between her lips when she walks up to the Lufthansa counter at Tempelhof Airport. She tells the woman at the counter she wants to take the next flight to Königsberg. It's a free plane ticket that belongs to Harro, but he can't use it because there's too much going on at the Air Ministry, where they are preparing the invasion of Poland.

It's the summer of 1939. Libertas sits in a window seat, looking down at the mouth of the Oder River and alongside it Stettin, the capital of Pomerania. The Baltic coastline has a certain boldness, swinging northward like a protruding chin. They fly over Peenemünde, where the scientist Wernher von Braun is building his rocket, then bank to the right and descend toward the city of Danzig (today Gdansk). *We kindly request you to extinguish your cigarettes in preparation for landing.* After a brief layover it's on to "a very nice evening flight" over East Prussia, which from above looks like a giant flounder.

The airport at Königsberg is the oldest civilian airport in Germany. Libertas catches the local railway there, and it shuttles her along the city walls to the old town and North Station, where the trains run to the peninsula of the Curonian Spit. She doesn't have much with her, just her portable Remington typewriter, her Leica camera, her accordion, and *no* bathing suit, because according to her travel brochure, "bathing is not limited by any regulations" in the town of Nidden, her final destination.

After the thirty-minute ride, she is first deposited in Cranz, the biggest East Prussian seaside resort. Its wooden buildings are whitewashed, the summer light glinting golden. Once, this town had been frequented by Jews from Germany, Poland, and Russia. Not anymore. The steamers that ply the Curonian Lagoon — a sheltered waterway between the mainland and the peninsula — leave from here. She must decide between a ship called *Memel* and the "highly elegant, double-turbine *Kurisches Haff*" (as one advertisement describes it), with its restaurant, smoking lounge, and promenade decks. The trip takes a pleasant three hours. There's a markedly high number of women on board, all of them heading to Nidden, this bohemian place for artists and travelers situated between lagoon, the Baltic, and the sky. The famous painter Max Pechstein can frequently be seen on the shore that summer of 1939, usually with his easel, painting a picture in bright South Seas colors: wooden boats on the water, a naked beauty running across the sand. Here in Nidden, on the far edge of the Reich, the cult of Nazism seems to have been kept somewhat in check; one can paint however one wishes, use whatever colors one feels like, and speak more openly than in any other part of Germany.

On her first evening, Libs sits on the veranda that stretches outside the "artist's room" of the popular Blode Hotel, a traditional haunt of painters. Her eyes take in the expressionist works lining the wall by Lovis Corinth, Max Pechstein, Karl Schmidt-Rotluff, and others — a unique experience in Hitler's Germany, where art is strictly regulated and expressionism is considered degenerate. There's a lot of chitchatting on the veranda, preferably about art, but also, of course, about the political situation. Weeks from a possible invasion of Poland, an excursion to the strategically significant Curonian Spit is a somewhat risky proposition — which excites some of the visitors, possibly including Libertas. War is in the air, even if nobody knows the timeline.

Libertas Schulze-Boysen, freelance writer.

Song breaks out on the veranda. It's an old tune from the Curonian region, with a melody that enchants Libertas:

*At twilight the elk step out from the dunes*
*And move from the moor to the sand*
*When night like a loving mother*
*Spreads her blanket o'er sea and land*

It's a dreamlike piece that reminds Libertas of her Liebenberg poems — as well as the poetic tasks ahead of her. She has her manuscript with her, based on the diaries from her long ship voyage on the Black Sea. Nidden is an ideal location to bear down and create something.

It's just a shame that it doesn't work out to stay in Thomas Mann's summerhouse, which he'd built in 1929 with the prize money from his Nobel, and which he'd last visited in 1932. Until recently the owner of the Blode Hotel, the painter Ernst Mollenhauer, still had keys to it and could with the approval of the writer allow artists to use the space. It's easy to believe that Libertas and Thomas Mann discussed this possibility when they met in Zurich the year prior. But just a few weeks before Libs's arrival, the reddish-brown structure with blue shutters and roof trim had been seized by the forestry service — which, ironically, her family friend Göring headed up.

Instead Libs has now rented a room in a fishing hut. It's a nice spot, and she sits there and loads paper into her Remington typewriter while the owner and her daughter mend fishing nets in the next room.

Nidden is an inspiring place, with all the famous artists who have worked or are still working here — and a beautiful, convenient one. Whenever Libertas wants to take a break from her writing, she simply hops up and goes outside, walks through the oaks to the wide beach, takes off her clothes, and throws herself into the breakers, which are far more powerful here than anywhere else along the Baltic coast of Germany. Or she rides her bicycle to the high dunes, called the "East Prussian Sahara," and takes photos with her Leica of this trackless landscape, the "Valley of the Dead," an elemental, primeval world that also enchanted Thomas Mann.

Libertas had learned photography the year before through an intensive course offered at the Berlin film and camera manufacturer Agfa. The most important aspect is choosing the motif, and one day she sees something unusual in the glimmering heat. At first she thinks it's an optical illusion, a Fata Morgana, just as perhaps Thomas Mann had experienced while writing his novel *Joseph and His Brothers,* which he worked on in Nidden during 1931 and 1932. It concerns the fleeing Israelites and their exodus from the sandy hell of Egypt, where they were persecuted. What Libertas sees is a heavily laden ship edging past the high dunes toward a mooring in Nidden — a lagoon steamer practically overflowing with passengers.

She wants to get a better view, and runs along the dunes to the little harbor. The people on board have lots of suitcases and bags with them, but they don't look like artists or tourists. They don't seem to be locals, either, as nobody disembarks. In fact, they are Jews desperately trying to reach the neighboring country of Latvia, where they believe they'll be safe. Latvia is also an authoritarian state, but there's been no racist persecution there. Not yet. Since the Memel Territory was re-annexed by the German Reich in the spring of 1939, many Jews have already fled to Riga, Latvia's capital, and the only major city in the Baltic region. To do so, they use the regular ship lines from Cranz to Memel, with a planned stop en route in Nidden. The regime tolerates this migration. Since there's no concentration camp in East Prussia, the Nazis are actually happy to have the local Jews hit the road of their own volition — and on their own dime.

Libertas gets out her camera as discreetly as possible. She wants to take one or two photos, not more. They'll be symbolic, with the high desertlike dunes in the background. Every person, regardless of where on earth, will immediately understand what's happening in Nazi Germany. The world will wake up and put an end to the anti-Semitic actions before it's too late.

Up to now it's always been Harro who gathers the explosive, confidential material from his workplace that's formed the basis of discussions in their circle of friends. Now she's bringing something to the table and can show that her involvement isn't just superficial, as a few others in the group, including Dr. Elfriede Paul, have claimed. She can prove that she, too, is important for the resistance and not just an appendage of Harro's.

She puts the viewfinder of her Leica up to her left eye and focuses on the Jewish refugees.

Harro will love her for it.

Click.

# 2

Libertas stows her camera again. The ship with the Jewish refugees heads off toward Memel. Suddenly a police officer is next to her, asking for identification. He has spotted her photographing something she should not have photographed. Libs is accused of espionage, arrested, and placed on the next lagoon steamer to Cranz. From there she is taken to the police headquarters in Königsberg, a redbrick fortress-like building overlooking Adolf-Hitler-Platz.

The police station is crawling with uniformed police. Libertas is led along the main wing, deeper and deeper into the huge building. Guard rooms and offices line both sides of the hallway; they turn sharply into a second wing, which wraps around another courtyard. Here are the cells. What she feared the most has now happened. Without Harro, without anyone to advise her, she's alone with police officers.

They confiscate her film as well as her Leica, repeat the charge of espionage, and ask her why she was photographing these unknown people at the Nidden harbor. Libertas hesitates to answer. What do they know about her, about Harro? Have they transmitted her personal information to Berlin already? Will they make a connection to Gisela von Poellnitz? How she would love to be sitting on the veranda of the Blode Hotel, chatting away right now, taking a dip in the ocean later.

Might it be possible to charm the officers? She's just a young, silly thing who was staying at the artist colony trying to write poetry. She had no idea it was illegal to take pictures of people in a boat. They just seemed so strange to her, with all their luggage. She had no plans to do anything with the photos, didn't even know who the people were, and had just found it an unusual sight.

Libertas instinctively refuses to admit anything, and it works. She's permitted to leave, though she is told not to return to the Curonian Spit. Relieved, but also worried and disappointed, she takes the train to the Königsberg airport, where she boards the next plane to Berlin, a new, four-engine Condor.

Harro picks her up, holding her tight after her dangerous adventure.

# 3

Rudolf Bergtel, a man in his late thirties with a receding hairline and melancholy look, has been sentenced to eight years in prison for actively supporting the banned German Communist Party. Since then he's been cutting peat in a swampy prison camp, where the mosquitoes aren't the only bloodthirsty entities. Drying out the land, draining the moors: hard work with poor provisions, not to mention the physical and mental abuse by SA personnel.

Dressed in a blue prison uniform, Bergtel manages to escape in the summer of 1939: with a bike to Bremen, from there onto a train to Berlin, all the while dogs searching for him in the bog. On the third day the manhunt is extended to the entire Reich, but by then he's already met Kurt and Elisabeth Schumacher through his girlfriend, Lotte Schleif, who heads up the public library branch in Berlin-Neukölln.

On August 15, 1939, two weeks before the start of the Second World War, another friend, introduced as "Hans" and dressed in a Luftwaffe uniform, takes him to Anhalter Bahnhof train station. Bergtel, still emaciated, is dressed like a proper hiker, with a backpack, walking stick, and Tyrolean hat with a tuft of chamois hair. It's a cloudy day, barely seventy degrees, with passing showers. In the busy main hall of the station, colorful movie ads decorate the walls; so too does a Wanted poster for Bergtel. The text asks for help in apprehending him: *a hardened criminal, considered dangerous.*

"Pardon me, where is the night train to Nuremberg?" The two men synchronize their watches. Crowds are jostling; Harro notices how quarrelsome and high-strung everyone around him is. There are constant outbursts of arguing, and even if the well-known jovial, funny Berliners haven't entirely died off, it's also clear that these are not cheerful times — which is confirmed by headlines blaring from papers at the newsstands:

LAST WARNING TO DEMOCRACIES — THE AXIS IS CALMLY LOOKING FORWARD TO GROWTH! INTERVIEW WITH REICH ECONOMY MINISTER FUNK: TRADE WITH USA BREAKING DOWN OVER DOGMATIC CAPRICE — NO SIGNIFICANT LOSSES FROM BOYCOTT — TARIFF WALLS NOT INSURMOUNTABLE — GERMANY PREPARED FOR COOPERATION — WE'RE BEING PUSHED TOWARD WAR.

Finally they find their way onto the correct platform. Harro puts the train ticket in Bergtel's hand: one minute left. Blond-haired Kurt Schumacher, one of Harro's closest friends, is already sitting on the train, also dressed as a hiker. The conductor's whistle blows, the signals switch to green. Harro bids farewell, lifting his left hand. As the train pulls out, he walks out of the station with an unhurried stride.

Kurt Schumacher and Rudolf Bergtel spend that night in a sleeper car, pretending not to know each other. Bergtel chats with other passengers in order to appear social despite his haggard appearance. In the morning they transfer in Nuremberg to a local train to Bludenz, deep in Austria.

There begins the arduous climb to the mountain pass called the Swiss Gate, beyond which lies freedom.

Kurt is a mountaineer, knows the region, and wants to reach the goal on that first day — but is Bergtel sufficiently fit? Every few hundred meters of elevation the escapee takes glucose tablets. It's a difficult climb: sure-footedness and a head for heights are definitely required.

Nearly half a day later, at 5,600 feet, they run into a shepherd, who seems suspicious to them. Is he watching the border of the Reich? As casually as possible they ask if he can recommend an alpine hut where they might spend the night. The shepherd tries to tell them they won't reach the shelter before dark, and starts to ask where they're heading. They continue their hike, and the shepherd watches them for a long time, until they take another path to get out of his line of sight. The result is that they miss the hut and end up overnighting in a cave.

They start off again at seven-thirty in the morning. Kurt wants to go faster. They gain elevation, heading toward the sun, and when they reach an emerald green lake after twenty-five kilometers of high alpine hiking, they've nearly made it. The Swiss Gate, the huge hole in the rocks, is within sight, close to 7,000 feet above sea level.

They leave the path and make their way haphazardly toward it: one last steep climb. At the top, they look down and see a Swiss train rolling through the valley below. Rudolf Bergtel takes his leave from Kurt Schumacher, asks him to send his best to Harro, and descends to freedom.

# 4

Not everything goes as well for Libertas as she'd expected upon her return from Königsberg. Instead of solace for the fear she'd had to overcome at the police headquarters, or perhaps praise for her clever demeanor in facing off with the officers there — or even for her courage in taking the photographs of the Jewish refugees in the first place — bitter criticism rains down on her.

The disciplined, ever levelheaded, and razor-sharp doctor Elfriede Paul considers Libertas's decision to photograph the transport ship "stupidity," pure and simple. Libs could have endangered the rest of them, and the fact that Harro is defending her now goes to show that he's too much under her influence. Elfriede's priority is — "given the gravity of the moment," so close to the attack on Poland — to establish unimpeachable standing and not create any scandals, in order to operate most effectively in case of war.

Then it's the last day of peace. Harro and Günther Weisenborn meet in a light drizzle at the sailing club Blau-Rot. Harro walks out to the pier, "slim, handsome, and neat, his profile cuts through the evening sky along the Wannsee," as Weisenborn writes. It is August 31, 1939, and Weisenborn is still suffering from a lung infection, while Harro has just finished thirty-two straight hours of work.

They sail out in the jolly boat *Haizuru*, which Ricci had given to Harro. The wind is refreshing; Harro sits at the tiller while Weisenborn crouches in the bow. "Tonight the attack on Poland will start," says Harro, as if talking to himself. "Up to this point, Hitler still had room to maneuver, but as of tomorrow the options narrow." The boat whizzes through the darkness, water splashing on the planks. For Weisenborn, who doesn't see well at night, Harro appears as a shadow against the moonlit water.

"He'll invade Russia next," Harro continues. "It's going to make history, but he won't be doing so on his own anymore. We're all going to be playing some small role. Now every nation and every person must show where they stand. It's going to be the biggest war in the history of mankind. But *he* will not survive it."

The water rushes past them. Weisenborn can no longer make out his counterpart, can only hear this clear voice in the boat that knows the big moment is at hand.

# 5

With the German invasion of Poland the next morning, rationing begins in Berlin. Clothing, food, drinks, tobacco, and many other daily needs are soon available only with a coupon. Driving cars is restricted, and Harro and Libertas's convertible Caesar is soon joined by two bicycles, christened Brutus and Cassius.

Antiaircraft spotlights scan the skies above the capital ever more frequently, and Harro and Libertas stay home most evenings. They've moved into a proper apartment, and with over 1,740 square feet, a roomy one. It doesn't have the bohemian flair of Waitzstrasse, but it's sunny and freshly painted, and the newly tiled bathroom has hot running water. In addition, there's central heating, so they no longer need to bother with coal bricks. They even have a servant's quarters, which could be a nursery when the war is over. Altenburger Allee 19 is the address, a penthouse in one of those perfect Berlin residential buildings in the fancy area known as Neu-Westend, near the Olympic stadium, boulevards of fragrant green-ery all around. And it's suitable for a lieutenant reserve officer, for that is what Harro has been for the past few months now, promoted on Hitler's fiftieth birthday.

They sit separately, each at a table, and the clack of the typewriter keys fills the room, the bell at the end of the line, the ratchet of the carriage. Most of the time only Harro's Remington can be heard, whenever he's "working on this or that, that makes him happy," as Libertas puts it in a let-ter. For Libertas, writing has become more difficult since the onset of the war. The arrest in Nidden destroyed her creative stay there, frustrated her attempt to deal with her ship diary in peace. The energetic support from the professional author Günther Weisenborn has also disappeared since the end of the affair. Even writing letters has become difficult for her. She's been trying for a while to compose a birthday greeting to Harro's dad but doesn't know where to start or end. Everything affects her far more than during peacetime, when she "had as an outlet the occasional private gaiety and carelessness" to divert herself.

Harro holds up better under the gravity of the moment. Since the in-vasion of Poland, he is more full of energy and on top of things than Libs has ever seen. He is "working himself to death, but he stays high-spirited and positive," she writes in one of her few letters to her father: "And he's full of hope. I'm not so hopeful. I lost much of my 'straightforwardness' this summer because I spent too much time thinking. But I shouldn't even write this to you . . . Sometimes it's not good to think too much because one learns to understand too much."

It sounds banal but isn't: Libertas is suffering. She grieves for the dead on the battlefields of Poland, and in contrast to Harro she doesn't have the ability to consciously control her emotions. As a result, the war doesn't afflict Harro the same way it does her. While she is saddened by "the sac-rifice of youthful, precious blood," Harro sees it as a necessity — even if an infinitely sad one — that finds its meaning in the struggle against Na-zism. She fervently hopes to be able to reach a similar approach, and soon: "Otherwise it won't be bearable."

Suddenly the phone rings, pulling her away from her thoughts. When Libertas answers and hears the voice of Elfriede Paul, who had criticized her so much about Nidden, she's initially alarmed — but when she listens to her words, she's saddened. She knew it all along: There was no hope for Gisela von Poellnitz. Now it's certain. Her cousin, she learns, died the day before, September 14, 1939, in a Swiss sanatorium as a result of the tuberculosis she contracted in Gestapo detainment. She was twenty-four years old.

# 6

Libertas goes to bed early while Harro stays at his writing desk late into the night. Then he too falls asleep for a few hours next to the four-tube radio.

In the morning, which comes too fast when the sun rises shortly after seven a.m. and its red light streams through the large windows, he stretches out his arm and switches on the multiband radio again. He puts on his uniform and the gray gloves his mother has given him for his birthday and descends in the wood-paneled elevator, which is still in service in Altenburger Allee 19 to this day.

From the door it's just a few steps to the subway: Neu-Westend, one stop from Adolf-Hitler-Platz, eleven stations to Potsdamer Platz, twenty-four minutes, then another ten on foot to the Air Ministry, the façade of which has been darkened by overnight showers. He uses the staff entrance and passes the monumental stone depiction of marching soldiers. He doesn't even have to show his identification before entering the empire of handrails made of aluminum, floors of Bavarian marble, the unusually fast paternoster elevator, the more than two thousand rooms where the conquest of Poland is being speedily organized.

Harro treats the military hostilities as a starter's gun for the next phase of his resistance activities. Now that the war is on, his time in the office is merely the first half of a much longer day. No matter how late he has to work during these hectic first weeks of war, it's only in the evenings that things really get going. It's then that he takes off his uniform, puts on sporty civilian clothes, and heads off to make connections with kindred spirits.

An important circle Harro gets to know centers around Heinrich Scheel, a resident of Kreuzberg who had attended the Schulfarm Insel Scharfenberg, a progressive school set up on an island in Tegeler See, a lake in the northwest part of town. He'd grown up in a Social Democrat household and his first pamphleteering experience was about the background of the murder of Ernst Röhm, the founding head of the SA. Later he studied history at Berlin University and is now a meteorological analyst for the Luftwaffe. Crucially, he hates the Nazis just as much as Harro does.

Scheel's best friend from his days at Scharfenberg is named Hans, last name Coppi: a young activist who was politicized early. Hans wears round glasses with thick lenses that magnify his eyes, and has plump curved lips and a dreamy gaze. Coppi's mother runs an ice cream shop in Tegel while he is a lathe operator in a metalshop — a fearless person who from the age of eighteen had spent time in youth prison and in the concentration camp at Oranienburg for distributing pamphlets. Coppi belonged to an illegal communist youth cell, and also had contact with a Catholic variation of the Boy Scouts, with whom he organized a campaign of posting handbills criticizing the rigged Reichstag election of November 12, 1933. Using a children's printing kit they had made hundreds of leaflets: *Isaiah Chapter 41 Verse 24: Behold, ye are of nothing, and your work of nought: an abomination is he that chooseth you.*

# 7

Scheel and Harro joining forces is the beginning of a process the Gestapo will never truly understand. It's not a group that's being formed, and certainly not an organization; it's a social network that spreads and morphs in a nonhierarchical way, surfacing here and there. An organic growth, allowed to evolve, the main point of which is the exchange of information.

Helmut Himpel, whom Harro knows via the Engelsings, connects to them as well. In his free time, the thirty-two-year-old dentist tries his skills as a goldsmith, loves to drink wine from the Baden region, and enjoys making music with his twenty-eight-year-old fiancée, the Catholic Maria Terwiel, known as Mimi, who plays piano and guitar. Because her mother is Jewish, Mimi had to break off her law studies, even though she had successfully laid out her dissertation in 1935. Being of "mixed race," she isn't allowed to marry Himpel, as it would be "race defilement." Mimi ekes out a living as a stenographer, far below her qualifications, and is full of hatred for the Nazis, as Helmut Roloff, a concert pianist who is friendly with the couple, describes it: "But that's how it was for all of us."

Roloff, for his part, met Himpel while playing music: "He was one of those guys whose face one can read and know exactly what he's thinking after a few sentences," he says of the dentist. When Himpel asks whether they might work together in the future, Roloff is surprised at first: "How would a concert pianist and a dentist collaborate?" After Himpel explains that with this question he is putting his life in Roloff's hands, a light goes on for the musician. "Sure, why don't we do that" is his immediate answer.

Even though the amorphous group is growing, there's still no strategy for how best to fight the regime. Indeed, resistance could hardly be more difficult that first winter of war and even more so during the spring of 1940, which is marked by the Wehrmacht's triumphs over Norway, Belgium, Holland, and especially France. The Germans find themselves flush with victory. The security service of the SS perceives "a previously unreached internal cohesion" in the population.

As a reaction, the friends around Harro tighten their close bond, doing many things together, including meeting at Günther Weisenborn's place for a "South Seas" party, where the women wear hula costumes and everyone dances. They also stage a spring party attended by Lale Andersen, the singer who scores Germany's first ever million-selling recording with "Lili Marleen," a sentimental song about a lantern, a loyal girl, and a young sentry.

On May 11, 1940, Harro and Libertas, Kurt Schumacher, Günther Weisenborn and his new girlfriend, Margarete — who goes by the nickname of Joy — as well as Dr. Elfriede Paul and Walter and his son Rainer Küchenmeister travel up to Liebenberg. Instead of sleeping at the castle, they opt for the outdoors, camping on the banks of the private lake, singing songs and playing guitar around a campfire. Libertas joins on the accordion, the sound of which floats across the water in the gathering dusk. It's not exactly a withdrawal into the private sphere, since at these gatherings they naturally talk of politics and the recent attack on the west, but initially a strengthening of personal relationships is the order of business.

Again on August 9, 1940, Harro and Libertas are at Liebenberg, making "raspberry preserves in order to be prepared for the next wartime winter." Harro is once more delighted by the water of Lankesee, which is "magnificently clear, aromatic, and the perfect temperature." But even here in the countryside, peaceful normality no longer exists. "There are swarms of prisoners of war, Poles and Frenchmen," he writes to his parents about the forced laborers working in the fields around Liebenberg: "Among the latter there are many who are educated . . . who apparently submit to their destiny with dignity." Though it's made sure that nobody speaks to them, Libertas cannot resist singing a French song that the prisoners can hear in the distance, while accompanying herself on the accordion.

During this summer of 1940, Libertas takes a new job. She starts to write film reviews for the culture section of the high-circulation *National-Zeitung*. It's no easy task, as all film productions are under Goebbels's auspices and have little to do with her own ideas about cinema. Nor can she write freely and openly criticize; rather, her texts must bend over backward to include language from the *Zeitschriften-Dienst,* a publication put out by the propaganda ministry. It is distributed to editors of all German newspapers and informs them in a paternalistic-friendly tone as to what they are to report on, what they are *not* to report on, and above all, *how* they are to write about things.

The existence of the *Zeitschriften-Dienst* is supposed to remain unknown to the general public. As a result, simply copying passages from it won't work, since then articles from all over the Reich would appear too similar. The reviews must conform to the dictates but also show originality — that is the hard part.

For Libertas there is another difficulty: Her pieces must always be smarter than those of her colleagues, because as a woman she constantly has to assert herself against the male journalists. In addition, the scope of the cultural section is shrinking as the availability of paper drops because of war-related shortages — space on the page is becoming ever more dear. Libs's strategy looks like this: When faced with obvious propaganda flicks, she reviews them in a pro forma way, doing the job as instructed. As for the few films she likes, on the other hand, her sentences take on another nature, her style becomes extravagant, reviews appear in verse or in the form of a love letter, and she tries everything to get across her true thoughts.

It's a method of compromise that is the product of the realities of her existence as a woman in the patriarchal Nazi dictatorship. Libertas decides to knowingly cooperate to a certain extent in the propaganda game in order to maintain influence, make money, and express herself. Even so, she never crosses certain boundaries, refusing for instance to write about *Jud Süss* or *Der ewige Jude,* the most horrid of the Nazi productions — anti-Semitic films that depict Jews as greedy and degenerate, fueling racist hatred in Germany.

It's the same sort of balancing act Harro is doing, a pragmatic, enervating approach that necessitates self-denial: the bitter reality of their so-called normal lives in the Nazi state. She'd wanted to become a poet when she was a child, and now she writes constrained reviews of censored films and is an editor whose thoughts are straightjacketed and who no longer has any illusions about the movie business in Germany. "Only in an authoritarian state and in such a centralized industry could the film world be so hastily and smoothly transformed for war purposes, as has happened in Germany," she writes in one of her articles.

There are also personal developments during this time: new acquaintances who inspire Harro and Libertas. At a dinner at their friends the Engelsings, they get to know Greta and Adam Kuckhoff. Adam is fifty-three, a broad-shouldered writer with calm, dark eyes who loves discussion and only gets skeptical when there are no differences of opinion. His historical novel, *Der Deutsche von Bayencourt,* is considered his masterpiece. At this point he's been working on crime novels for a while. They manage to skate by the censors because they aren't taken seriously as literature; as a result, he's able to hide subtle subversive messages against the Nazi regime in them. Kuckhoff is also interested in film, but has just turned down the largest German production company, UFA, to adapt *Der Deutsche von Bayencourt* for film because he fears the story will be distorted to suit the Nazis.

Kuckhoff's wife, Greta, is thirty-seven, a translator with a narrow, somewhat pale face who worked on the first complete translation of *Mein Kampf* into English — in order to warn the American people against the dictator. Prior to this translation, the only edition available in the United States had been a version scrubbed of the anti-Semitic passages. Greta and Adam have a two-year-old son named Ule.

The Kuckhoffs and Schulze-Boysens hit it off immediately. Adam is pleased at the directness with which Harro discloses his political stance over dinner. Harro doesn't sidestep the burning questions that are on everyone's mind. Instead he hurls himself into them in order to find answers. Greta also likes the dashing, ready-for-action fellow who sits at his desk at the hub of the Air Ministry. Libertas, too, appeals to her, and she especially enjoys the way the elegant pair complement each other during discussions, how they both put even complicated explanations succinctly and in plain language, and thereby exude a confidence that they are at home in the most disparate places and circles.

But most important, via the Kuckhoffs, Harro and Libertas receive an invitation to the home of another couple critical of the regime, Mildred and Arvid Harnack. The two of them live on the top floor of a beautiful old building in Woyrschstrasse, near Tiergarten park — a large apartment without a phone line so as not to be listened to. Arvid is an intellectual, with wire-rimmed glasses and a sharply receding hairline, though he's only in his late thirties. He comes from a distinguished Baltic-German academic family whose most prominent member is Adolf von Harnack, a theologian and church historian, privy counselor and founder of the Kaiser-Wilhelm-Gesellschaft — later renamed the Max Planck Institute — one of those men who contributed to making Germany's research institutions among the best in the world. On a Rockefeller grant, Arvid had studied economics in the United States, where he'd met the love of his life, Mildred, a honey-blond Midwesterner and whip-smart literary scholar who was personally acquainted with Thomas Wolfe as well as the best-selling German writer Hans Fallada.

When Harro and Libertas visit the Harnacks in the spring of 1940, it is Mildred who opens the door, her big blue eyes beaming. The foyer of the apartment is lit by candles, and several vases with fresh lavender sit on an antique table. Beautiful old carpets from Arvid's family cover the exquisite herringbone wood floors, the pale yellow walls are broken up by light blue and green ornamentation as well as paintings by Arvid's mother. The table is set festively, with old family silver: bread, cheese, tomatoes, and liverwurst. Exactly as one would expect from a well-to-do family of scholars.

After the light meal, Arvid guides Harro into the back wing of the place, which he and Mildred use for work and where their library is. Harro scans the bookshelves and sees *Das Kapital* by Karl Marx. Arvid confirms that he believes a planned economy to be the best system. As far as he's concerned it offers the only way to disempower the corporations and cartels whose influence otherwise threatens democracy. He imagines Germany as a state aiming for social equality, organized as a centrally planned economy, and balancing East and West in its foreign policy.

Mildred and Libertas also get on well. Libs has brought old photos of Liebenberg because she thinks they might impress the American. And she's right. The black-and-white pictures of the enchanted castle meet Mildred's childhood images of Germany as a sort of fairy tale, a land of forests, lakes, and castles.

It's a highly charged meeting that night, first and foremost because of Arvid and Mildred's activities. Since 1938 they've been in touch with an American couple by the name of Heath, with whom they exchange confidential information. Donald Heath is the first secretary of the U.S. embassy in Berlin, a financial attaché who is also responsible for intelligence operations. Since Arvid is deputy director of the American department of the German Trade Ministry, his meetings with Heath seem totally innocuous. The two couples have become friends, spending weekends together going cross-country skiing in Grunewald. As members of the American community in Berlin they maintain an unforced association, made even easier by the fact that Mildred is the president of the American Women's Club of Berlin and the Berlin representative of the Daughters of the American Revolution. Mildred also tutors the Heaths' son in English and American literature. On these occasions, Donald Heath Jr. functions as a courier.

Arvid's news about the war economy and rearmament of the Nazi regime arrives via Heath on the desk of Henry Morgenthau, the American Treasury secretary, and then moves on from there to the Oval Office. "An interesting example of how the secret opposition to the Nazi regime continues to exist," Heath writes to the secretary. These weekly Harnack reports cover the operations of the German central bank, foreign trade statistics, Nazi debt, gold, and exchange policies, the financial results of IG Farben, or massive Nazi assets hidden in American banks, which could be confiscated by the United States. Arvid is involved in almost all significant economic political activities of the regime, including secret trade agreements with the Baltic republics and Iran. A perfect source for the United States.

But the Russians, too, are interested in him. Already in 1935 Arvid had contacted the Soviet embassy in Berlin and handed over copies of secret trade contracts, documents concerning the exchange policies of the Reich, and other materials on the financing of German espionage. This cooperation ceased in 1937 as a result of Stalin's purges, when Arvid's contact person was recalled from Berlin.

In the early fall of 1940, the Russians wish to reactivate the cooperation. Though officially Germany is a Soviet ally, there is someone at the embassy on Unter den Linden who doesn't trust the peace between the two countries.

On September 17, 1940, the Harnacks receive a visit. Their bell rings that evening, and as Mildred opens the ornately carved wooden door of their Tiergarten apartment, there's a good-looking man in his early thirties standing there, with thick, light-brown hair, smiling. In fluent German with a Viennese accent, since he learned his German in Austria, he introduces himself as Alexander Erdberg. In reality his last name is Korotkov and he's an envoy for the director of the field office of the People's Commissariat for Internal Affairs, or NKVD, the Soviet intelligence agency. Korotkov knows that Arvid is critical of capitalism, and is also informed about his earlier contacts with the Soviet Union. Perhaps one could revive the cooperation?

Arvid doesn't need to think it over for long. To him the visit offers a long-desired chance to maintain two channels and function as a bridge between the United States and the Soviet Union. Wouldn't such a connection be a first step toward an agreement between the two power blocks for the period after the war? Couldn't it be useful for the German resistance to create ties to the West *and* East in order to advocate for continued independence for Germany once Hitler is gone? This orientation toward both sides conforms with Arvid's political views: socialist economics in a free system. In his view the American president, Franklin D. Roosevelt, whom he admires, also strikes this balance with his economic interventions that could be termed socialist, such as regulating the banks, and the large-scale public-commissioned projects that stimulate the American economy in the wake of the Depression. It is also true that the United States has yet to enter the war, while the Soviet Union, on the other hand, is under potential threat, which in Arvid's opinion makes working with the Russians sensible.

His colleagues have no idea what's on his mind:
Lieutenant Harro Schulze-Boysen at the Air Ministry.

Arvid Harnack learns during this fall of 1940 just how serious the threat is to the Soviet Union from a colleague who has contacts to the Wehrmacht high command. The word is that Germany will start a war in the east in the coming year. The goal: the separation of the European section of the USSR along a line running from Leningrad to the Black Sea. In this area a vassal state is to be created, fully dependent on the Reich, and in the rest of the vast territory the plan is to set up a German-friendly anti-communist government.

During the final weeks of 1940 Harro also receives evidence of a change in posture toward the Soviet Union. His Russian knowledge has improved to the point that he can now read the Russian classics in their original language. But when he tries to borrow Dostoevsky from the library at the Air Ministry, he realizes that all Russian literature has suddenly been removed. Tolstoy, Pushkin, Gogol — none of it is available anymore. Shall members of the Wehrmacht no longer be able to read about the demise of Napoleon's army in Russia's vastness in *War and Peace*?

On December 13, 1940, Hitler signs the highly secret directive that sets in motion the attack against the Soviet Union. As a result, Harro is moved at the beginning of January 1941 from Wilhelmstrasse in the center of Berlin to a forest on the Havel River, near Potsdam, called Wildpark-West. There the general staff of the Luftwaffe is housed, including Göring's command bunker, with its own rail station for his four specially chartered trains. From one day to the next, Harro no longer lives at home with Libertas on Altenburger Allee, instead staying in a room in the woods, his window looking out on the bleak shapes of bare trees, looming out of the frozen ground like giant thorns.

His work duties change as well. He is now the contact point for German Luftwaffe attachés from around the globe, and receives confidential reports about sensitive military topics from all the important world capitals. What Libertas initiated with her chat with Göring at Liebenberg is bearing fruit: Harro is now sitting at a nexus of information of the German war machine — and at the exact moment when his new acquaintance Arvid Harnack is making closer contact with Moscow.

# 8

The first concrete evidence of the Wehrmacht's planned attack on the largest country in the world comes across Harro's desk in January 1941: secret aerial photos taken from six thousand feet by a plane flying out of Königsberg. The photos of Leningrad and the nearby island Kotlin, of important rail junctions and ports, are so clear that individual buildings can be made out. At the same time the so-called Russia department is transferred to the active staff of the Luftwaffe, which prepares the war plans.

Every weekend Harro takes the S-Bahn into the city, though he uses his precious time not necessarily to be together with Libertas but rather to take walks with his new friend Arvid through the ice-cold Tiergarten park. Each man brings to these secretive meetings news from his field of work. A detailed picture of the Wehrmacht plan takes shape — valuable information that could be used by the other side to prepare. Arvid, this exciting new contact, sends a jolt through Harro. Together they form a two-component explosive: alone, each was of limited effectiveness, but now the otherwise so dissimilar men are like hot wires creating a spark.

Harro knows that his information ends up in Moscow through Arvid, and it doesn't bother him. On the contrary. Even if it is morally questionable to support the Soviet Union because of the red dictatorship's brutality, gulags, show trials, and countless political victims, he still considers it his duty to inform the great neighbor to the east — a country that Germany has a nonaggression pact with — about the invasion plans. The Soviets are still not at a level of military preparedness to be able to withstand a German surprise attack. What could be worse than if Hitler, as feared, managed with another Blitz to get all the way to the Ural Mountains and into the Caucasus and were able to access the vast resources there, especially the gas and oil? At that point the Nazi regime's global domination would be all but assured. As Churchill recognizes, Harro also knows that the giant communist empire, with its inexhaustible supply of raw materials and powerful steel industry, offers the most effective — and perhaps the only — military option to stop Hitler's expansion and suppress Nazism.

Harro is also pursuing another strategy to sabotage Operation Barbarossa, which is the code name of the planned invasion. He hopes to use a pamphlet, his first since *Der Stosstrupp,* to convince his comrades, the officers of the Wehrmacht, of the senselessness of an attack on Russia. In every free and unobserved moment in his monklike work cell in Wildpark-West, he works on a text about Napoleon Bonaparte and his failure in his attempt to conquer the huge eastern realm, including plenty of barbs that any German can see are aimed at Hitler. Bonaparte wasn't born in France but rather in Corsica, the piece explains. Just like Hitler was born in Austria, not in Germany. Initially Napoleon had claimed that war was only about restoring the country's natural borders — another parallel to Hitler's expansion of German territory even before the start of the war. But then French troops got bogged down all over Europe. Most people at that time were convinced that he'd be successful in the conflict with Russia. Likewise in Germany, many are convinced Hitler is invincible. "But when the victor of so many battles retreated in defeat, he realized that he had incorrectly evaluated the land and people of Russia. The war was settled politically, not militarily. The emperor was abandoned by the 'society circles' of his own people," Harro says in his six-page essay, which forecasts a similar outcome for the Nazi dictator.

This time helping him write is the eighteen-year-old Horst Heilmann, the son of a professor from Dresden, who wishes to become a diplomat. Horst is Harro's best listener in the foreign policy department at Friedrich Wilhelm University, where Harro had taken up his studies again in January 1940 in order to have an academic credential and thus meet the requirements for a higher pay grade. Since then Harro has taken over teaching several seminars because there's a shortage of assistants. Initially a committed member of the Hitler Youth, and even a Nazi Party member, Horst Heilmann has turned away from fascism under Harro's influence. He's co-author of the Napoleon piece, with which Mimi Terwiel and Elisabeth Schumacher also help. Printed at postcard size, the essay reaches opposition circles as far away as Munich.

Harro has no illusions about the perils of these activities. To his parents, who seem to sense how risky his life has become during that long, cold winter of 1940–41, he writes:

> Dear Mama — Papa and you both write that I should "beware." It should be clear that I'm not doing anything frivolously. But there's no guarantee of any of our lives during this time of war. As concerns my person, you must always know that the length of a life is no measure. I believe that in my 31 years I've lived more intensely and have experienced more than many other people combined. Given that, how could anything sad happen? So please do not worry on my behalf!

The danger for Harro rises when Korotkov wants to meet Arvid's contact in the Air Ministry. Arvid says he'll ask whether the individual is willing to have a meeting, cautioning that Korotkov needs to be careful. He suggests it is "advisable to keep up the appearance," that Harro is meeting the person "to whom his information has been passed, but who isn't necessarily part of a Soviet agency." Otherwise there is a risk that Harro will interpret the get-together as a recruitment to work as a spy and turn it down on principle. After all, while Harro is actively working to undermine the Nazi regime, he also considers himself a German patriot.

Thursday, March 27, 1941, is the last day it snows that winter. The trees are still bare but are beginning to come to life, poised to blossom. Harro takes the S-Bahn in his officer's uniform from Wildpark-West to Wannsee, where he switches trains and heads to Schöneberg. It's below freezing, fresh white snow covers the space between the rails, and at the Harnacks' apartment on Woyrschstrasse, logs are flickering in the fireplace.

Harro is introduced to a good-looking man called Erdberg. The Russian starts the conversation with his Viennese accent. He doesn't wish to stick to small talk and wants to focus on the main point. There is one difficult aspect he addresses right away. As much as he would value Harro's general engagement in the resistance, he also knows that his superiors in Moscow will be highly skeptical. The distribution of illegal leaflets, for example, is just too dangerous, and should therefore be stopped. Moscow is interested in only one thing: information about possible German attack plans. Otherwise it would be best if the sources lived completely conventionally, not raising any suspicion.

Harro thinks about this — and shakes his head. He makes it clear that he aims to create a "counterpublic" against the Nazis and that the "work of his group, which consists mostly of artists" will be continued "without being reduced to mere intelligence work." If this condition is accepted, he is willing to keep the Russians apprised of things going forward. He has no intention whatsoever of holding back or concealing anything. In closing Harro pulls a sheet of paper from the pocket of his uniform and reads from it a list of railway main lines that are to be paralyzed in an initial attack.

Later that evening, Alexander Korotkov looks out the window of his office inside the Soviet embassy on Unter den Linden, the city's main boulevard, which is swathed in black-white-red swastika flags. It's no longer snowing, and he types out a report for his director. To Harro he assigns for internal use the code name Starshina, the Russian word for "sergeant." The courageous German — who knows what he wants and showed up prepared for the meeting — made a good impression on him. Korotkov taps on the Cyrillic keys: "He is, it appears, a fierce man of inimitable enthusiasm and passion when it comes to discussing the situation in Europe and the world — and ponders the need for action to attain these goals."

# 9

Through his contact with Korotkov, Harro has committed, as he is later accused, *Landesverrat*, or treason. It is the most ignominious crime that a Prussian officer could commit, and that's what Harro is: an officer, and the kind there won't be any more of in the country soon. Yes, his great-uncle Admiral von Tirpitz had built the navy for the Kaiser, and now Harro Schulze-Boysen believes to have realized as a first lieutenant of the Luftwaffe that the institution to which he has devoted his life, and to whose commander in chief he has sworn allegiance, is betraying itself and has become an enemy of Germany. And he, as a soldier, must do what he is duty-bound to do: fight the enemy. Other people, specifically his commanders, have betrayed the country in that they are facilitating an illegal attack on the Soviet Union. He, on the other hand, is risking his life to save Germany, which is threatened with utter destruction by a two-front war. And in order to liberate the country from this system that is turning upright citizens into murderers.

On April 2, 1941, less than a week after Harro's initial meeting with Korotkov, the Soviet account of the events surrounding Arvid and Harro is stamped SOVERSHENNO SEKRETNO, meaning top secret. "It is essential to activate the work with Starshina to the maximum extent," it has been decided in the Lubyanka, the central intelligence office in Moscow.

The sort of activity that is meant becomes clear on April 18, 1941, when Korotkov opens a vulcanized fiber case that has been sent by diplomatic post. Inside is a portable transceiver. It's a battery-powered radio device that can be used outside — on a boat, for instance. "A spare battery," it says in an accompanying leaflet, "as well as instructions for making contact with us will follow."

In the eventuality that it indeed comes to war against the Soviet Union, Harro and his friends are supposed to be able to share military information at any time, through the ether, directly from Berlin to the East.

# 10

It is Sunday, April 20, 1941, Hitler's fifty-second birthday. Harro is enjoying a bike ride through the woods of Wildpark-West, first along the Havel River, then the lake Zernsee and the river Wublitz. He inhales the fresh air deeply, thankful for every ounce he can get into his body. Spring. After half an hour he reaches Marquardt, a fishing village north of Potsdam. There he leans the bike on a park bench. Libertas and Elisabeth Schumacher are coming by train, as is Korotkov, though independently of the other two.

It's around fifty degrees, the sun appears sporadically, lighting up the woods and shimmering across the water as the three young Germans and the equally bohemian Russian stroll along the banks of the river.

How far along are the plans for the invasion of the Soviet Union at this point? Harro has discovered that the heads of military-economic administration for various soon-to-be-occupied districts of Soviet territory have already been selected. For Moscow, for instance, it will be a Herr Burger, who up to now has served as the chair of the chamber of commerce of the city of Stuttgart. Burger, like other top-ranking officials, has already received his conscription notice and is preparing to leave for Russia. All of which Harro reports to Korotkov.

They head for a kiosk. There's a radio blaring, an international soccer match: Germany versus Switzerland. Coming out of halftime it's tied at one goal apiece, a disappointing start for the team of German national coach Sepp Herberger. Harro orders a round of beers, and they sit at a square table with cast-iron legs. Korotkov used to play soccer, on the youth squad of Dynamo Moscow. "The German team advances forcefully," exclaims the radio announcer excitedly, "but they hesitate in front of the goal. Their technical superiority may not be enough to overcome the situation." Suddenly a surprise: The Swiss take a two-to-one lead. How can it be, the team of huge Germany losing to that of tiny Switzerland? Korotkov smokes a cigarette, sips his beer, looks across the water at the woods on the other side. It all looks so harmless, two men and two women meeting and enjoying drinks while in the background a soccer match plays, this beautiful sport where even an outsider has a chance.

So who should take the transceiver? Elisabeth? She's dependable, and because she's a freelancer, she's flexible. And her husband, Kurt, could be the radio operator. For Harro, the risk of handling the broadcasting is too high. He's too heavily exposed by his work in Wildpark-West, and his apartment in town, on Altenburger Allee, is also a poor choice as a radio base, since it is the meeting place of his oppositional group of friends. Also, the somewhat spacey Libertas is less ideal as an operator of the device than the more purposeful Elisabeth, who is stalwart and ever more hard-edged in her engagement against the Nazis.

As she demonstrates on this April day, Libertas is indeed the most erratic in her actions. She comes willingly to a meeting with a Russian agent, enjoying it as an unusual social event, something titillating. But she's restless, subject to mood swings — and sometimes becomes caught up in her own concerns.

These last few months before the invasion of the Soviet Union, which will cost millions their lives, she spends time "with obligatory fecklessness such as looking for an apartment for [her] brother, putting in moth-balls, writing articles about film," as she herself reports. These are exactly the things she feels like doing — but of what value are they in her life with Harro? For that there's only one thing of import, and even if she agrees with it, it's not her true passion, not always at least. It's already led to tension, fights, which have been more frequent of late — and in the stressful period leading up the war in Russia, it's led to Libertas looking for a way out, a "new fulfilling activity . . . that will preferably free me from Berlin."

Sometimes the marriage with Harro really is not easy, particularly when he seems so aloof, when his head and perhaps his heart aren't with her but somewhere else. It's a complicated, extreme situation to fall head over heels in love with somebody who, because of his experiences, particularly those nights in the torture chamber, might no longer be capable of unobstructed love. It hurts Libertas again and again when she is unable to get close to him during the rare intimate moments they have together, and to have to observe him only from outside, to gaze upon the façade of his perfect Prussian officer's face. What is she supposed to do?

It's not an easy period for Libertas. She's given up work on her ship's journal, too, which had meant so much to her. "As a result of the shortage in paper and diminished labor, novels are no longer being published unless they can somehow be justified military-economically or as propaganda," she writes to her mother-in-law, Marie Luise, in frustration. Tough times for a book about a woman's self-discovery and self-realization on the global seas. Where is her way forward now? How can she be free to fulfill her own mission of leading a truly artistic life?

# 11

On June 17, 1941, during a meeting in the Kremlin, information provided by Harro to Korotkov about the finalization of military preparations for the invasion of the USSR is brought to the table. But Joseph Stalin shakes his head: *Propaganda!* He is convinced that his pact with the Third Reich will endure through the rest of the year. "Send your 'informant' from the staff of the German Luftwaffe back to his whore of a mother," he scribbles with his notorious green pen in the margins of the top secret classified report 2279/M: "He's not an informer but rather a disinformer. J. St." The red dictator still regards Hitler as a dependable, staunch ally — not as his most dire enemy. Stalin, the distrustful control freak who sees treachery behind every hedge, believes the despot in Berlin will truly stick to a pact.

On the evening of this same seventeenth of June, Günther Weisenborn is at Harro and Libertas's, sipping wine with them. "Marriage problems," notes the author in his diary laconically. An observation that is perhaps tinged with Schadenfreude — but in this case, one that is also strikingly perceptive.

As a result of her efforts, Libertas has several job offers during these precarious days, all of them outside Berlin. The editorial staff of the *National-Zeitung* in the western German city of Essen has held out the prospect of her taking over the cultural section, a newly founded news agency has promised her the position of bureau chief in Geneva or Lisbon, and Agence Havas, the largest French news agency, which has recently been taken over by Germans, is interested in Libertas for a post in occupied Paris. She now has the possibility to be independent — and also to extricate herself from the mortal danger of the illegal activities — and to function out in the wide world, making money, and to advance as a woman. It's all within reach. But can she bring herself to leave her husband in this precarious situation?

She decides to consult the discreet Greta Kuckhoff, at the Kuckhoffs' place, where it's possible to relax on the roof terrace while their turtle crawls around and their little boy, Ule, takes a nap. Having chosen a sunny spot, Libs sits on the terrace with her eyes closed as Greta serves coffee and cognac and asks if everything's okay, noting that Libertas looks tense. Libertas opens her eyes and tells her she's worried. There are such huge political events unfolding at their doorstep that she feels paralyzed and ill equipped: events "that on the one hand cripple one's strength, but on the other spark the heart and the entire person, and put everything else on hold and render all private plans meaningless . . . And rush decisions, making it demonically difficult to make the right choices." She smokes one cigarette after the next and drinks coffee greedily. Greta shouldn't misunderstand her: She sees the importance of doing everything — doing even more than she has up to now. But she doesn't believe that, in a worst-case scenario, she can hold up under an enhanced interrogation by the Gestapo. Unfortunately she's from a family that, since the scandal that embroiled her grandfather and the Kaiser, hasn't been equipped with robust nerves.

Greta listens to it all. In resistance one can burn out, get exhausted, have doubts about success — tire of the mortal risk. Ask oneself too often whether it's enough or what will happen next. It's an enervating existence. Greta understands: Libs is young and hungry for life, and perhaps it is wrong for people who like to follow their impulses and senses to undertake such serious work. But she also knows that Libs's sense of belonging to the network is strong. Her love for Harro defines her life. And besides, she is an aristocrat, the one among them who can pass in the uppermost circles. Wouldn't it be better if she stayed?

Whether what restores her mettle is the cognac, the stimulating coffee, or the spirited advice that it is always good to recognize one's own short-comings, after the discussion with Greta, Libertas turns down all the out-of-town job offers. She will stay with Harro, attempting to find her liberty in the fight against evil, which at this point has almost all of Europe in its claws.

# 12

On the evening of June 21, 1941, Alexander Korotkov is dining splendidly with a colleague from the Soviet embassy in the restaurant at the Kroll Opera House, as he so often does. Six young Wehrmacht officers are sitting at the next table, in high spirits. *For how much longer?* the Russian asks himself, as he observes their merriment.

At the same hour, in Moscow, the dreaded chief of the Soviet secret police, Lavrentiy Beria, sends a note to Stalin condemning Korotkov's boss for relaying the information he has provided from Harro:

> I once again insist on the recall and punishment of our ambassador in Berlin, Dekanozov, who as before is bombarding me with "disinformation" that Hitler is allegedly preparing to attack the USSR. He stated that this "attack" will begin tomorrow . . . But I and my people, Joseph Vissarionovich, firmly remember your wise prognosis: Hitler will not attack us in 1941!

Even that night a freight train rolls over the border of the German Reich from the east, laden with Ukrainian wheat. The Soviet Union dutifully fulfills the agreed-upon quotas in the Hitler-Stalin pact.

At three in the morning, a light is still burning in the German Foreign Office on Wilhelmstrasse. A black Mercedes with a driver and an SS escort is sent to the Soviet embassy, and Wladimir Dekanozov is forced to get into the car. The German foreign minister greets him coolly and informs him of the attack that is now under way. Dekanozov can smell schnapps on von Ribbentrop's breath. Suddenly this man is no longer one of his most important allies but his worst enemy. The Russian is told that his embassy on Unter den Linden will be barricaded.

In Moscow, the Soviet foreign minister reacts with disbelief to the bad news, which is conveyed to him by the equally concerned German ambassador, von Schulenburg: "We didn't deserve this," splutters Molotov. "One could have negotiated!" Only Stalin still believes he can negate the truth, by not accepting it and trying to downplay things: "Hitler does not know about this."

Out at Wildpark-West, sirens ring out at six in the morning on June 22. Screaming and grandiloquent, a voice announces over the loudspeakers that the German armies have crossed the Russian border in order to liberate the world from the scourge of communism. The sun is up, light pressing through the forest; it is the longest day of the year. At midday the sun is at its highest point, and the Germans celebrate it with fire. According to the Nibelungen saga, Siegfried, the radiant hero in armor, is killed on the solstice by his dark counterpart, Hagen.

Even if none of it is a surprise to him, Harro senses the historical gravity of the moment. The war against the Soviet Union will represent a change of era: the beginning of the end of the Nazi dictatorship. Now the largest country on earth is fighting the criminals in Berlin. He's convinced that the friendly contacts he maintains with Moscow will be helpful for the period that comes next, and create an opportunity to protect the national autonomy of Germany, to hinder a second Versailles. Harro hopes to be a respected negotiating partner by that time.

Life in Berlin goes on quite normally on this day that is anything but normal. The German soccer championship finals take place as scheduled. Ninety-five thousand fans cheer feverishly and celebrate in the Olympic stadium. Libertas hears each goal live, the noise floating in through the open window of the apartment on nearby Altenburger Allee.

Meanwhile, on Unter den Linden, a heated crowd presses toward the cordoned-off Soviet embassy. Someone points to the smoke coming from the chimney. Those dirty fumes, he yells, prove that they're burning all the evidence of disgraceful Bolshevik warmongering. We should repeal the extraterritoriality! Immediately!

It surprises Korotkov how quickly everything happens, though he should have known. Had he not sufficiently trusted his own sources? After the hatches are battened down, he still sits at one of the transceivers — of which there are now two. He's been due to deliver this one to Elisabeth Schumacher for more than two months. Korotkov knows it's crazy, but he

119

has to go back out into what is now the enemy capital. But how can he get past the SS guards carrying a radio device — and encryption key codes — without being caught? The situation in the embassy is ominous: The telephone line has been cut off, so there's no longer a connection to Moscow. Supplies are low, and it is supposed to take several more days before an evacuation. Only the First Secretary, Valentin Berezhkov, is allowed out, because he has been invited to a meeting at the German Foreign Ministry and will be escorted there by an SS officer by the name of Heinemann.

With pipe and pistol: Harro takes aim. Pictured here with
Dr. Elfriede Paul and Kurt Schumacher.

Korotkov comes up with a plan. Berezhkov will treat the German to the last of the caviar and Crimean champagne from the depths of the embassy cellar. And indeed, Heinemann takes the bait, becomes trusting, and indicates he's having money troubles. The Russian offers him one thousand marks that he's been saving in order to buy a music box. He doesn't need the money anymore because he won't be permitted to take it out of the country anyway. The SS officer accepts the bribe. There is more of the caviar, along with all sorts of smoked fish, vodka, and beer, while Berezhkov invents a romantic tale about one of the embassy employees named Sascha and his German fiancée, whom he may never see again at this point. Heinemann offers to smuggle Sascha out during Berezhkov's visit to the Foreign Ministry so that he can say goodbye to his lover.

The moment arrives, and they drive in the embassy vehicle, an Opel, to the guarded perimeter. Heinemann sits woodenly in the front next to Berezhkov, while Korotkov is hidden in the back with his vulcanized fiber case. The guards don't notice. At Wittenbergplatz, in front of the entrance to the department store KaDeWe, Korotkov is let out. He gets on the nearby subway and heads to Elisabeth Schumacher's place.

The next day they repeat the whole thing, and Korotkov meets for the last time with Adam Kuckhoff, with whom he has become friends over the past few months. But now that the attack has begun, there is discord between the two men. In order to stop the German war machine, Korotkov suggests to the dumbfounded German that he scatter nails and shards along the arterial roads of Berlin in order to hinder the columns of vehicles and tanks heading east. Kuckhoff stares at him stone-faced with his dark eyes. Doesn't Korotkov know that the Wehrmacht has staggered positions all through Poland? And that you can't stop tanks with nails? When the Russian notices Adam's annoyance, he tries to conciliate him: It was just an example. What he meant was that one needs to do everything possible to hamper the German advance. "Believe me, we are robust and strong," says Korotkov, full of conviction: "The war will be over relatively quickly." As a going-away present he hands Adam a packet of coffee, whole beans so it can be kept for a long time. Then they agree to an apartment swap after the capitulation of the German Reich — in order to come to a better understanding of each other's culture in the future.

# 13

Not long afterward, with the Wehrmacht already deep into Belorussia, a vulcanized fiber case is opened in a Berlin apartment: "A thousand greetings to all our friends," goes the coded test message that Harro broadcasts into the ether. The encryption is handled by Arvid, who has set up a room in his apartment specially for this. It's not so easy, not even for a superbrain like his, and demands full concentration. The Russians are notorious for their complicated codes and use a method involving a word order from a random book to create a key code. Only when the listener has the same book and knows which sentence is being used can he decipher the message.

If the enciphering isn't difficult enough, operation of the radio transceiver represents its own challenge. The fact that the promised professional instructions never materialized in the rush and excitement of the moment doesn't make things any easier. It's true that Harro took a course on radio communications as part of his military training and knows how to set the right wavelengths; nevertheless, he waits nervously after sending the "thousand greetings," awaiting a reply that proves the message has reached its intended recipient. And sure enough a reply does come. The Russians have received and deciphered their test broadcast.

But who shall be the radio operator going forward? Harro doesn't wish to take on the duty because of his position, and the person he'd imagined handling it, Kurt Schumacher, is unexpectedly unavailable. As a result of the Russian campaign, the sculptor has been conscripted and is guarding prisoners of war in Posen.

Harro quickly seeks a replacement. His choice is Hans Coppi. Since he's been detained in a concentration camp before, he's considered "unworthy" of duty and isn't conscripted into the Wehrmacht — so he can be depended on to be around for the task of broadcasting. In Moscow they're not happy about the change and express doubts due to Coppi's inexperience. Nevertheless, the central office demands of Korotkov that the decision be stuck to.

There's no record of how many attempts at communicating take place in the next few months. But the Soviets do not receive the secret military reports from Berlin they feverishly anticipate — and at a time when the Wehrmacht is making huge territorial gains as Fedor von Bock, supreme commander of Heeresgruppe Mitte (Army Group Center), encircles and decimates the Soviet Western Front under the command of General Dmitry Pavlov near Bialystok and Minsk. Hundreds of thousands of Red Army soldiers end up in prison camps, and shortly thereafter the Wehrmacht takes Smolensk and heads on a direct course toward Moscow.

Where's the news from Berlin? Korotkov, who is now the Moscow chief of the German division of the foreign intelligence service of the Interior Ministry — the People's Commissariat for Internal Affairs, abbreviated NKWD — could answer the question. He knows the backstory: The radio operator needs to learn his job first. It's complicated, and Hans Coppi is struggling to figure everything out. It's essential to broadcast on days of the month that produce multiples of four and seven, and from 2:00 a.m. to

3:15 a.m. German time on the wavelength 52.63 meters, as well as from 4:15 p.m. to 5:30 p.m. on the wavelength 42.50 meters, and from 10:30 p.m. to 11:15 p.m. on 46.10 meters. For a call signal he is to use the fourth, first, and sixth letter of the German name of the day of the week when the connection is made. If he calls out into the ether on a Thursday, which in German is *Donnerstag*, the call sign would be NDR; if he sends a signal on a Monday, or *Montag*, it is TMG.

As hard as Hans Coppi tries, no connection is made during this crucial second half of 1941. At the same time, Arvid is informed about the German line of attack at the Trade Ministry, and Harro learns just as much at the Air Ministry. The two of them see ever more clearly that the Nazi strategy is built on sand, because the German war economy isn't able to support the simultaneous campaigns against the British Empire and the Soviet Union for much longer. The Reich has overextended itself, and even if the Soviets have their backs up against the wall, there will be a reversal. Massive logistical problems are already appearing for the Wehrmacht during the autumn of 1941. Soon the Germans will be short of fuel — without gasoline, there's no advance. There aren't enough aircraft for the Luftwaffe, and the production of ships is also lagging. With the exception of brutality and Pervitin, the methamphetamine pills distributed by the million to soldiers to give them an artificial boost, nearly everything is in short supply. These critical actualities, substantiated by data from Harro and Arvid's offices, could steel the resolve of the Allies. The psychological effect of successful, consistent communications via shortwave radio could be highly valuable.

In Moscow the military leadership is calling ever more urgently for information from the in-house intelligence service, the Soviet Main Directorate of the General Staff of the Armed Forces, referred to as the GRU, as well as the civilian intelligence service, the NKWD. The head of the NKWD, Pavel Fitin, decides to reactivate the channel to Berlin, leaving his office on Lubyanka Square and walking through the ice-cold rain to a meeting with his counterpart at the GRU. The idea they cook up together will change the course of Harro and Libertas's lives.

The Soviet military intelligence service has a man in Brussels with the code name Kent and a taste for adventure. Despite all the risks, the idea is to send Kent to Berlin in order to "clear up the situation, gather and transmit urgent information to Moscow, as well as to figure out why the radio contact isn't working," as it states in a secret Soviet file. That is how the following message, formulated by the NKWD, is sent via GRU channels from Moscow to Kent in Brussels:

In Berlin find Adam Kuckhoff or his wife at Wilhelmshöherstrasse 18, telephone number 83-62-61, second staircase to the left, top floor, and explain that you were sent by a friend of "Arvid" and "Choro" whom Arvid knows as Alexander Erdberg. Remind him of the book Kuckhoff gave him before the war, and of the theater piece "Ulenspiegel." Suggest to Kuckhoff he arrange a meeting between yourself, and "Arvid" and "Choro." If possible, then figure out from Kuckhoff:

1. When will the radio connection be made and why isn't it working now?

2. Where are all the friends and how is their situation?
. . .

In the case that Kuckhoff cannot be found, seek out the wife of "Choro," address Altenburger Allee 19, telephone number 99-58-47, and explain to her that you have been sent by someone whom she met together with Elisabeth in Marquardt. This mission is applicable even if you are able to meet Kuckhoff.

By "Choro" the Russians, who don't have an "h" in the Cyrillic alphabet and transliterate it as "ch" instead, mean Harro. This message, born of necessity, is hurriedly sent as a series of numerical codes on August 26, 1941, wafting over the antennas of the German radio-defense forces. The inclusion of names, addresses, and telephone numbers in this wantonly negligent transmission is likely due to the anxiety of the situation.

One thing is for sure: The only thing separating Harro and Libertas, Arvid, and Adam from the executioner now is Russian encryption, supposedly the best in the world and impossible to crack.

# 14

In September 1941, the man the GRU calls Kent — the name comes from a British spy novel — is preparing for his Berlin visit. In real life, if he can be said to have one at all, Kent is named Anatoly Gurevich. He's Jewish, studied tourism in Leningrad, was spared in Stalin's bloody purges because he was too young, took a quick course in espionage when there was a desperate need for intelligence personnel, and in his first mission worked as an interpreter in the Spanish Civil War. Kent is not too tall, has protruding ears, the forehead of a thinker, and, whenever possible, a pipe in his mouth, which is why his lower lip is somewhat deformed. At this point he lives in Brussels using a fake Uruguayan passport under the name

Vincente Sierra, has fifty suits in his closet, and lives with a Jewish woman named Margarete Barcza, who fled Czechoslovakia with her family from the Nazis. The thin, blond Barcza has no idea who her husband really is, but actively takes part in the social life he leads as a successful business-man. At twenty-seven, Kent is the head of Simexco, a Belgian trade com-pany that is actually a cover operation and that, interestingly, specializes in working with the German occupation forces, supplying tools and other material for everything the Nazis are building in occupied Western Eu-rope. That is how their connections are made, how genuine trust is built, while militarily significant information is collected along the way.

In Brussels, the German communist Johann Wenzel, known as *Profes-sor,* is responsible for sending the gathered data to the Soviet capital via shortwave radio. And Brussels is just a branch of a larger entity. The main operation is in Paris, led by Leopold Trepper, a Polish Jew and commu-nist, a legendary figure feared and hunted by the German security forces as *Grand Chef.* Trepper had initially headed up a clothing firm with the ro-mantic name Foreign Excellent Raincoat Company, but he too has tran-sitioned into the construction business. In the French capital the con-nections are particularly good to Organisation Todt, a German civil and military engineering organization that is building the Atlantic Wall in France for the Nazi regime. Wherever a new bunker is constructed or new barracks for the Waffen-SS are erected, the Soviet agents not only know about these projects, but are also making money from them.

On August 28, 1941, two days after he has received the radio message, Kent, the *Petit Chef,* waltzes into the Brussels office of Oberfeldkomman-dantur 672 and submits his request for a Simexco business trip to Ger-many. He quickly receives a document confirming the military-economic interest of the trip, and on September 24, the German chief of security police and intelligence confirms the travel visa for the Uruguayan citizen Vincente Sierra for the territory of the Reich and Bohemia and Moravia — the name given to German-occupied Czechoslovakia.

A month later, on October 21, the Wehrmacht is so close to the Rus-sian capital that the tank general Heinz Guderian can see with his scis-sor-scope the goings-on at the end of a Moscow tram line. The same day, Kent is on a train from Brussels to Cologne, where he has a one-hour lay-over, smokes a pipe, takes a look at the famous cathedral, and then gets in a sleeper car to Nuremberg, and at ten-thirty the next morning contin-ues on from there to Prague. Still using the name Sierra, he checks in to a room at Hotel Skroubec on Wenceslas Square, does some business for Si-mexco in the hours that follow, appears at the chamber of commerce, and then tries in vain to make contact with a fellow agent who has, it turns out, already been nabbed.

On October 28, a Tuesday, he heads from occupied Prague to the capital of the Reich. The train chugs through the Elbe valley, with its wooded hillsides and castles, all dusted in an unusually early snowfall. As they pass a factory, Kent pulls out a notebook and writes down the location and name, using invisible ink. Every time they come through a town he looks, as ordered, for signs of bomb damage. He's also to keep a lookout for possible chemical weapons production sites. This is, however, difficult to do while riding past on the train. The light snow makes him happy: If it is this cold in Germany at the end of October, it could be a sign of a hard winter, and that means the Wehrmacht will be freezing in the Russian expanses.

Arriving in Berlin — at a time when the deportation of the Jewish population has begun in the entire Reich — the agent checks in to the room he'd reserved by telegraph at the Excelsior Hotel at Anhalter Bahnhof, an establishment for businessmen and with six hundred rooms the largest hotel on the European continent. As he lies on the bed smoking his usual pipe, he realizes he's entered the lion's den. Exhausted, he falls asleep.

The next morning he gets up early, studies the congratulations in the *Morgenpost* newspaper to Joseph Goebbels, who has turned forty-four that day, and reads with a heavy heart the news of the situation in Leningrad, his hometown. Anatoly Gurevich bites into a fresh roll baked by the hotel's bakery and looks around for the waiter. He's already ordered the same breakfast twice and is still hungry. The villages around Leningrad are burning. Artillery rumbles from morning to night. Even if it doesn't say so in the paper, Gurevich knows: The people in his hometown are starving. They huddle together at night in the cold. In the morning, frozen horses lay in the street and are gutted on the spot. Men's beards have ice crystals hanging from them; women wear scarves that are frozen to their scalps.

Snow has fallen again overnight.

Anatoly Gurevich, alias Vincente Sierra, brushes the crumbs from his jacket, signs the check, indeed two of the same meal, a whim of his, even if it is against the clandestine code because it stands out. He puts on his winter coat that, alas, won't keep him all that warm. As a would-be South American in wintry Germany, he constantly feigns freezing. Next he enters a phone booth, transforming again into Kent, and dials 99-58-47. It rings in an apartment in Neu-Westend.

"I got your number from a friend of yours named Elisabeth," he says when Libertas picks up the black Bakelite phone.

They meet in front of a U-Bahn station. There's not a minute of sun that day: A mix of snow and rain falls — cold, unpleasant Berlin weather. She sees him as she comes up the stairs: He looks levelheaded, friendly, almost cheerful, which makes Libs, whose heart is beating wildly, relax.

"Could we take a walk?" asks Kent as people stream around them toward the U-Bahn station. "It's good to walk in the cold." His German is passable, she thinks, looking him in the eye. She nods. Though her character might seem erratic to some because she oscillates between exaggerated self-confidence and total insecurity, at this moment with the Russian agent her extroverted side takes the upper hand, something that makes her irresistible to most men. With her gloved hands she takes a Johnny brand cigarette out of the packet and shoves it between her lips.

"Are you and your friends doing well?" asks Kent.

"They're all well."

"Why are they not being heard from in Moscow?"

She inhales deeply. She's not fully informed about all the activities concerning the transceiver, though Harro has mentioned that they are having technical problems. "I believe the device is defective."

"Can I see Choro?"

"I've alerted him to your visit. He's stationed outside Berlin and can meet you tomorrow afternoon at the same hour at the S-Bahn station Heerstrasse. Does that work?"

When the tall, slim Harro, with his blond hair and blue eyes, turns up the next day at Heerstrasse station in a glistening Luftwaffe coat, Kent thinks for a moment he's been set up. What does this officer want from him? But Harro is alone and makes it clear he is a friend. Together they stroll along Preussenallee toward Altenburger Allee, and after a quarter of an hour reach the apartment. Kent puts down his hat and coat in the foyer, which is decorated in Japanese style. Libertas comes out of the kitchen, where she has prepared a few small bites. They sit together at the table and eat, breaking the ice, which is helped when Harro pulls a bottle of vodka from the refrigerator and glasses from a brown sideboard that also holds the Rosenthal Chippendale china, a gift from Marie Luise.

Afterward, Harro and Kent retire to the fireside in the parlor, sitting in the tall, plush Kaiser-era chairs Libertas had scrounged from Liebenberg. Kent practically disappears into his, stretching out his feet on the brown bouclé carpet, staring at the old Swedish cabinet grandmother Augusta had fobbed off on Libs because you can fit so much stuff in it. He fills a pipe and lights it.

They begin their conversation with a question, specifically why the communications have failed up to now. Harro explains that for some reason they are unable to receive messages or any confirmation of their attempts to transmit.

Nothing has arrived at their end, Kent says, and agrees with Harro to a new wavelength of forty-seven meters where the Berliners can hear headquarters. Next, while they continue to chat, he writes in invisible ink Harro's summary of the information from recent weeks. The main thrust of the German invasion won't be Moscow but rather the Caucasus; the attack is to occur in the spring next year. The Reich is suffering fuel shortages; the offensive toward the southern Russian city of Maykop is supposed to change that.

As the conversation continues, Harro places importance in explaining the shortcomings of German production. He wishes to give a boost to Russian morale, since in Moscow, as he learns from Kent, they are worried about the formidable combat strength of the German armies. Harro reports that the mass production of aircraft in the occupied countries is lagging. Up to now they've first and foremost performed repairs in those areas, and there are only 2,500 or at most 2,700 combat-ready planes available. Significant losses have been documented of late, even in special units. The growing relief shipments from England and the United States to the Soviet Union substantially complicate German operations. Hitler's power is not nearly as great as one supposes. Part of the Wehrmacht's leadership has ceased to believe in a quick victory.

After more than two hours, the two men return to the Japanese foyer. Kent takes his leave from Libertas as well.

"Nothing much new here," Harro writes to his father after the explosive meeting. But in fact, the Russian's visit has put him in an extremely good mood. Finally a channel is open. They are in demand in Moscow.

# 15

Jägerstrasse 26, on Berlin's Gendarmenmarkt square, is home to the Deutsche Kulturfilm-Zentrale, or German Documentary Film Institute, which is part of the Ministry of Propaganda. Founded in August 1940, this agency organizes the production of the ten- to fifteen-minute short films that run before the feature presentations at theaters big and small. Documentary film production is flourishing, and there is a constant need for new content to fill the prominent slot before the feature. Countless documentaries are made each year by production firms, many of them small, and the wide variety of styles, varied approaches, and diversity of subject matter are a nightmare for the control-obsessed Nazis.

The Kulturfilm-Zentrale is trying to change this. Under the leadership of Senior Councillor Carl Neumann it is meant to become the "central manager of production for all of German documentary filmmaking." The goal is to review every film in production and require every producer "to first submit his project to the institute for approval."

When the search goes out for someone to head up the department for *"Kunst, deutsches Land und Volk, Völker und Länder"* — art, German land and people, other peoples and countries — Libertas applies. Whether it's the recommendations from MGM and the *National-Zeitung* or her being on such good terms with Engelsing, the influential producer at Tobis — she gets the job. She starts on November 1, 1941, one week after Kent's visit, and her salary is an excellent eight hundred Reichsmarks per month — far better than Harro's, who even since his promotion to first lieutenant makes only five hundred marks.

Libertas is a special kind of censor: What she considers too close to the Party line she leaves "hanging out to dry" — she simply doesn't let it proceed on account of production difficulties. Meanwhile, filmmakers who dare to do something new, something ambitious, receive her passionate support.

It's been clear to Libs for a while now that she has to stop merely writing about film and finally start making them herself. The job at the Kulturfilm-Zentrale seems like an important step in this direction.

But again the war gets in the way. On her very first day she finds herself presented with an entirely different kind of challenge. Her new desk is piled with envelopes filled with horrifying photographs, voluntarily sent in by soldiers. Suddenly she is looking at snapshots, some of which show the so-called *Sonderbehandlungen* or "special treatments": task forces in action carrying out the mass murder of Jews.

Libertas has no idea how these images got from inside Goebbels's propaganda ministry to the Kulturfilm-Zentrale and from there of all places to the department for *"Kunst, deutsches Land und Volk, Völker und Länder."*

How will she react?

# 16

In these wintry days Harro is transferred from Wildpark-West back to Wilhelmstrasse, back within the limestone walls that during the sudden cold spells, when at night the temperature drops below freezing, crack so loudly it sounds like gunshots.

It is December 20, 1941, a week since Hitler declared war on the United States as a result of the Japanese attack on Pearl Harbor. Libertas's new boss, propaganda minister Goebbels, has called on the German people to donate winter clothing for the men on the Eastern Front, who are snowed in. Their leaders, expecting a quick victory, supplied the troops with only summer uniforms.

On this evening shortly before Christmas, Harro and Hans Coppi walk along the twin rows of young bare trees in the middle of Reichsstrasse until they reach house number 106, right on Adolf-Hitler-Platz. They enter the building and step inside the spacious elevator, its interior painted light gray.

Harro has the key to Oda Schottmüller's dance and sculpture studio on the top floor. Oda isn't home; she's touring through France and Holland with her dance program, entertaining the German troops. Her place is a fabulous loft with windows that offer the visitor a sweeping view to the north. It's spacey and high up, and thus ideal for what the two visitors have planned.

Hans Coppi sets the vulcanized fiber case on Oda's desk and snaps open the locks. His gaze passes over the yellow walls with Oda's self-made masks: a golden one with a bald head called "The Hangman," another, uncannily lifelike, with bulging red lips, bright, deep blue eyes, real hair. It is icy cold in the large room. A gramophone sits next to a record collection — chamber music; music from Japan, India, Bali. On a clothes hanger is a meshlike gold-colored gown that Oda wears for one of her new dances: it bears the title "Gold" and its choreography is meant to convey the absurdity of capitalism. Next to the gown hangs a gray-green cape and a leotard with a skeleton painted on it that she uses for "Last Man Standing," a dance about death on the battlefield.

Harro looks at his wristwatch. He is wearing gloves. It is twenty past ten. He pulls out the envelope that Arvid handed off to Hans Coppi. Typed columns of numbers listed in groups of five. 10:29 p.m.: In a minute it will be time to start transmitting. Hans has set the wavelength: 47 meters. He places his right index finger on the Morse key. Harro has calibrated the tension spring so that the contacts that switch the current on and off are spaced neither too closely nor too far apart. It is possible to send eighty to one hundred letters per minute.

At precisely 10:30 p.m., Hans Coppi's elbow rests on the table. He knows by now: The melody comes from a *loose* wrist. Every radio opera-

The melancholy of resistance: Oda Schottmüller,
sculptor and mask dancer.

tor has his own *handwriting,* which is why for those sitting on the other end it's normally not enough to simply know the call sign. They have to recognize the *handwriting* of their counterpart — but Hans Coppi hasn't had the chance to develop a recognizable signature, since they still haven't managed to send a successful transmission.

His thumb and forefinger rest on the knob at the end of the lever. Don't tense up now — it's like playing the piano: Be too tight and you can develop tendonitis. Three times he taps the knob. Three times the contacts switch the current on and off, on and off . . . three times . . . then *once:* That should be the call sign. Pause. It is quiet in the room. Three . . .

Eight . . .

Five . . . five . . .

After the war, former members of the Wehrmacht's Radio Defense Corps will claim that German agents caught these impulses with their sensitive antennas. There isn't proof. In a densely inhabited city like Berlin, tracking a signal down is anything but easy. In this case the indicators would have pointed west: The cars would speed off in that direction. Minutes later they would stop. They would repeat the technique for getting their bearings, send the results back to the command center, and receive the updated coordinates, stalking ever closer to this place where the masks hang on the walls and two men are attempting to unmask the German war strategy.

After fifteen minutes the slender, muscular, by now seasoned fingers of Hans Coppi can no longer hold the knob, though only half of the sets of numbers have been transmitted. A short break — then the wrist again loose, elbow on the table, index finger and thumb tap the knob. It swings up and down on its lever as Harro walks left and right past the windows to stay warm — swinging on a lever of his own. Isn't it brazenly beautiful, the starry sky tonight over Adolf-Hitler-Platz?

The cars from the Defense Corps would be parking now if they had picked up Hans and Harro's trail. Men outfitted with the newly developed close-range direction finders, which can fit inside nondescript suitcases with barely visible cables leading to miniature earpieces, would get out and move quickly, but not too quickly, through the streets. They wouldn't have the exact address yet.

Disappointed, Harro shakes his head. Again they don't receive any confirmation from the other side. Hans turns off the transmitter. The latches of the suitcase snap shut. They switch off the light, lock the door behind them, step into the elevator, and ride down.

The streets running out from Adolf-Hitler-Platz form a star, pulling cars toward the square from all directions, including the alleged vehicle from the Radio Defense Corps, which would have been about to reach its target, but just lost the signal.

# 17

Whether the transmitter is broken or the signal simply didn't make it through, they will need to try again — albeit from a different location, for safety's sake. But where should they take the radio now?

Recently Hans Coppi met the thirty-year-old Erika Gräfin von Brockdorff, who lives in the same complex of buildings as Greta and Adam Kuckhoff.

Erika and her husband, Cay, have several friends who are opposed to the regime, like the dramaturg Wilhelm Schürmann-Horster. They lead an open marriage, and Cay has been called up to the army, leaving Erika behind with their four-year-old daughter. Even more dynamically than others, Erika personifies the kind of rebellion that Libs and Harro have created: a resistance that proceeds from life itself; the natural impulse, unstoppable in some people, to profess unconventionality, to *be* unconventional.

Erika is a sensual woman with short blond hair. In most of the photos taken of her she wears a faint smile, but from the look on her face it is clear that she can also let loose and laugh wholeheartedly. She fears no one and knows the impression her free spirit and curvaceous figure make on men.

When, after the latest misfire at Oda's, an alternative location for transmitting is needed, Erika offers up her handsome studiolike rooms. Right up to the end she will provide a place for sending transmissions and repairing broken devices.

Erika von Brockdorff enjoys her new role, savoring each moment of her new clandestine existence to the fullest.

# 18

Around Christmas, 1941, when the fortunes of the Wehrmacht turn with their failure to capture Moscow, Harro meets the forty-two-year-old psychoanalyst and psychotherapist Dr. John Rittmeister, head of the outpatient clinic at the German Institute for Psychological Research and Psychotherapy.

John comes from an old Hamburg merchant family, a slight, sensitive, highly intellectual man. For Rittmeister, defying the dictatorship comes as naturally as supporting those who suffer under the regime. He has helped several of his Jewish patients to emigrate, and aided his homosexual clients by providing favorable reports. John's wife, Eva, is fifteen years younger than he. She wants to be an actor and is studying to get her diploma at the private night school run by Dr. Wilhelm Heil in Schöneberg, where an anti-regime circle has come together, made up of young blue-and white-collar workers and female students. Often they all meet at the Rittmeisters' place after class, discussing subjects like psychotherapy and politics and talking about what can be done against the regime.

When John Rittmeister meets the irresistible, radiant Harro, he considers it a kind of deliverance. Harro is well informed and has an interesting take on the situation in Germany. Suddenly John has someone he can talk to at his level — who completes him. And just like that, Harro's circle grows to include the entire group circulating around John Rittmeister.

It seems an ideal moment to become active again. For the first time since the war began, the news from the front is not good. The Germans sense that things are going south: Hundreds of thousands of young men have already fallen. The divisions that were just outside Moscow at the end of October have been pushed back as far as three hundred kilometers by the Red Army.

It's a good moment to come out from hiding, seek publicity, make contact with as many people, as many potential sympathizers, as possible. Together, Harro and John come up with the idea for a comprehensive essay meant to awaken the forces of resistance lying dormant in the population: to reach those who despise the Nazis but who up to now couldn't bring themselves to do something — and there are lots of people like this in Germany.

A text that will rouse the crucial strength of the citizenry and give them the courage for a new beginning — now, when the light has appeared at the end of the tunnel.

# 19

Even as success remains elusive on the Eastern Front, the Nazi regime pushes full steam ahead with the persecution of the Jewish population in Europe. Beginning on January 3, 1942, Jews are no longer permitted to leave the Reich; on January 16 the deportations begin from the ghetto in Łódź to the extermination camp in Kulmhof (Chełmno). Starting on January 17, on Goebbels's orders, Jews are no longer allowed to buy newspapers at kiosks; subscriptions are also prohibited. On January 20, 1942, in a villa on the same Wannsee where Harro and Libertas met and where they still like to go sailing, the details of the "Final Solution to the Jewish Question" are worked out. Under the leadership of Reinhard Heydrich, the head of the Reich Main Security Office, which also contains the Gestapo, systematic mass murder — genocide — is made the task of the state. Every single person in the giant machine of the Reich who gains knowledge of this and nevertheless continues to participate thus becomes a murderer.

There are hundreds of thousands of such people in Germany — while those who do something to *oppose* it can be counted off on a few hands.

Every day in the Deutsche Kulturfilm-Zentrale, Libertas learns more about the mass murder of the Jews in Germany and throughout Europe.

Strange as it is, more and more snapshots from the east keep landing on her desk. If for a long time she didn't know how to react to this material, now she has a plan. She archives the horror — and she does more than this. She gets in touch with the perpetrators, some of whom even brag about their crimes. She answers the letters that sometimes accompany the photographs, asks for full names, troop companies, addresses back home. She wants to collect as many details as possible, evidence for the big trials she expects when the war is over and the Wehrmacht has suffered ultimate defeat. Her collection anticipates the controversial exhibit *Crimes of the Wehrmacht* put on by the Hamburg Institute for Social Research, which more than half a century later will reveal to the German public for the first time the extent of the military's participation in the genocide.

In one photo that Libertas archives, a little girl can be seen with her older brother, their mother, and an infant. All four of them are to be shot together. Ordered to line up, the girl has taken her rag doll and stood it up in position next to her.

Libertas does the lion's share of this oppressive work at home — gluing photos in an album, writing captions, and keeping up the correspondence with the perpetrators. To her mother-in-law, Marie Luise, she writes in January 1942: "Much of the time I am deeply melancholy . . . I don't know how one can keep one's wits and still endure all that is happening in the world every single day. But of course the end must be coming soon. I have a firm belief that it will."

She sits intently at her desk while from the other side of the parlor come the comforting clacks of Harro's typewriter keys. The two of them might spend less time with each other and sleep together less often than Libertas would prefer, but they *are* a couple. They love and understand each other. Harro pushes the carriage to the right — new paragraph. The heat in the building is out of order or shut off on account of the war; he types quickly so his fingers won't freeze. He plugs away at his new pamphlet, drawing inspiration from John Rittmeister. He writes: "The infamously stupid state bureaucracy is hardly capable at this point of fulfilling the tasks that fall to it. The corruption in the administration, in the economic realm, in the Wehrmacht, but above all within the branches of the party, has reached sickening proportions."

Influenced by Thomas Mann's radio addresses, which the writer has been broadcasting over the BBC from his exile in California since 1940, Harro wants to denounce everything there is to denounce about the Nazi regime: the atrocities in the east, which he finds out about from Libertas, the ever-worsening supply situation at home, the corruption of the Party and of the institutions they control. It is a full-on assault that calls for a socialist renewal of society, for peace on all fronts and the punishment of those who have committed crimes.

Often it's hard to concentrate on the work — again and again it is interrupted by the wail of sirens. Sometimes the Royal Air Force bombs the Mitte neighborhood, then Steglitz or Tempelhof. Harro and Libs have volunteered as air raid wardens just so they can prevent a warden they don't know from storming into their apartment while they're down in the cellar. This way they are allowed to stay upstairs, go into the unused nursery, turn on the electric heater, snuggle up under the sheep's wool blanket and watch the blazing sky through the skylight — the exploding flak, the play of light above the clouds. The flares hang in the sky for minutes, and they can physically feel the concentrated sound of the approaching enemy planes, wreathed in the flashes of bursting shells.

"It's rotten luck of course if a bomb catches you in bed" goes Harro's laconic commentary on their decision not to go to the air raid shelter. "But if the bomb falls one meter farther along the side of the building, then it detonates in the cellar and it's time's up for the people down below — if they haven't already succumbed to flu, kidney infection, lung infection or whatever else (which can't happen to us up above)."

When talking to his parents he likes to downplay the issue, which only shows how normal the madness has become: "The risks of bombardment are really no greater than what you experience on a normal weekend in Berlin using any modern means of transportation . . . For now it's really not even worth mentioning. You can't make yourself crazy, after all. We'll get used to the noise." Even when in the middle of Reichsstrasse, just around the corner, the shell of a heavy antiaircraft gun that initially failed to detonate comes down and explodes with such force that it blows countless holes in the facades of the surrounding buildings, shatters a number of windows, and leaves a cavernous hole in the pavement, Harro takes it lightly. Maybe he's even secretly happy, because he knows the British bombing raids are taking an ever-larger toll on the Reich.

The centuries-old brick Gothic architecture of Lübeck and Rostock collapses in the blink of an eye, and Cologne is about to face Operation Millennium, in the course of which, for the first time ever, one thousand bombers will attack simultaneously. Kiel, Harro's birthplace, has already been destroyed. On February 14, 1942, Harro's "colleagues" in the British Air Ministry give the *Area Bombing Directive*, which orders the large-scale bombing of civilian areas, meaning city centers and residential neighborhoods. Over 90 percent of the old town in Munich, where the National

Socialist German Workers Party, the NSDAP, first originated, soon no longer exists. Industries important to the war effort — BMW, Krauss-Maffei, Dornier — are severely hit.

Based on the production statistics available in the Air Ministry, Harro assumes the air attacks will be successful and will bring about the end of the war. Among colleagues there are discussions as to whether from a military perspective the Allies' commitment of so large a part of their industrial capacity to the production of bombers is a mistake. But Harro is convinced that an intensified air war will prove to be completely unsustainable for Germany. He does not think that the English "will call off the attacks out of concern for architectural treasures, theirs or ours. Their whole materialist war plan is based on bringing their supposedly superior production capacity to bear to an ever greater extent, and their best opportunity for doing so is in the air." For him it is clear, as he writes to his father: "Germany, because of its raw material shortage, will not be capable of making up the discrepancy — and for that reason the other air forces, who don't have these difficulties, will win one day. But how many more irreplaceable cultural treasures will go down the drain before then?"

It really is an ideal time for preparing the new pamphlet he is working on with John Rittmeister. Its title will be *Concern for Germany's Future Is Spreading Among the People.*

# 20

Libertas has a new friend: Cato Bontjes van Beek. The two met at the fair in Leipzig and drove back to Berlin together. In the car, a safe place, they could speak freely. Since then they have gotten together a few times, playing table tennis or listening to audio recordings of Thomas Mann smuggled out of Switzerland. Cato, whose button nose is sprinkled with freckles and who wears her red hair tied back, is as impressed by Libs's having met the author of *The Magic Mountain* in Zurich as she is by her contacts in the film world. And so when Libs asks her to help out at the Kulturfilm-Zentrale, she immediately says yes. Libs needs a hand writing things up for the secret photo collection of the crimes of the Wehrmacht.

Cato has no problem acting on her anti-Nazi stance. She's been doing it already. For some time now she and her friend Katja Casella have been hiding people from the Gestapo; Katja makes her painting studio available for the purpose. They call it *"reinterment."* The people they're helping are no longer safe under their own roof and need a place to stay where the police can't find them, usually for a day or two, sometimes longer. Things get tricky during air raids, when Katja's studio, like all other homes and apartments in Berlin, can't be locked, since the air raid warden has to have free entry everywhere to be able to check whether the air defense regulations are being kept. Because of this, Cato and Katja drum it into their guests that once the sirens go off they should deposit the key in a place agreed upon beforehand, leave the house as soon as possible, and not come back for a while — and in the meantime, don't talk to anybody.

There's another thing Cato does to improve conditions in Germany under the swastika. This concerns the countless forced workers whose labor the regime exploits in order to maintain the war economy, well over a million people from France, Poland, the Soviet Union, and several other countries — the number keeps climbing. Together with her sister Mietje and their friend Sibylle Budde, a "half Jew," Cato has developed a system for making contacts among French prisoners of war. The young women head to the Witzleben commuter train station. There the young Frenchmen board the train in small groups with their guards to ride to Westkreuz, where they are forced to work for the Schering pharmaceutical company. Every morning their primitive wooden clogs clatter on the stairs and in the tiled corridors of the train station. The Frenchmen always ride in the very last car, as per regulations. Cato, Mietje, and Sibylle get to the platform just late enough that they have to run to catch the train — and end up on the last car. As soon as they are in, two of them distract the guards while the third distributes messages and presents to the French prisoners with a silent smile.

It doesn't take long until Cato, Mietje, and Sybille are passed requests: for medicine, pencils, sewing supplies, fruit, matches, tobacco. Once they bring the Frenchmen a soccer ball for their downtime after work in the prison camp. These are dangerous operations that can easily go wrong, for which reason the prisoners implore them to stop. But Cato wants to keep it up. She enjoys these little adventures, even if they mean putting her life at risk.

The perfect comrade-in-arms for Libertas.

# 21

In these early weeks of 1942, a true network develops in Berlin. It is formed of the connections between friends. Only a few have any idea of its size. Overlapping within it are Hans Coppi's Scharfenberg circle; Rittmeister's conclave of young people; the colorful troupe centered around Wilhelm Schürmann-Horster, which meets mainly at Erika Brockdorff's apartment; Arvid Harnack's discussion group, with students from the Berlin night school handpicked by Mildred — and also the communists the American-German journalist John Sieg knows in Neukölln.

Another circle emerges in the apartment of the former Prussian minister of culture, the religious socialist Adolf Grimme. To this group belong his school friend Adam Kuckhoff, Arvid Harnack, and again John Sieg. Not everyone knows about everyone else. Harro is one of the prominent voices, but not the leader — there is no leader. But he does join together many of the diverse strands to make the network stronger.

By this point more than 150 artists, writers, doctors and academics, blue- and white-collar workers, soldiers and officers, and students have banded together: conservatives, communists, social democrats, even former Nazis, but the vast majority of them unaffiliated with any party. Catholics and Protestants, women and men of Jewish origin, atheists, aristocrats and poor folk, high school students and grandfathers — and an astounding number of women, almost half the group. Out of a total of seven Berlin friend and resistance groups is woven an amorphous meshwork, a movement with no organizational principle determined from above, and no controlling principle, no statute, no formal membership, no structure. Thirty years later, in the 1970s, the poststructuralists in Paris will find a term for this kind of form: the *rhizome*. It is a gradually developing means of organizing knowledge, a non-hierarchical diffusion, and it might finally be what Harro had imagined all the way back in the Weimar days: an organic community of *Gegner,* adversaries, who are comrades and friends. An "alliance of unbound joie de vivre," as the university teacher Werner Krauss calls it, the boyfriend of Ursula Goetze from the Rittmeister circle.

Things don't always go smoothly when these diverse characters get together. The colorful mix of education levels, ages, genders, and sexual orientations produces friction. "Enemy territory!" grumbles Heinrich Scheel's class-conscious girlfriend when she first arrives at Altenburger Allee 19, which because of its unobstructed sixth-floor views is called "the Italian apartment": "This neighborhood! This apartment! And there's a ladies' fur coat hanging in the wardrobe!" Scheel's companion exclaims in shock.

It is Harro's task to move between the different groups and to stimulate the rhizome of resistance to further growth: to bid anyone welcome who has the courage and wants to do something. This calls for the tact that he learned from his father, the authority he inherited from his mother, and his own inborn sense of camaraderie. He is the driving force and determines the intellectual direction. It's about assessing the political and military situation, and for this purpose he contributes classified information from the ministry. But it's also about private cooperation, an openness outside of the gender roles prescribed by the regime's propaganda. "So, enough chitchat, now let's get to work" — the line becomes Harro's catchphrase, his way of dispensing with the nonessential. At times there are larger gatherings that resemble parties, at others smaller meetings — in the dentist's office of Helmut Himpel, for example, or the practice of Dr. Elfriede Paul, where Harro, Libs, Kurt, Elisabeth, and Oda get together at irregular intervals.

Through Libertas a man named John Graudenz comes into the picture. He looks like Cary Grant, only a bit rougher around the edges. Soon he becomes an indispensable friend, above all to Harro, and also helps write the pamphlet *Concern for Germany's Future Is Spreading Among the People,* which for all of them is meant to be a kind of political manifesto. Graudenz had spent four years as a reporter for the Berlin bureau of the *New York Times;* in the twenties he had reported from the Soviet Union for United Press and was the first to bring the news of Lenin's death to America. Thanks to his unflinching reports of the famine on the Volga — which he had seen firsthand, traveling downriver on a steamer — the Soviet Union had kicked him out of the country. Now the tall Graudenz, who often has a stubborn forelock hanging over his intense dark eyes, is a successful businessman and works for the Wuppertal automobile manufacturer Blumhardt. Through his connections he has for years been helping Jewish acquaintances leave the country — his friend Sophie Kuh, for example. John Graudenz's wife is named Antonie, their two daughters, Karin and Silva, are teenagers.

Harro and John Graudenz visit Cato Bontjes van Beek's small apartment on a gloomy day in late January 1942. With them are Hans Coppi and another new acquaintance, twenty-five-year-old Fritz Thiel, who works at the Zeiss Ikon factory as a precision engineer, has experience as a radio operator, and belongs to John Rittmeister's circle. At Libertas's suggestion they want to check whether Cato's place is suitable for transmitting, but the first order of business is *Concern for Germany's Future Is Spreading Among the People.* They've brought a six-page draft of the essay, which Cato and her boyfriend, Heinz Strelow, a poet, are meant to type up for use as a stencil. Harro encourages them to make improvements to style and content in the process. The duplication is done by means of a mimeograph machine that John Graudenz has obtained.

But it is all moving too quickly for Heinz Strelow. After the visitors have left, he criticizes Cato for being too trusting: Who were these other people whom Harro introduced under false names? He assures her that, generally speaking, he too sees the point of putting out pamphlets. But here there are too many people involved; the danger is too high. His girlfriend dismisses this. She has already reached for *Concern for Germany's Future* and reads:

> It is no longer enough to "gripe" or make stupid jokes. When you have to wait in line for every little thing, protest! Get louder and louder! Stop putting up with all of it! Stop letting yourselves be ordered around! Oppose this fear all around us! We will save ourselves and the country only when we find the courage to place ourselves on the front line in the battle against Hitler.

When the text is printed Graudenz goes to Helmut Himpel's apartment with a stuffed suitcase. There, with the help of the phone book, Mimi Terwiel is putting together the list of recipients and has already started addressing envelopes with a typewriter. When they don't finish stuffing the envelopes that first night, they pack everything in a cupboard in Himpel's living room and meet up again the following evening, this time with Harro and Hans Coppi.

It's not easy to mail such a large quantity of letters without drawing notice. In purchasing stamps, envelopes, and paper at great volume it is important to be careful — the same as when putting them in mailboxes. For this reason they distribute the load among themselves and send it off here and there in small batches.

This time their target audience isn't just their fellow Germans but also the foreign correspondents in Berlin and and important diplomatic missions. People outside the borders of the Reich should be made aware of the network's existence, a network that wants to establish contact with the *entire* anti-Hitler coalition, seeking a cease fire on all fronts, west *and* east.

The Wehrmacht's local district recruiting headquarters, as well as Nazi functionaries like Roland Freisler, state secretary in the Ministry of Justice and later president of the People's Court, also receive copies of the single-spaced missive. They are all meant to find out that resistance exists, that this is what the people are thinking. Alois Hitler, the half brother of the dictator, who has cadged a house for himself on Wittenbergplatz, also finds a copy in his mailbox. Everyone who reads *Concern for Germany's Future* receives an unvarnished impression of the situation, a sober stocktaking, combined with a passionate appeal:

> Send this letter out into the world to as many as you can! Pass it on to friends and co-workers! You are not alone! Fight on your own at first, then as a group! TOMORROW GERMANY WILL BE OURS!

Not everyone answers this call to conspiratorial dissemination. Instead, 288 copies make their way to the police and the Gestapo. The latter, in a daily report, speaks of a "Communist movement," although evidence of such an alignment cannot be drawn from the text. "The pamphlets, produced on the typewriter and mechanically duplicated, were sent in sealed envelopes to various Catholic parish offices and a number of fellow citizens in intellectual fields, such as professors, doctors, graduate engineers." The report continues: "The texts refer to the situation that has been worsening with each new month and which they claim has been caused by National Socialist politics" — a sore point, it seems. Goebbels, who as minister of propaganda is especially incensed, sends a letter to the head of the Gestapo, Müller:

> The enclosed pamphlet, which is put together in a clever sophistic manner, is being forwarded to me from all corners of the earth . . . Today I laid hands on a copy that was mailed from the Berlin-Charlottenburg 2 post office. It occurs to me that the blue envelopes are all of the same type. Maybe that's a clue.

But the Gestapo has nothing to go on. The investigations reveal only that the text was copied using a "single-drum device, probably an older model," with absorbent and branded paper with the watermark of the Geha company. A review of the businesses that stock this paper reveals that it is sold exclusively to government institutions, in particular the Wehrmacht.

The investigation of the envelopes likewise yields no success for the search. During wartime only four varieties are allowed in Germany, but the pamphlet was sent in *fourteen* different envelopes that vary in color, size, and quality. "The envelopes differ from one another and have no distinguishing feature that could be helpful for further investigations."

The Gestapo has to admit its failure: "A review of the recipients, research into the origins of the paper type and envelopes used, forensic investigation of the text and examination of the letters have up to now yielded no information that might be used for further conclusions . . . Several letters were obtained and forwarded to the State Police by the administration of the Reichspost Berlin. These letters were delivered, unopened, to the Reich police records department for the purpose of searching for fingerprints. Treatment of all letters with iodine steam likewise yielded no success."

Harro and his friends have done their job well.

# 22

Cato's boyfriend, Heinz Strelow, still believes, however, that it's only a matter of time till they all get busted. He seeks Harro out to air his criticism that their talent for conspiracy is on the whole limited and they have been too careless in their choice of friends. It's true that a lot of goodwill had been shown, but the whole thing was just a prolonged improvisation, Heinz claims. Sooner or later, the inhuman pressure bearing down on them would inevitably lead to catastrophe. He also thinks the combination of sending radio transmissions with the production of informational material could be disastrous. Therefore, he tells Harro, he'd like to stop working together.

The sources don't show whether Harro takes Heinz Strelow's criticism to heart, but for him this is what is essential about their network: that there are no distinct structures. That the fabric isn't prevented from growing, but rather allowed to expand, to remain flexible. Any person who is critical of the Nazi system, eager for contact, cosmopolitan, if possible artistically talented and open to intellectual challenges is welcome. Anyone who wants to lead a self-determined life can be part of this resistance. Anyone who in some manner believes in this diffuse surplus value that arises when the most diverse thoughts come into contact with one another and cross-pollinate, develop dialectically. And if someone wants to leave, he can do this as well — as Heinz Strelow now wishes to.

Initially the person who suffers most from Strelow's departure is Libertas, since it means that Cato Bontjes van Beek also drops out. Now Libs has to find someone new to work with her on her secret photo collection of the horrors on the Eastern Front.

# 23

It doesn't stop at the *Concern for Germany's Future* pamphlet. Things are moving fast now.

One warm, almost summerlike evening, Adam Kuckhoff pulls black cotton gloves over his strong fingers. He has never done this when writing before. The desk at which he sits is massive, with several drawers for his various projects. It dates back to Weimar days, when Adam had it built. But the illegal text he's working on tonight is especially charged. This he will hide in a secret chamber in the wall with a door next to the desk that is covered up by an old gothic rug.

The writer has brought a co-author on board for this undertaking, the German American John Sieg, born in 1903 in Detroit, where he once stood on the assembly line at Ford. In the late 1920s Sieg was a freelance writer in Berlin and editor of the culture section for the *Rote Fahne* newspaper. In 1928 and '29 his stories from America appeared in the monthly *Die Tat,* which Adam Kuckhoff edited; he also wrote for the *Berliner Tageblatt.* John Sieg is a powerfully built man with a mischievous smile, long active in the workers' movement, unshakeable in his hatred of capitalism, and driven by the dream of building a better world. His time as a beat reporter has sharpened his eye for details and helped him develop an ear for dialogue. In 1933 he declined an offer from the head of the SA in Berlin to work as a journalist for one of the Nazi newspapers. After that he was no longer permitted to publish and in 1936 he started working for the state railroad. But he doesn't want to give up writing and since 1940 has edited the multilingual *Innere Front,* an illegal magazine for foreign prisoners of war who are damned to forced labor in Germany. The goal is to encourage them to revolt.

In his gloved hands Adam holds the photo with the little girl and the doll that Libertas passed on to him. Libertas's photo collection has put him face to face with the apocalyptic madness of Operation Barbarossa. His idea is to pose questions to the reader of his text in a direct, personal address. He hopes in this manner to coax out answers — and to do so on a deeper level than that of reason.

Kuckhoff and Sieg's *Open Letter to the Eastern Front* is addressed to soldiers and officers as well as to the units of the regular police force, the Ordnungspolizei — more than twenty thousand policemen, many of them with families, who after receiving deployment orders were suddenly torn from their normal lives and are now taking part in the mass shootings, overwhelmingly of Jews, in Poland, Ukraine, and Belarus. It is a text that seeks to communicate with its readers' unconscious and to appeal to the deep-seated sense of honor common among all men. A "Police Captain" character who serves as an imaginary conversation partner, who in principle could be any German soldier throughout the expanse of the war in Russia, is told the fictional story of a colleague who murdered a mother with three children, one of which, a girl, also lined up her rag doll to be executed:

> But then something happened, and his nerves have been shot ever since: he had to do away with a young woman, a peasant, along with her three children. "Why?" He shrugs his shoulders: "Orders." The woman held an infant in her arms, it was bitter cold, and she kept trying, futilely, for what would be the last two minutes of her life, to wrap the crying child in pitiful rags to keep it warm. With a helpless gesture of apology she attempted to convey that she had nothing else, they took everything from her. To the right, next to the woman, kneeled her six-year-old son, to the left a girl about two years old, who at the last minute, before the order came to kneel, toddled back to grab her doll. Well, sure — "the doll gets it too." Like I said, it was a ridiculous, pitiful thing that doll, nothing but rags. The little girl, after kneeling herself in her awkward, little-kid way, also set the doll up in a kneeling position next to her in the snow, or tried to, anyway. "So who did you shoot first?" I asked ... Yeah, and then suddenly the six-year-old boy jumped up and started running towards the shooter. From what he told me it must have been a real bitter struggle between him and the kid, just for a few seconds of course, but that's where the bite wound in his stiff finger comes from, and it took him two shots, since the first one missed. The other got the boy in the eye, turned it into a dripping mess. The little girl on the other hand was very quiet and tumbled down next to the doll without a sound. Really though there's nothing else to say about that silly doll except that for our murderer it became a kind of "tic" — the doll of all things.

The description of this gruesome occurrence isn't all. Adam and John write about the psychological consequences, and their so innocuously titled *Open Letter to the Eastern Front* leads directly into the hell that this tour of duty unleashes in the psyche of the perpetrators:

I visited a few fellow police officers at the State Hospital recently. They had been sent there from the East on account of nervous breakdowns — all of them. You know what hospitals are like. That special kind of quiet. They had tried to brighten the room up with flowers, the patients were allowed to listen to music — laughably simple touches meant to heal the spirit, plus there were even a few beams of sunlight, it was just like a novel. Anyway there's a ward there where they put the worst cases, the brother officers were telling me about it with a kind of fearful relief: former beat cops who used to radiate strength, now they can only hop around. Others crawl around on all fours, slowly shaking their heads, their hair falls wildly in their faces, and the look in their eyes is like a St. Bernard's. The boys told me a lot of horrible things. The quiet in the ward was deceptive; the furies were raging within. Whispering, eyes wide-open, hoping I would give them a word of absolution or justification, they told me about mass shootings, about extreme cruelties, about blood and tears beyond all proportion, the brutal orders from the SS, really more like ultimatums, how unbelievably calm many of the victims were ... Naturally I didn't offer a word of consolation to any of the patients, something to help them in the horror-tormented twilight hours of their evenings, and all the more eagerly did they reveal to me their crimes. Am I of all people supposed to drive off the ghosts of the murdered, am I supposed to grant a kind of absolution to someone who confesses after the fact, albeit racked with torment, that for months, as his daily quota, so to speak, he followed orders and shot up to fifty people a day? One of these nevertheless pitiable executioner-creatures — and this will interest you as a criminologist — says he can't rid himself of the image of a small, dirty rag doll. He also added, feverishly, hastily, that his finger had grown stiff on account of a nasty bite wound ... Of all things the doll, the last and most helpless thing of all that was left behind, of all things this was now his "illness," and soon he'd probably have to go "down there" with the St. Bernards. Tell me, Captain, what is the difference between those who murder from degeneracy, out of a sense of duty, or out of cowardice? In any case, this one story has stuck with me only on account of the absurd doll detail — but does there exist anywhere in the world a mind, a person, a book, anything with the capacity for remembering, for setting down all the horrors committed against the Soviet people?! ... The terrible thing is simply this: that Hitler has managed to turn countless ordinarily honest and law-abiding people into accomplices in his crimes!

It is an early, harrowing account of what is going on in the east. But what can the individual soldier on the front do to oppose it? The *Open Letter to the Eastern Front* has an answer, and doesn't shy away from voicing it. Resistance to the Germans' mass murder *does* exist: not just in the form of the Red Army, but also of women and men everywhere in Russia who take up arms and hide in the forests to fight as partisans — an effective form of struggle that the Prussians themselves practiced in 1812 against the invading troops of Napoleon:

> Can it be that difficult, Captain, when placed between one kind of death and another, to choose between the proud, honorable tradition of Prussia, which appeals to your conscience, and the base brutality of the SS rabble that has terrorized you into carrying out the "duty" of cowardly murdering Russian patriots?! I myself — I would join the partisans. I would go over to their side without a second thought. Let whoever belongs with the "St. Bernards" go join them, out of lack of resolve, out of pure cowardice.

A clear call to action, to switch sides, to desert, to go over to the enemy. But is it answered? The authors don't have exaggerated hopes that a large number of officers will have a radical change of heart. Nevertheless, Adam and John, armed with typewriters and black cotton gloves, don't want to leave anything untried. Their last paragraph reads:

> There are moments when what is called for is not so-called shrewd behavior, or silence, or cowed caution, but rather initiative, daring, and, if one must, the ability to sacrifice oneself.

There is no record of how widely distributed the text was among the troops. What is known is that the "Open Letter," through Kurt Schumacher, who received copies in his barracks in Posen by way of his wife, Elisabeth, and John Graudenz, made it on into Russia and did in fact reach the Eastern Front.

It might be just a single flame of words with a glow that disappears amid the countless flashes of rifle muzzles and tank guns, just a soft voice in the rage and thunder of artillery. But it is the first time in this war that the executions at the hands of the task forces that are operating behind the front lines are singled out in such a way.

This too is part of that fabric of dissent, of a will to inform and exhort the public, in the rhizome growing around Harro and Libertas.

# 24

Young Alexander Spoerl, son of the celebrated German novelist Heinrich Spoerl, receives a mysterious telegram this spring of 1942 in a village on the Tegernsee lake in Bavaria. He is to present himself at the Deutsche Kulturfilm-Zentrale in Berlin.

Clueless but curious, the twenty-five-year-old takes the train to the capital, gets out at the Anhalter Bahnhof, and makes his way on foot to Gendarmenmarkt, where at Jägerstrasse 26 he registers with the porter and is let up to the second floor. There he receives a surprisingly good offer from some man he doesn't know; is introduced to still more men; makes the Nazi salute, even if he doesn't care for it; and after shaking hands is finally led to a room at the end of a hallway.

The woman who opens the door has a dreamy, friendly gaze; her light brown hair, fashionably cut, falls to the left side of her forehead. She is scarcely older than Alexander and asks the other men to leave her alone with him. She closes the door and asks if he'd care for a cigarette.

Alexander runs a hand through his tousled hair and wishes he had taken more care in combing it. "I have to tell you," he blurts out, "I don't have any experience in filmmaking and I don't know the first thing about documentaries." He tells her that he studied mechanical engineering, but his real goal is to be an author. He plans to write books about women and sports cars, finding both subjects fascinating.

"Are you still running your *Antiwelle* [anti-wave]?" Libertas asks him with a friendly smile.

Alexander looks at her, baffled. How does the woman know about his anonymous resistance project, his pamphlet against the Nazis that is circulating in film circles?

To reassure him, Libertas tells him that she found out about it from her friend Herbert Engelsing and that Enke's recommendation is the reason he is here.

Now Alexander smiles. In an instant his shakiness gives way to a feeling of recognition, "the silent understanding of those who are opposed to National Socialism" and *have* to trust each other, because their lives depend on it. "The *Antiwelle* is still active," he says, and takes a good look at Libertas, who, as he will later so effusively write, "unites in perfect measure the instinct, the naïveté and the passion of the woman with an intellect that seems fully male. She was, to use a very silly expression, an enchanting person."

But what she is asking of him is no light task. Soon his job will be developing the images of targeted killings coming from the Eastern Front in the Kulturfilm-Zentrale's on-site darkroom. Quickly Libertas sets to training him for her secret archive.

It would be hard to find a more interesting boss. Or a more dangerous one.

# 25

Harro, too, makes an interesting acquaintance this spring of 1942. The sources don't say where and when she walked into his life, but things moved quickly, and the woman got what she was after with such finesse that it's almost as if someone had put her up to it.

Her name is Stella Mahlberg, and Harro never planned on an encounter like this one. It was never his intention — he never sought extramarital affairs. And yet it has happened.

Stella Mahlberg is a "half Jew," an actress at the Deutsches Theater, up to now only known for minor roles, one of the two maids in Kleist's *The Broken Jug* for example. "I still tremble deep in my soul when I get close to you," Harro writes to her in early April: "A very silly, but wonderfully rare condition, like a sunrise."

There are reasons for this sudden outpouring of emotions, and maybe they have less to do with sex, which has never been his main concern, than with the attempt to feel anything at all again. After the nights of torture in the SS basement he had lost Regine, his girlfriend at the time, because he couldn't open up anymore. Later he had been drawn to Libertas because he believed she would be his saving grace, spurring him on to move his life in the right direction — and she had, too. But his relationship with her, his wife, who by now is just as wrapped up as he in this struggle that for him is life itself, is for that very reason also a product of the SS torture chamber and thus inextricably linked with it. With Stella things are different. A sensual person with raven-black hair, she lives in an unpolitical world. She knows nothing of his activities, and this is precisely what makes her so alluring to him.

His pet name for her is Fix, for *Fixstern* — fixed star — and that's exactly how he sees her: as a separate world, where different laws apply — unsullied, still intact. A counterpoint to the state of things on *this* planet, which so taxes his strength. It does him good to have this place of refuge, a point of contact outside his group of friends and outside his work. It is the artistic world, out there somewhere, where he himself would like to live, which he knows from his *Gegner* days but lost a long time ago. Stella Mahlberg — this he realizes after just a few meetings — allows him to be *intimate*. "Only rarely do you find someone else whom you can open yourself up to," he writes to her. She is no casual fling; his time is too short for that, his work too serious. She represents something that he hopes will change him, help him to lose control, to rediscover the side of himself that has been lost in the fight against Hitler. "I am too close to you to face you," as he puts it, somewhat bluntly, in a love letter to her: "That which I can say to you will be something different than what I say to the rest of the world. They can only be conversations with myself."

Hardly a meaningless affair — so how can he *not* clue Stella in on his illegal activities? Harro is aware of the walls that have grown up around him, and he could only tear them down by coming clean with her, ending the game of hide-and-seek and opening up about himself. But this would make her an accomplice, and he would lose her, just like he lost Regine.

Can it work — can he learn to feel again *without* destroying their fragile connection in the process? Maybe it can't be more than a limited thing, but that doesn't make it any less intense. Harro and Stella enjoy it, plain and simple. They meet up at the Zoologischer Garten train station and do something fun together. It is a mutual impulse to flee the world that is falling apart around them, and it makes them feel human, like heroes, if only for a day.

But what does Libertas have to say about it?

# 26

This Easter, 1942, Elisabeth Schumacher experiences something horrible. It involves a cousin's elderly Jewish parents, the blind musicologist Dr. Richard Hohenemser and his wife, Alice. The two of them live at Havensteinstrasse 6. The building borders a park; around the corner is Kaiser-Wilhelm-Strasse: an excellent location, much desired, the apartment itself spacious, with crown molding on the high ceilings. An SS man has made a claim on the apartment, and the older couple can count on exchanging their home for two bunks in separate barracks in a concentration camp. All the Hohenemsers can think to do is to lock themselves inside. When Elisabeth gets word of this, she fears the worst. With her husband, Kurt, stationed in far-away Posen, she asks for help from Dr. Philipp Schaeffer, a Tibetologist trained at the Heidelberg Institute for Buddhist Studies. Philipp can read Sanskrit, Tibetan, and Mandarin. With his shaved head and ascetic frame, he makes a monklike impression. He is also Elisabeth's lover.

Philipp doesn't hesitate to accompany her. He is five foot seven, slender, wiry, and very agile — and suddenly he needs to be, because when they get to the apartment door they can already smell the gas that the elderly people have turned on to end their lives. To their shock, however, the building's caretaker won't allow them to break down the door. Acting fast, Philipp decides "to use the air raid rope to climb down from the fourth floor and through the window on the third," as a report of the incident later states. The attempt has to be made secretly so the caretaker won't notice — and it has to happen fast.

As Philipp is rappelling down, the rope breaks. He falls more than thirty feet and lands on the pavement of the courtyard below with a severe concussion and a broken forearm, pelvis, and femur.

Elisabeth gets him to a hospital, where his hip is repaired with a nine-centimeter-long nail, but the doctors are unable to adequately mend his complicated fractures. In one of his ankles ankylosis sets in beyond healing and Philipp is only able to walk on crutches. Constant pain will accompany him to the end of his life.

He was not able to help the Hohenemsers with his efforts. Two days later, on April 8, 1942, they succeed in committing suicide.

Afterward, the SS man moves into their pretty apartment.

# 27

On May 8, 1942, three years to the day before the surrender of the Wehrmacht and the end of the Second World War in Europe, the British foreign secretary Anthony Eden gives a speech in Edinburgh and calls on Germans to resist:

> The longer the German people continue to support and to tolerate the regime which is leading them to destruction the heavier grows their own direct responsibility for the damage that they are doing to the world.
>
> Therefore, if any section of the German people really wants to see a return to a German State which is based on respect for law and for the rights of the individual, they must understand that no one will believe them until they have taken active steps to rid themselves of their present regime.

Eden hits a sore point. Up to now little is known abroad of German resistance activities against National Socialism. The images that are public show the opposite: cheering masses; unconditional, fanatical support for the dictator.

On May 10, it is a summery seventy-one degrees in Berlin. Harro and Libertas pick up Dr. John Rittmeister and his wife, Eva, and drive out to Stahnsdorf, near Potsdam, where Antonie and John Graudenz live with their daughters, sixteen-year-old Karin and fifteen-year-old Silva, in a small villa with a large garden next to a small wood.

The Graudenz family has well established itself in their community. They've become friends with the mayor, and Graudenz, the successful businessman, drives a Mercedes, has a valuable library, a fine wine collection, and a chic Blaupunkt radio. He also boasts a stately income of thirty thousand Reichsmarks a year. They keep a goat at the house for fresh milk, have an aviary full of songbirds and a watchful German shepherd named Tasso, who was trained as a mine-sniffing dog.

This Sunday, Harro lies on the grass and reads the *Pravda,* Moscow's largest newspaper. Libs enjoys the admiration of the teenage girls, and the pianist Helmut Roloff converses with the host — who sits shirtless at his Remington typewriter at a table in the garden — about the losses on the Eastern Front. Harro chimes in with his usual keen eye for geostrategical developments: This year they'll let them get as far as the Volga, since Stalin apparently intends to "wait to win his biggest victory in the region near Stalingrad that is so steeped in tradition."

Later they are joined by Maria Terwiel and Helmut Himpel, and someone else is there, too: Horst Heilmann, co-author of the Napoleon text, who has recently turned nineteen. Heilmann has a near-angelic look to him and is always snappily dressed. Today he has interesting news: After voluntarily enlisting in the Wehrmacht and being assigned to the Twenty-Third Reserve Division of the Signal Corps here in Stahnsdorf, he has successfully completed the test for placement with the decoding service at army high command. The very next day, May 11, he is to report for duty and begin wrestling with English, German, and Russian radio transmissions. Without knowing it, since he has not yet been informed of Hans Coppi's radio attempts, he is now in a crucial position with the very Radio Defense Corps that is potentially so dangerous for the network.

This afternoon in the Graudenzes' garden, where every now and then a green woodpecker flits into view, there is plenty to eat, a rarity in this phase of the war, which devours so many resources. John had a pig slaughtered in the garage a short while earlier; Karin and Silva had to sing loudly in two-part harmony on the garage roof in order to cover the squealing. The slaughter wasn't strictly legal, but it sure tastes good now.

They all sit around the table, enjoying themselves and discussing their next operation, meant to be directed against a propaganda exhibition that opened two days earlier in the Lustgarten in Berlin. It bears the name *The Soviet Paradise* and stretches across more than nine thousand square meters to show the "Poverty, Misery, Depravity and Need" in the Soviet Union, as it is described in the exhibition catalog. In a giant tent that rises almost as high as the museum behind it, the German people are shown their archenemy, the giant "Bolshevist" empire, depicted as a Jewish conspiracy that wants to subject the world to its yoke. Perfectly located between the Berlin Cathedral and the National Gallery, the easily accessible open-air exhibition is meant to become the most successful propaganda exhibition of the Third Reich.

Captured Red Army artillery pieces and armored vehicles are posted in front of the hall, pointed menacingly at the Berlin Palace. Large-format photos show grim-looking men with daggers, knives, axes, and scythes who are meant to depict Soviet soldiers.

The heart of *The Soviet Paradise* is the purportedly true-to-life reproduction of a neighborhood in "Minsk, the City of Lies," the Belarussian capital: dilapidated buildings that have been shipped to their present location exactly as is. Display boards list in detail which of the "real objects secured and removed from the Soviet Union" belong to which tavern or which institution. So-called *Schmutzwege* — "paths of filth" — outfitted with monuments of Lenin lead the flood of visitors to shabby hovels that lack any trace of culture, with dreary-looking niches full of dirty icons and ridiculous-looking Communist propaganda images. A grocery store with nothing but a few vodka bottles behind dusty panes of glass; a dirty, poorly supplied hospital room; even the reproduction of a so-called execution cell — tiled and complete with a hose for washing away the blood: shock value. Then more sober statistics on the partition walls that seek to prove how the German invasion had brought about an upswing in the economy in some places thanks to reprivitization and the takeover of farms by Aryans.

The reason for the bizarre horror show is simple: The war in Russia that has already cost so many young Germans their lives is becoming ever more unpopular among the people. The number of casualties has passed the million mark. More and more families between the Alps and the Baltic are mourning a loss. "This promises to be a first class achievement and to argue on the grandest possible scale that our war against the Soviet Union is justified," hopes Goebbels in a diary entry. In *The Soviet Paradise,* the good German is meant to learn the truth about the beastly, depraved enemy; turn away in disgust; and support with even greater resolve the master-race politics of the National Socialist regime — and to be prepared at any time to sacrifice their own child for it.

This time, unlike with their pamphlets *Concern for Germany's Future Is Spreading Among the People* or the *Open Letter to the Eastern Front,* Harro and Libertas and their friends don't want to use subtle arguments. They want to act in a bold and eye-catching manner, to deliver a broadside, so to speak, to broadcast slogans that make an impression. For their medium they decide on stickers. But how are they going to put them up in prominent places — and on as many posters for the propaganda exhibition as possible — without drawing notice? Harro has an idea. Whether his new romance with Stella Mahlberg makes him think of it is hard to say, but: Why not use love as camouflage? His suggestion is to work always in pairs, disguised as couples. While the two kiss, one of them casually puts up a sticker. The prudish Germans, so his thinking goes, will turn away from this public display of affection, so it should be a safe method. On May 17, exactly one week later, they should get started on the operation.

Later that afternoon Horst Heilmann reports on something he's learned in the Twenty-Third Reserve Division. Germany's Radio Defense Corps is now capable of decrypting British radio transmissions concerning the dispatch of convoys to Murmansk. Using these ship convoys the Western Allies are supporting the Soviet Union in its fight against Hitler, filling the gaps in Russian production in 1942 with urgently needed food supplies, combat vehicles, aircraft fuel, and raw materials. Millions of tons of cargo, 5,000 tanks and 7,000 airplanes, 350,000 tons of ammunition, and 15 million US boots for the sore feet of their Russian comrades have already reached the Soviet Union by this route. At the direction of the White House these North Sea convoys have been given special prominence in US media. The idea is to underscore the country's alliance with the Soviet Union in this war, which but for this aid might have taken a different course. Compared to the other two transport routes — the land route through east Siberia or the Persian Gulf — the route through the North Sea is the shortest and quickest, but also the most dangerous, since it passes closely by German-occupied Norway.

Right away, Harro sees it as imperative to warn London of the danger: If they don't, the soldiers of the British and American navies, on their way from Scotland or Iceland to the northern coast of the USSR, will be sitting ducks. As it happens, the most feared German warship stationed in the North Sea, which by its very presence threatens the Allied convoys, bears an all-too-familiar name. It is the *Tirpitz,* next to the *Bismarck* the biggest battleship ever built in Europe. Unless the British learn that their code has been cracked, they'll fall prey to his great-uncle's namesake. But how is Harro supposed to make contact with the British?

Johnny Graudenz knows Marcel Melliand, an influential textile manufacturer and publisher who has a subsidiary in New York and lives in Heidelberg. Melliand, who is married to an American, is a liberal citizen of the world honored by the Heidelberg Academy of Sciences, and a fierce opponent of the Nazis. He does business in Switzerland; the system tolerates this because he brings hard currency into the Reich. In Zurich, Melliand has connections to London. Graudenz proposes a meeting with him in southern Germany to arrange everything.

On this lovely evening in May in the Graudenz family garden, the temperature stays warm, while an almost forgotten feeling of satiety sets in.

What would the British foreign secretary Eden, who in his speech two days earlier had been so pained to note the lack of a German resistance, have thought of these people if he could have seen them? If he had realized for what they were risking their lives, heard that they wanted to protect the ships in the British convoys?

Would he have acknowledged and supported them?

# 28

On Wednesday, May 13, 1942, Harro and Stella meet on Ku'damm in the morning and go to the Deutsches Theater. At this time of day no one will bother them there. The affair is getting more intense. Harro wants to enjoy life to the fullest, and not just with Libertas, but with Stella, too, whether there's a war on or not.

On May 16, Libertas, who doesn't know anything about the relationship yet, travels to Vienna for four days for meetings with Wien-Film, which is responsible for almost all film production in Austria and is subject to the control of the Kulturfilm-Zentrale.

It is a Saturday evening. She couldn't get a ticket for the sleeper car, and it worries Harro, who takes her to the train station, that she is traveling in such "poor" conditions. But Libs is clever enough to at least rent a bed for half the night ("till three a.m."), "so this way it's somewhat bearable."

At least these uncomfortable travel arrangements spare her the danger of the next few days. Because of this trip, Libertas doesn't take part in the group's operation against *The Soviet Paradise*.

On Sunday night, half a dozen friends meet in an attic room at Nürnberger Strasse 33, near Kurfürstendamm, to go over the last details. Around the corner are the KaDeWe department store and the renowned Femina-Palast, with its "Tea and Dancing" on Sundays. Fritz Thiel, the precision engineer, lives here with his pregnant wife, Hannelore, just seventeen years old. They all sit around the living room table. On it are the stickers, fifteen by four centimeters. John Graudenz was responsible for the design and production:

Ständige Ausstellung
Das NAZI-PARADIES
Krieg Hunger Lüge Gestapo
Wie lange noch?

One of the stickers produced by John Graudenz. It reads: "Permanent Exhibit / The NAZI PARADISE / War Hunger Lies Gestapo / How much longer?"

What they're planning is as spectacular as it is risky. Because of this, a few of the friends, Günther Weisenborn, for example, have refused to participate. Here in Fritz Thiel's apartment there is also some last-minute criticism. The chance of being found out is just too high, says Ursula Goetze, the twenty-six-year-old student from the Rittmeister circle. She suggests they call the whole thing off.

At this moment Harro arrives, late because of Stella, still wearing his Luftwaffe uniform. He immediately senses that the mood in the room is about to turn and it's up to him to allay the doubts. To his thinking it would be fatal to cancel at the last minute. It would rob them of the verve for later operations. Besides, everything was ready: The stickers were already distributed. The eagerness to convince his comrades is awakened, his joy at verbal sparring, the parry and thrust of argument. Now this aspect of Harro's character comes out, this "certain fanaticism in organizing things that I care about," as he once described it in a letter to his mother.

With his inborn authority he explains that he considers it important not to give in now, despite the dangers and even though some believe the political impact of the operation will be negligent. They have to impart to the people of Berlin the sense that forces inside the country are ready to act. That there *is* resistance. If they didn't do something today, they would never do anything again. He looks around at his friends. No one argues, not even Ursula Goetze. It is now shortly after ten o'clock. Next door at the Femina Palast things are in full swing, and snatches of music come through the open windows.

*Over the roofs of the great big city*
*My song finds its way to you*
*Calls you back to me*
*Because I love you*

Some people would rather party than risk their life against the dictatorship.

# 29

An hour later Harro is holding his service weapon, a 6.35-millimeter Haenell-Schmeisser, under his long Luftwaffe coat, ready to fire. It's just over fifty degrees, the Ku'damm bathing in a play of light and shadow — though it's more shadow than light. The city is hiding from its enemy in the skies and has gone dark, as it has every night since the war began.

Ahead of Harro walks Maria Terwiel, her hair melting with the shadows of the imposing Wilhemine buildings across the street from Kaiser Wilhelm Memorial Church. From the entrance to a cabaret the late show crowd pours out. Next to Maria is Fritz Thiel; arm in arm they steer toward the entrance of a building. Fritz embraces her, his face moves close to hers, and he reaches into his coat pocket and takes out one of the stickers. Pedestrians everywhere. If someone notices the two of them, Harro will shoot into the air to draw attention to himself.

As he watches the make-believe love scene, does he think of Stella Mahlberg? He allowed Libertas great liberties with Günther Weisenborn and has himself always been faithful before now. For this reason he feels no guilt; rather, he has to admit to himself how much he enjoys the change of pace with Stella, the woman with the pretty name, the high cheekbones, the raven-black hair. Harro peers through the darkness. Fritz's lips are close to Maria's, his hands on her shoulders.

Eight couples are in action tonight. They lean against bus shelters, streetlamps, advertising columns, trees; they hug and kiss, like in the movies, like in a song by Lale Andersen — distributing the "Nazi Paradise" stickers.

Four neighborhoods of Greater Berlin are covered; Ku'damm is hit twice, because it's where the major cinemas are and the people should have something to talk about on the way back home to bed. The half Jewish electrical engineer Helmut Marquart is also taking part. Acting alone, he decorates the display windows of the exclusive shops on Kurfürstendamm.

Hilde and Hans Coppi, who actually *are* in love, who are married and now even pregnant, have set out for Moabit. From there it's on to Wedding, where people still get their water from pumps on the curb and the workers are sitting and eating, drinking and smoking behind the open windows. When they have successfully distributed their allotment, they ride their motorcycle back to their bower in Borsigwalde. There they kiss again, and Hans Coppi caresses his wife's swelling stomach.

Elisabeth and Kurt Schumacher are pasting stickers too. And Ursula Goetze, who grew up in the Communist youth movement and considers solidarity self-evident. Whatever doubts she had before, she is now fiercely resolved and about to head out. At home she calls her boyfriend, the teacher of romance languages Werner Krauss, to tell him that despite her reservations she's going to take part. In the end, this is the decision they came to as a group, and that was that.

"There's no way I'm letting you go alone," answers Krauss, though he doesn't like the idea one bit. To think of all the academic writing he had to do that evening! On the other hand, he is always up for wild nights out with Ursula, who is fifteen years younger: "I'll pick you up."

Shortly after eleven p.m., paler than usual, he arrives, fresh from the barracks, at her four-room apartment. "Fritz offered me a pistol to take with us," says Ursula by way of greeting. She refused it, though. They could discuss the rest on the way. Before they set off they look at a map to figure out the best way to get to Sachsendamm, a busy street south of Schöneberg, their assigned turf. Many workers pass along the route in the mornings and can read the stickers then.

Ursula Goetze and Werner Krauss, an unlikely couple with a difficult but sexually intense relationship, take the circle line to Papestrasse. They walk through the station's yellow-brick tunnel, their steps echoing, and reach the suburban train platform, which has already been widened as part of Speer's planned transformation of Berlin into "*Germania, Capital of the World.*"

Past the security guards' office, a waiting room for passengers, and an outhouse, they reach the Sachsendamm exit. The few passengers who left the train with them have dispersed, and the street looks deserted, no light shining on account of the blackout regulations. They pause for a moment to wait and see how many people might turn the corner and come walking up at this time of night, but it remains quiet. Could someone be watching them from one of the dark windows in the surrounding buildings? Once the area looks clear, Ursula, who finds the kissing idea silly, decides to distribute the stickers alone.

Werner Krauss follows her at a distance of thirty meters. Such a magnificent starry sky is spread out over Berlin — one would never have thought it possible before the war. The operation seems more and more absurd to him. He lights his pipe, lets his mind wander, and thinks about "the psychology of boredom." Maybe he'll write an essay on the subject. Ursula paces along Sachsendamm, posts her stickers, turns a corner and disappears down a side street. Werner hurries after her and is relieved, a short while later, to catch sight of her by the phone booth at the station. "Are you finished?" She nods. They step onto the platform. The train arrives and takes them to Anhalter Bahnhof, where they get off and go to the Thüringer Hof hotel, which Ursula's parents own. There they drink a bottle of wine to calm their nerves. Then Werner Krauss heads back to his barracks.

Permanent Exhibit
The NAZI PARADISE
War Hunger Lies Gestapo
How much longer?

The next morning, this will be read by thousands of Berliners.

# 30

A few days later, in a memo concerning "important national-political incidents," the Gestapo states for the record that "inflammatory Communist writings" have been disseminated throughout different neighborhoods of Berlin. Yet again their investigations yield no results. Again the spooks on Prinz-Albrecht-Strasse 8 have nothing to go on.

For Harro and his friends the operation is a huge success. They dared to leave their mark in public spaces. With their messages they have over-written the topography of the capital of the Reich. Even after the cleaning crews of the Municipal Waste Removal Authority have scratched away the last traces of the "Nazi Paradise" message, the mood among them is excellent. They have stared death in the face, felt its taste on their tongue — and they're still alive. They have gone from the uncertainty in Thiel's apartment to a feeling of triumph, have carried out their work against tyranny using the finest means possible, namely the embrace, the kiss. They have broken through the silence, loosened the monotone brown of Nazi Berlin, and nothing has happened to them.

No one was caught or arrested, and maybe there are a few people in this city who felt emboldened by their actions.

# 31

Libertas is eager to know if it all went smoothly. Somewhat earlier than planned and pleased with what she considers a successful trip, she comes back from Vienna, unlocks the door to the apartment on Altenburger Allee, steps inside, and hears suspicious noises coming from the parlor with the fireplace and the large chaise longue.

"You pig!" she screams at Harro as Stella Mahlberg hurries to get dressed. Stella too is surprised — by Libertas's surprise. "No deception where Libs is concerned. She knows the score and hasn't heard any lies from me. We don't do such things," Harro previously wrote in a letter to her. But it seems this itself was a lie. Once Libertas sees Stella's reaction and realizes this, she really loses it, and gives full rein to her anger: "I'm getting a divorce — now!"

"You can't do that!" is Harro's impulsive reply. "You and I know too much about each other!" For safety reasons alone a divorce filed in anger is unthinkable for him. He laughs, somewhat helplessly, which she takes as yet another affront. She announces she's going to talk to Engelsing to get legal advice for a separation. At least *she* still slept with him when she had others. *Her* sexual appetite was stimulated by her affairs, so he had profited from them too. But here things are different. Now there's something going on between the dark Stella and her blond Harro that Libertas has no part of, that excludes her and weakens her.

Couldn't he stand by her *now*, when she is sacrificing everything for him, has turned down every job offer, is building up the photo archive of Wehrmacht crimes and so urgently needs his emotional support?

# 32

Possibly as a means of fleeing the conflict, but mainly to meet Marcel Melliand, Graudenz's friend with connections in England, Harro leaves the city shortly afterward. In order to make the trip look innocuous, he first travels to Freiburg for a few lovely days. Marie Luise is there taking care of his brother, Hartmut, who is laid up in a sanatorium — tuberculosis is suspected. When their sister Helga comes as well, bringing her two small children, it becomes an impromptu family gathering. Only Erich Edgar is missing, who despite his sixty-one years has been returned to active duty by the navy and is stationed in Holland.

In Freiburg, Harro can breathe easy. The air is sweet, and it does him good to be with his family. Besides, the surrounding nature in late May is paradise. Everything is in bloom. It reminds him of the two peaceful years he spent here as a student in the late 1920s, before he went to Berlin and all this madness began. His time here had been carefree. He went for walks to the castle, along the river and into the nearby valleys, where he visited traditional taverns, and on summer evenings devoured large quantities of strawberries with whipped cream. Yes, they were two magnificent springs that he spent here as a student, living off his parents' money, and he realizes that he never thanked them enough for it. He just took it all for granted.

But times have changed, and things can't be as carefree as they once were. The war, now in its third year, weighs heavily on all of them. Around his mother, Harro makes no effort to hide where he stands. In Germany, he says when they're all sitting together, things will only start to get better when enough people are prepared to die for their convictions. Hitler might be able to have hundreds of resistance fighters murdered, but there is a limit.

And was he one of these fighters? his mother wants to know. Harro looks at her with his clear blue eyes and draws himself up: "Why not me?!"

"Once, in 1933, I was able to save you," Marie Luise heatedly replies. "I won't be so lucky a second time."

"Oh, Mom, the Gestapo isn't much more clever than I am."

Later, after a walk, Harro and his ill brother are sitting on a bench. As they look down into the green sloping valley, Hartmut asks him, though he has only a vague idea of his brother's activities in Berlin, if he too can take part.

Harro doesn't answer at first. A calm lies over everything, there is only the occasional sound of a bell ringing, the cry of a peacock from a nearby farm, a swallow flying overhead.

It's enough, Harro says, to have one person in the family risking his life. No more — they can't do that to their mother.

From Freiburg, Harro travels to Schloss Stetten, a castle built in the High Middle Ages, where he has arranged to meet with John Graudenz and Marcel Melliand. The Allied convoy situation has come to a head, the battle in the North Sea has broken out in earnest. The Germans are throwing everything they've got at the convoys to put a stop to the aid coming to the Soviet Union from Great Britain and the United States: U-boats, battleships, fighter planes — and they are succeeding. In the last few weeks the West has suffered devastating losses. Just recently a British merchant ship en route from Reykjavik to Murmansk was sunk by the German U-boat *U 403;* German destroyers had sunk two more, and an additional four had been bombed by German planes.

Schloss Stetten is the right place to lie low and discuss defensive measures. Harro, John, and the fifty-one-year-old Marcel are able to feel safe behind the castle moat and the outer wall with its round flanking towers. It even seems like a well-earned vacation, the sun tickling their noses in the morning and a summery warm breeze drifting through the half-open window. They meet in the shady courtyard of the inner bailey and sit under a blooming maple tree where the breakfast table is set with real coffee, hot chocolate, bread, butter, marmalade, and eggs.

Marcel Melliand, who even in his free time likes to wear pinstripe suits, understands the urgency of the matter. He promises to get in touch with his contacts as soon as possible and to apply for the necessary travel authorization. He hopes to visit Switzerland in August. Unfortunately, things can't move any faster.

Together they walk along the escarpment down into the village of Kocherstetten and from there to the river. They take a refreshing swim in the churning weir. "A natural bidet!" Graudenz cries exuberantly. "Natural, yes, but not so much the latter," Harro says, and enjoys the "full body massage in the rushing water." There's almost something ritual-like about it, cleansing, and Harro senses how much he needs nature to "rediscover a little of what I am."

After they've dried off, they lie in the hay in the sunshine. A pretty young woman joins them, but Harro's attitude is "utterly harmless," as he cheerfully writes to his parents. He's not here for love affairs — he has enough of that in Berlin right now — but for something else, his work.

And so, later that day, he starts on a new scholarly text that eventually is meant to become a book. It deals with the structural reasons for the outbreak of the two world wars. Horst Heilmann is again intended as co-author. Perfectly content, Harro sits there and writes. Maybe as he does so he shows himself what his life should really be. Here, back straight like his father's, sits the young, intellectual statesman of tomorrow, who even in the gloomy present is risking so much for his people — and will achieve even more for them in the future. Here he is, who in his country's name extends his hand to the British, Americans, and Russians and seeks to unite their hands on Germany, to parry the sword of Damocles that hangs over his homeland and threatens to pierce its heart.

For three long weeks he stays in the castle and writes, a luxurious, wonderful time. No wonder then that he is annoyed by the letters from Stella Mahlberg that reach him here — demanding, emotionally intense. She's always trying to play Elektra, he writes back to her — and not just on the stage. Nothing but drama.

Not so with Libertas. From her come letters in which she writes as "sweetly as always," and Harro looks forward to going back to her so she can "see him in a condition fit for a human being for the first time in years," well-nourished and well-rested.

Thus he has arrived at the personal decision that his stay in southern Germany was meant to guide him toward. Libertas is the love of his life, plain and simple. And this might be the most important result of this trip.

# 33

On June 30, 1942, Johann Wenzel, Kent's radio assistant, receives uninvited guests in his Brussels garret. He has just sent two transmissions when his colleague downstairs — not Kent, this time — shouts something he doesn't understand. Military boots are thundering up the stairs. Quickly he lights the packet of reports he hasn't yet transmitted with a match, desperately blows on the flames, and once the fire is finally strong enough throws the packet into the oven. But the paper burns poorly, and the boots are already at his doorstep. Quickly Wenzel takes the two messages he just sent, which are still lying on the table, and flees through the hatch onto the roof, where he tears them up and tosses them into the chimney. Heavy pistol-fire opens up from below. In a fit of rage — and to avoid dying without a fight — he starts ripping tiles off the roof and hurling them at the soldiers shooting at him from the street. Then he takes off running, trying to get past the soldiers' perimeter. He leaps from roof to roof, his black silhouette sharply outlined against the night sky. After running about three hundred feet he is stopped by a firewall, climbs down a ladder mounted to a chimney, and flees into a building, where he runs up the stairs to the top floor and hides in a corner of the attic.

Several times the Germans soldiers walk past him.

Then an officer pulls him out of his hiding place by his leg.

Johann Wenzel, once a confidant of Ernst Thälmann, head of the German Communist Party, is a big catch for the Nazis. He is brought to the Gestapo detention camp in Breendonk, a fortress near Brussels. There they intend to get him to talk, to find out the cipher so they can decode the messages sent between Western Europe and Moscow — which include the broadcast to Kent about Harro and Libertas. But Wenzel is a trained fighter and can't be made to speak that easily. When they tell him they already know everything, so he might as well confess, he knows it's just a trick — and he doesn't say a word. When the interrogator claims others have already confessed, he simply doesn't believe it; and if they really have talked, he calls them liars and keeps denying everything. Most of the time incriminating evidence from a third party won't be enough to find you guilty. As it says in the *Eleven Dictates for the Conduct of Prisoners,* which is circulating in Communist cells: "I will never confess to the crimes I am accused of, not even when all manner of evidence is served up against me, because they will fabricate evidence and construe facts in such a way as to obtain my confession and convict me."

But in Breendonk, Wenzel learns the hard way what the Gestapo men call *Verschärftes Verhör* — lawyers at the Nuremberg Trials will call it *third-degree interrogation* — and just how much use all his rules and good intentions are going to be to him. It starts with an orgy of beatings that lasts for five days and goes far beyond any of the poundings he has taken before. He is initially subjected to conventional mistreatment with clubs, whips, and rubber batons, but when he still refuses to talk, more refined methods are brought to bear. Particularly unpleasant is being struck with either a ruler or a round or rectangular rod as thick as a finger behind the ears, in the neck, on the eyelids, and on the jugular vein, which inflicts severe damage to Wenzel's vision, hearing, and balance. While being tortured in this way he sometimes starts seeing double, whether it's the Gestapo officers interrogating him or other objects in the room. Voices sound far away. He has massive swelling around his eyes; his corneas are damaged. He loses sight in one eye.

These "beating interrogations," led by the Gestapo officer Voss, are followed by a period of quiet and ordinary interrogations that are conducted with Wenzel in the so-called *Krummschliessen,* or "bent buckle." Using a special set of manacles, his arms are twisted around and pinned to his back. This procedure is especially agonizing. After a certain amount of time it leads to cramping and in some cases paralysis of the muscles in the arms, back, and stomach. Wenzel has to vomit and loses consciousness. But he doesn't talk.

One night after several weeks in Gestapo custody he tries to open the veins in both wrists by rubbing them against his sharp eyeteeth — also enlisting the help of a nail broken out of his bunk — until the blood is gushing out of his veins in spurts. When he comes to again his forearms are as swollen as rolling pins and the blood has turned adhesive, sticking together the wounds and the ropes cutting deep into his wrists.

He isn't dead, though; instead, he is taken to Prinz-Albrecht-Strasse 8 in Berlin. Breendonk was just the beginning. From now on, Libertas's and Harro's lives depend on his ability to hold fast.

# 34

They know nothing of the mortal danger they are in now that Johann Wenzel, a stranger to them, is sitting in Gestapo custody. The GRU, the Soviet Union's military intelligence service, doesn't inform its competitors in the NKWD intelligence agency about his capture, and for this reason Korotkov is never able to warn his contacts in Berlin.

Harro and Libertas have redone the interior of their apartment so they can work better, moving the bedroom to the room by the door, which they let out until last year. Now the second room is free for Libertas to write in, while Harro continues to use the parlor with the fireplace. There he has built himself a low wall of bookshelves. The renovations were expensive, but now they're finally finished. Now they each have their own space. True, they sit apart from one another, but they are connected through the open doors, each hearing the clatter of the other's typewriter. They continue to leave the little room to the right of the long hallway unused. Still a potential nursery.

Harro's writing collaboration with Horst Heilmann grows more intense this summer of 1942. Harro believes they've "got all sorts of things cooking," and the nineteen-year-old Heilmann is getting to know his old teacher better and better — and Libertas, too. For the sensitive young man the two of them represent the ideal couple. They are people for whom honor is more important than conformity. He falls platonically in love with *both* of them, but especially Libertas, who returns his feelings. It never becomes physical between them, but their souls seem to speak the same language. Heilmann is also finding out more and more about their illegal activities. Because of his position in the Wehrmacht's code-cracking division, Harro wants to shield Heilmann from information that would be delicate for him — for as long as possible, at any rate. But the young soldier is presented the Wehrmacht photo collection, which shows him that the horrors on the Eastern Front are real. This further strengthens his resolve to emulate Harro and Libertas in their defiant stance against the Nazis.

It rains a lot in these first weeks of August 1942, during which Johann Wenzel continues to be interrogated at Prinz-Albrecht-Strasse 8. Still, every morning from seven to nine Harro is on the Havel River, in the *Duschinka*, his new sailboat. It has replaced the *Haizuru*, which Weisenborn now uses.

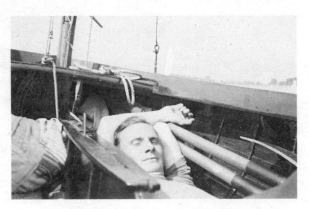

Still relaxed: Harro on the *Duschinka*.

Harro doesn't care if it's storming or raining; not even hail bothers him, and rough waters won't scare him off. It becomes more and more clear to him that he really must end the affair with Stella, which is still smoldering. On August 5 he writes her a farewell letter: "The two of us: horribly adrift. If I could I would fall out of love as quick as I could and come back to you when the war was over to try my luck then." His reason for the breakup is typical Harro: He doesn't want to subject the "so rare and dear feeling" that he has for her to the thousand trials of their current existence. Like with Regine, he contends that precisely *because* he cares for her he cannot see her anymore. "I intend not to write to you any more, nor to call you anymore." Period.

Meanwhile his relationship with Libertas is on the mend, and on top of that, starting on August 9 the sun is shining every day. It's almost like before: They sail on Wannsee, talk about everything and nothing, swim, cook, and sleep together. They both know that life is short and could be over tomorrow: Fate has cast them into hard times. Neither of them wanted this. They are just people who want to live and love. They drive out to Liebenberg, where the air shimmers in the dry heat and they "tan nice and brown and jump into the water over and over again. The Lanke has such magnificently clear, blue water — very rare for Brandenburg."

It's all far from carefree. There isn't much to eat, not even in the countryside. The economic situation of the manor house and surrounding estate has grown even more precarious. The hopes Uncle Wend had put in Adolf Hitler have not come to fruition. The Fürst complains that the cold winter will mean considerable damage to the coming harvest; come fall they will all have to tighten their belts even further.

As they sit on the terrace, the neglected tennis court in front of them, to their left the outbuildings, which could use a new coat of paint, Harro and Libertas can see it is Polish and French prisoners of war who are keeping the estate going. They are busy everywhere, but above all in the fields; many of the recent arrivals are captured Red Army soldiers. "The people, who before now only knew of them as *Untermenschen* [subhumans] from propaganda, are now finally getting a proper look," Harro writes his parents. "Everywhere you go the talk is of the Russians." By now there are more than ten million forced laborers in Germany; men in the prime of their lives who have to work as slaves for the enemy.

In Berlin as well, the food situation is getting ever more miserable. "One really is hungry all the time," Harro writes in a letter to his father. Now, though they no longer have to squeeze every penny — above all thanks to Libertas's salary at the Kulturfilm-Zentrale — there isn't "even the kind of food that could keep a person healthy." In the shops, in exchange for ration stamps for bread, meat, cooking fat, eggs, marmalade, sugar, and other items, the most meager amounts are doled out, which over the course of the first six months of 1942 are cut even more drastically. The bread ration goes from 9.6 kilograms per month down to 6.4; an adult receives only 300 grams of meat per week, 206 grams of cooking fat. Each bite takes something away from the next meal. Where are the joys of life that the two of them are so fond of, and that were always the basis of their relationship? When are they still able to experience the magic moments when they can share something lovely together, eat well, go to the movies, or dance? Cultural life withers, shops close, every night the blackout. Dancing is widely prohibited. The Resi dance hall, with phones on the tables and its own pneumatic tube mail system that the guests can use to send each other presents, is closed. The war devours everything, eats up their reserves, chains them to a draining day-to-day existence that offers little satisfaction. Could this be the "overreaching capitalist system of government" that Arvid Harnack predicted, "the final result" of which is "to turn the people into an army of slaves"?

As far as the city's restaurants go, it helps at least that Harro and Libertas don't need to scrimp financially and can go out to eat every now and then, "where it costs a whole pile of money." But even assuming they can get a reservation — which is hardly easy — they still have to bring ration stamps. At Horcher, at Lutter & Wegner, or Borchardt they can still eat quite decently and drink a passable wine; on an especially lucky day at Borchardt for example they get wild boar haunches in cream with sauerkraut cooked in wine for 2.40 RM. The waiter collects ration stamps for fifty grams of meat, fifteen grams of fat, plus a twenty-gram bread stamp for dessert.

But they no longer stay out into the small hours of the morning; instead they take an early subway back home. There is loads to do in the office, even on the weekends. Due to the war situation, work on Sundays has been instituted all around, "a heavy burden for everyone with any sort of family life," as Harro writes to his parents, voicing his objections to this "unregenerate" treatment: "But of course it is typical for the present time that you protect and care for motors and machines while at the same time expecting the extraordinary from people without any such consideration." Still, he jokes, hinting that he and Libs aren't just talking about having children, "in every respect, having to stay home every night leads to a distinct upswing in family life."

No different from Libertas, who spends all day plowing through work at the Kulturfilm-Zentrale, Harro's day starts early in the morning. After waking he rubs his tense, stiff body with alcoholic liniment, mixes a few grains of cocoa powder with dried milk, and swallows a spoon of *Biomalz,* a vitamin mixture, to stave off malnutrition. Then it's off to the Air Ministry. After a few hours in the office it's time for lunch in the casino of the *Haus der Flieger,* the pilots' house, across the street from the Gestapo building — where Johann Wenzel is still being worked over. There isn't much on the plates, though. Even at a meeting with high-ranking Croatian officers, Harro reports, there is only "synthetic tomato soup, potatoes, and peas (no sauce, no meat), synthetic ice cream, bread with curd cheese (no butter)" — and this on a non-meat-free day and for a festive occasion. The large quantity of alcohol doesn't help either. It certainly continues to flow, "but with so little in your stomach it hardly sits well."

A friend of Harro's sees him around this time, sitting at a table outside a restaurant in a bombed-out street, looking haggard and gamely eating up every last bit of the modest meal served to him. "Here we're all 'starved' to a certain extent, that is to say somewhat weakened by undernourishment," Harro writes to his father, and adds, acidly, but inconspicuous to the censor: "But this can't diminish our faith in the Führer one bit. It's just annoying, because it so often happens now that you can't keep slaving away like you of course want to."

This August 1942 is a month full of tension and strain — what's missing is relief. Harro waits feverishly for news of whether Marcel Melliand has made it into Switzerland to warn the British, while in the heat of southern Russia the situation at Stalingrad comes to a head.

Then the shoe drops. After several weeks of "thorough interrogation by the State Police," as the official language would have it, the detectives on Prinz-Albrecht-Strasse achieve the "divulgence of the encryption method." Johann Wenzel has told them the sentence used in the cipher, and now the investigators set to work decoding the Soviet messages they have fished out of the ether. Work begins in the decryption unit on Matthäikirchplatz, not far from Bendlerblock, the seat of the army high command. There sit the young math geniuses, the cryptographers of the Wehrmacht. Horst Heilmann is one of them, even if he doesn't hear about *this* particular activity right away — it's all too secret for that. But some of his colleagues are amazed. Before now they have labored in vain, staring at comparison charts and calculating probabilities, trying to make sense of the jumble of numbers from the Russians. Now, suddenly, here comes a flood of intelligible messages. And one of them contains the real names of Berlin citizens — an address at Altenburger Allee 19 and even the telephone number for Harro and Libertas.

Dr. Wilhelm Vauck, mathematics, physics, and chemistry instructor and head of the decryption unit, gives word to the high command of the Wehrmacht. Admiral Wilhelm Canaris, the head of military intelligence, is informed. He himself is secretly part of the resistance and collaborating with the army officers who want to get rid of Hitler. But he won't intervene in a case like this one, where it seems contact was made with the Bolshevist enemy. The men he is conspiring with, like Ludwig Beck, Hans Oster, and Henning von Tresckow, are like himself strict anti-Communists and in favor of a clear Western alignment for Germany.

Thus at a meeting between Canaris; the leader of his Radio Defense Corps — and later a co-conspirator in the coup attempt of July 20, 1944, when Stauffenberg planted a bomb against Hitler in Operation Valkyrie — Fritz Thiele; the leader of Military Intelligence, Third Division, Lieutenant General von Bentivegni; and SS-Oberführer Schellenberg it is decided that the Gestapo will conduct the investigation of First Lieutenant Harro Schulze-Boysen of the Luftwaffe.

# 35

At the headquarters of the Gestapo, since 1939 part of the Reich Main Security Office and known as Amt IV Gegner-Erforschung und -Bekämpfung — Division IV — Researching and Combating the Enemy — a thirty-man special commission is called into action and dubbed Rote Kapelle or Red Orchestra — a term that has already been used once before in Belgium. The name reflects the direction the investigators have chosen for their pursuit: alleging a link between the Berliners and the Soviet spy network. It also reflects the fact that in intelligence jargon the radio operator is known as a "pianist," who translates signals into notes that are received acoustically by the person on the other end.

After Georg Elser's singlehanded attempt to kill Hitler with a bomb at the Bürgerbräuhaus brewery in Munich on November 8, 1939, and the successful assassination of Himmler's deputy Reinhard Heydrich on June 4, 1942, in Prague, this is the third special commission in the Gestapo's history.

The thirty-nine-year-old SS-Obersturmbannführer and senior councillor Friedrich Panzinger — nickname Panz — an old Munich companion of the Gestapo chief Heinrich Müller, is called upon to head the Berlin commission. Panzinger wears nickel-frame glasses and is a cold bureaucrat. He is barely involved in the day-to-day investigative work; his job is to keep Himmler up to date.

The investigation itself is led by the reserved but diligent Horst Kopkow, a thirty-one-year-old specialist in sabotage who holds the ranks of Kriminalrat and SS-Hauptsturmführer and is head of the Referat IV A 2 subdepartment. Even before 1933 Kopkow had "proven himself through his active efforts in the SA and SS," as one of his service evaluations indicates: "With exemplary composure and rare nerve he always helped lead the charge in tavern brawls. He personifies the qualities of limitless focus and strong force of will." In short, a first-class Nazi.

Kopkow picks the thirty-four-year-old Kriminalkommissar and SS-Hauptsturmführer Johannes Strübing, his most clever senior officer, to be lead detective in the case.

The work of the special commission is designated a *Geheime Reichssache* — secret Reich matter — the highest possible level of classification. No one in the Reich Main Security Office is permitted to have any knowledge of the proceedings unless it is of absolute necessity. Even the initiated tend to learn only what they need in order to carry out their particular task.

The Gestapo officers have observation work ahead of them. Listening in on phone calls, shadowing people, putting Harro and Libertas under the microscope. But it is also *narrative work* that has to be done, weaving a story together that will fit the paranoid worldview of National Socialism and justify the cost of a special commission. Amt IV Gegner-Erforschung und -Bekämpfung needs *Gegner* — adversaries — and they have just been offered an excellent opportunity.

# 36

That summer, in Munich, a student group called the White Rose is distributing leaflets against Hitler's crimes. At the same time, Harro is also planning a new pamphlet action with John Graudenz. It is meant to outdo everything before it.

Graudenz suggests establishing an illegal print shop. He can obtain the necessary machines from his company. It would put them in a position to react quickly, to produce large volumes of material, to flood the country with sensitive information about how the war is going and bring about a popular revolt.

But on August 14, 1942, something else happens. Two people meet again, two individuals involved in a passionate affair during a difficult time. Though he had already split with her, Harro makes another date with Stella Mahlberg.

Libs doesn't like this rekindling business one bit. Her nerves are frayed as it is. Recently it seems like someone is following her. Or is it just paranoia? Is there really a clicking sound on the telephone line? Is there an echo that wasn't there before? When they go sailing, is there a man standing over on the shore with binoculars? Is he watching the birds on Wannsee, or is he watching the *Duschinka*? And just who is Stella Mahlberg, anyway? How can Harro jump back into bed with this woman he barely knows?

The more Libertas thinks about it, the more furious she gets, and she decides to leave for a few days, to visit relatives in Bremen. Let Harro get caught in his own web of illegal and clandestine activities, let him stray deeper and deeper into the traps this world has set. Let him tighten the noose around his own neck.

She has to put Caesar's roof up before she gets on the highway. Heavy rain is falling that day, painting a camouflage pattern on the limestone of the Air Ministry, where Harro sits in his office and looks out the window at the blurred façade of the by now "Aryanized" Wertheim department store. Screened by this heavy downpour, the threads of the Gestapo spiderweb are working silently and secretly, winding ever more tightly around him.

But as closely as Horst Kopkow has been watching Harro, he still can't figure him out. What kind of person is this? First lieutenant in the Luftwaffe, his great-uncle the legendary Tirpitz ... and a Bolshevist agent? Then again, why else would the Soviets have ordered their man in Brussels to meet with him? And what role does Libertas play?

Kopkow, the sabotage specialist, has dealt with communists before. He knows how they tick, where their weaknesses are. Russian agents he can deal with; German communists he can torture until he gets the desired result — or until he's killed them. But these people he has his sights on now work differently. Live differently. They have affairs with pretty young actresses. Go sailing on Wannsee. Ride horses at a castle north of Berlin. Libertas's family knows Göring; they once hosted him for a deer hunt. Her grandfather was the Kaiser's closest friend — though he had a dubious reputation. They can't be communists. These are Berlin bohemians. Kopkow is confused.

On this day when it rains so hard and Libertas speeds toward Bremen in her Fiat, the detective observes Harro walking through Tiergarten with a stranger. Harro's unknown companion wears nickel-frame glasses and has a sharply receding hairline — a bureaucrat type in his mid-thirties. Because of the pounding rain, Kopkow can't understand what the two are saying, and neither can he see them particularly well, since they keep disappearing under their umbrellas. There's really nothing suspicious about it. Two men go for a walk in the park in bad weather, nothing more.

Arvid, by now in a senior position in the Economics Ministry, believes he is being followed. He has moved his study into his bedroom, which seems more secure to him, has searched his apartment for bugs but found none. His younger brother, Falk, begged him to try to flee the country, but Arvid refused. "How is one supposed to lead a resistance movement from abroad? Our biggest enemy is here," he told his brother. "And if we leave, who will be left?"

Whatever it is that Harro and Arvid discussed in this heavy rain, there is no record of it. It's possible they talked about their mutual friend Carl-Dietrich von Trotha, who is also building up an ever more active resistance network — the one the Gestapo will call the Kreisau circle. Von Trotha is a colleague of Arvid's: economist in the Reich Economics Ministry, expert on the energy industry, a democratically inclined, highly educated man. The "circle" thinks of itself as a kind of think tank for the German resistance, and is working collectively on initial ideas for a new constitution for postwar Germany, which will later meet the approval of the would-be Hitler assassin Claus von Stauffenberg. An alliance of European states would include Germany and its wartime enemies Great Britain and the Soviet Union: a crucial point that also matches up with Arvid and Harro's ideas. A new world is meant to emerge that places individual people at its center and not the masses.

But that's still a long way off. The Second World War isn't over yet, and it is taking an ever more horrible course. Every single day of this summer of 1942, thousands of soldiers die on all fronts and thousands of people perish in concentration camps — every single day. Thousands of civilians, including women, children, and the elderly. At his desk Harro learns that on August 23, six hundred bombers of Luftflotte 4 launched a devastating attack on Stalingrad. Because of the Soviet dictator's orders, the people of the city that bears his name weren't evacuated. More than forty thousand civilians are killed.

The sun is shining on August 30, a Sunday. There are late-summer days when Berlin is incandescent. The sandy Brandenburg soil is hot between your toes, and the sky hovers so high above that you feel its blue is part of the universe. At these times, in this city where so much is happening all the time, life becomes cosmic.

The heat hangs brutal over Wannsee, the temperature climbs to ninety degrees, in late afternoon the wind rises: sailing weather. Harro had ridden his bike from his apartment to the Blau-Rot sailing club that morning. Hannelore and Fritz Thiel arrive in their paddleboat and tie up at the dock. Weisenborn comes too and brings Joy, who is now his wife. Exactly three years ago he was sailing here with Harro alone. It was raining then, it was the start of the Second World War, and Elfriede Paul had just given him an earful on account of his many affairs.

Weisenborn has grown wise; he is focused on Joy. But what about Harro? Libertas is still in Bremen, and the entrancing person strolling toward them all on the dock is a thirty-year-old woman with high cheekbones and a new pet name, which she received two weeks earlier at their last rendezvous: no longer the loaded *Fix*, but rather the ironically distant *Stellizitas*.

What is Harro thinking about as he helps Stella on board for this last sailing tour of his life? Is he angry that she came because he misses Libertas, who he first met in this very place? Is it possible he didn't even invite Stella? That she, after hearing of the outing, simply headed over here in order to seize her chance, with Harro's wife far away? Was she thinking, how could Harro resist her, once the sun has set, the starry sky has spread out above them, the others gone, and she is there to sweeten the night for him on board the rocking boat?

Harro can't be pleased with her presence, since there is another guest on board with whom he has something urgent to discuss, something strictly confidential — Horst Heilmann. Harro wouldn't have to be shy around Weisenborn; he could speak freely, confer with his close friends about what he should do as he senses ever more clearly that he's in the Gestapo's sights.

Now he is paying for never having confided in Stella. On a small sailboat it is impossible to carry on a long conversation without everyone on board overhearing. It is a tragic excursion for Harro, who has so much weighing on his heart but who — on account of the woman whom he could not open his heart to, but whom he nevertheless seduced — cannot speak freely. He can't form an escape plan, can't determine what their strategy should be, how the group should behave in the event of an arrest.

It is no exaggeration to claim that if it weren't for the affair with Stella Mahlberg everything would have been different — Libertas, more than anyone, would agree. Now there is confusion, mutual distrust, just as Elfriede Paul predicted and warned them about. And if the doctor had always assumed that it was Libertas who would jeopardize everything with her amorous escapades and her romantic view of life, now it is Harro of all people, the coolest head among them, who at the crucial moment is distracted.

He doesn't send Stella away, as he might do — does this seem too dangerous to him? Does he think she could give him up? — but rather asks her to sit in the bow, where she just has to be sure to duck when the sail whirls around. True, with Stella Mahlberg on board, the sailing party does look unsuspicious to the outside observer. But the price Harro pays is high. On his crucial last day of freedom Harro can confer with neither Weisenborn nor Heilmann, the only ones whose advice could help him now.

It is a ride into ruin. Even the dip in the Wannsee is no longer refreshing. At the same time the *Duschinka* plows its way through the waves of the Havel River, so, Harro knows, do the steel prows of the Allied warships and merchant vessels split the ice-cold waves of the Arctic Sea, while the *Tirpitz* moves its guns into position. The German authorities — this Harro has learned from Graudenz — have denied Marcel Melliand permission to enter Switzerland.

After sunset they sit in the Blau-Rot clubhouse, looking out over the water. The storm that was threatening doesn't arrive, not yet. When, finally, the chance arises for a private conversation, Harro pulls Horst Heilmann aside and tells him about his contacts abroad and that he's not sure whether someone has gotten wind of them. Heilmann stares at him wide-eyed. Most of the radio ciphers from Moscow are known to the decryption unit, he tells him, shocked. He promises to do some digging while on duty the next day.

Harro is a bit too solemn as he bids them all goodbye after sunset, including Stellizitas. If it was her plan to spend the night with him on board the boat, it doesn't work. Alone, he cycles back through the warm woods. He doesn't want to go home yet; he's too restless for that. He thinks of Carl von Trotha, his good friend; Harro is a constant guest at his house in not too distant Lichterfelde.

He gets there around ten p.m. What the two men talk about remains unknown. Whether it is the possibility of fleeing or getting a warning to Arvid in the Economics Ministry (though he has already left for vacation with Mildred), or maybe just about basic economic questions — we don't know. But that night Harro does borrow a book from Carl, a book he won't have the opportunity to read: *Die europäischen Revolutionen und der Charakter der Nationen* by the Jewish scholar Eugen Rosenstock-Huessy, a work of universal history, later published in English as *Out of Revolution: Autobiography of Western Man,* that sees European history as a continual conflict between religious and secular powers — a balance, so claims the author, that finally works in the service of freedom.

# 37

On August 31, 1942, General Paulus's Sixth Army has reached the outer limits of Stalingrad. It is at this point in time that Hitler's power reaches its fullest geographical extent: The Wehrmacht has all but reached the oil fields of Baku in Azerbaijan, and on Mount Elbrus, the highest peak in the Caucasus Mountains, the swastika flutters in the icy cold.

But Germany has overextended itself. This has been true for some time now, and finally the moment has arrived: The wind has shifted, the pendulum swinging back the other way. The Third Reich has reached the apex of its dizzying parabolic ascent, has taken its turn and is veering toward its inevitable end.

At the Radio Decryption Unit on Matthäikirchplatz, Horst Heilmann asks his superior, Alfred Traxl, for information about decoded Russian radio transmissions. Traxl gets out a folder labeled "*Rote Kapelle*" and hands it to him. Heilmann reads about an officer in the Luftwaffe. His name is Harro Schulze-Boysen. He and his wife, Libertas, have been unmasked, revealed to be agents of Moscow.

The ceiling fan spins tirelessly, moving the humid air around. Horst Heilmann turns the pages with trembling fingers. He doesn't find his own name. What should he do — flee? If he did he would rob Harro of his last chance to escape. No, he will remain loyal to him, must warn him, to save him — or to go down with him. Even if it could cost him his own life, Horst Heilmann reaches for the phone.

It rings, but his friend doesn't answer, only the secretary in Harro's department. Would he like her to pass along a message?

Heilmann thinks. Then, even though it's risky, because it will leave a record, he asks her to have Harro call him back. He gives her his number and puts the receiver back on the hook. Waits for Harro to call. The heat grows more and more unbearable.

Libertas drives back on the highway from Bremen to Berlin, pedal to the floor.

# PART IV

# THE BLACK CURTAIN

*(Fall 1942)*

If it should devour us, I'll say this: it's sure been grand.

— HARRO SCHULZE-BOYSEN

# 1

Horst Heilmann's phone finally rings. Only now of all times he's not at his desk. On account of the heat the doors are open on Matthäikirchplatz, and since a ringing telephone has to be answered, Dr. Wilhelm Vauck, head of the Fourth Intelligence Division of the army high command, steps into Heilmann's office and picks up.

"Schulze-Boysen here . . ."

It takes Vauck a moment to regain his composure. Could it be that he is hearing the voice of the *very* man who has been his obsession for weeks — the state's most wanted enemy, if he understood the Gestapo correctly? But why is he calling Heilmann's extension?

"Do you spell Boysen with a *Y*?" is all that Vauck can come up with in the moment as he pretends to be making note of the name to leave a message for Horst Heilmann.

"Of course," Harro answers, confused. Suddenly he regrets having given his name, and hangs up.

A short time later the phone rings in his office. Heilmann? Or is Libs finally back? Full of expectation, Harro picks up. The man on the other line introduces himself as Colonel Bokelberg, the commandant for the offices of the RLM chiefs of staff. He asks Harro to come down to the lobby — it's urgent. Harro puts the receiver on the hook and sets down his fountain pen. He hesitates a moment, then he stands up. A cold fire burns in his eyes, and the muscles in his large, gaunt jaw are tense.

As he walks down the stairs, his fingers trail one last time over the aluminum handrail. He takes the paternoster, and it brings him quickly downstairs.

Bokelberg is waiting in the lobby. He escorts Harro to the exit. Blazing light streams inside as the black ebony door with the thick brass handle is opened.

There is a car waiting in the driveway, motor running. Two men step forward and place themselves on either side of him. They all sit in the back seat. One of them introduces himself as Horst Kopkow, Geheime

Staatspolizei. Slowly the car drives off. It is a short drive, but it lasts an eternity.

## 2

Libertas calls the Air Ministry, but Harro doesn't answer, just the secretary, who tells her he is traveling on official business. She doesn't know when he will be back. Then she adds that his silver sword knot is still hanging on its hook in the wardrobe.

No Prussian officer travels without his sword knot. Libertas knows this.

That afternoon she picks her brother up at the bus station and shares her fears that Harro has been arrested. They hurry to the apartment on Altenburger Allee and consider whether they should flee. But surely the building was being watched? What to do with the photo collection, all the materials that are kept here?

## 3

If he stands on the chair he can see a little sliver of sky. In cell number two, the first on the left down the right hallway, there is also a small table and a bunk that can be flipped up in the daytime. Four horizontal and two vertical bars form its iron frame, on it a thin, bare straw mattress that is so saggy he is constantly having to balance on one of the iron bars or else slip between them — a torment. There are two wool blankets, covered in bedbugs, about which a guard offers: "Yeah, 'fraid you'll have to help us feed a few critters while you're here."

From the courtyard Harro hears cars, doors slamming, shouted commands. At four o'clock the guard on duty shouts into his cell that he's about to be taken up for interrogation. Harro sits ramrod straight, like his father taught him: resolved, full of energy. He feverishly goes over his plan of attack: And if they ask about *this* — and *this* — and *this?* Then you say *this!* And if they try to dig into *that* — or *that?* Come up with an answer! Be quick. Credible. They're about to come get you. In his head he goes through every possibility, every scenario over and over again.

At six p.m. there is bread and black coffee. Still no interrogation. He paces in the cell, his thoughts run in a circle: around and around. He gets tired. That's what Kopkow wants.

It's eight o'clock. Haro lies on the bunk, ready to jump up immediately. At some point he hears a clock strike ten. A bare lightbulb in wire, like a caged bird, shines on the ceiling. Above his door there's a small rectangular pane of glass so the guard can check that the light is still on.

Eleven o'clock. He still hasn't been picked up for questioning. All the energy he's wasted has left him numb. He lies on his back, eyes open, stares at the dirty ceiling. How is Libertas doing? Has she been arrested too?

Finally, keys clatter in the door. Exhausted, he gets up. An officer stands before him. With a practiced, gentle motion he puts the special steel handcuffs on Harro's wrists, snaps them closed, and locks them with a tiny key, which makes a clicking sound.

He is taken upstairs, down a wide corridor with a domed roof adorned with crown molding. There are large semicircular windows with curved benches set in front of them. Here and there sit informal groups of men in ill-fitting suits, conversing in hushed tones. Some briefly lift their heads as Harro, still in his Luftwaffe uniform, is led past and taken into a long room, up to a lectern-like stand: fingerprints. There's a yellowed light-brown stool that swivels, like something you'd find in a schoolroom. Harro is ordered to sit, the back of his head is pressed against a metal bar, and to his right at shoulder height a sign with number and date hangs on a latch: *Gestapa42Aug.173*.

He looks at a camera; it flashes. His pupils instantly constrict. An officer to his left pulls a long lever connected to the stool and with a creak and a sudden jerk it spins to the right. A second flash illuminates Harro's profile, and then with another rough motion the stool lurches into semi-profile position. Another flash.

# 4

Three days after Libertas called his office, on his thirty-third birthday, September 2, there's still no news from Harro. So as not to draw suspicion, Libertas goes to work this morning at her office in the Deutsche Kulturfilm-Zentrale at Gendarmenmarkt. What is she supposed to do in this moment of greatest danger? Warn the others? But wouldn't that make her look even more suspicious?

A day earlier, on September 1, 1942, exactly three years after World War II began, it is summery and warm in Königsberg, the capital of East Prussia. Mildred and Arvid Harnack arrive at the main train station and walk to the Pregolya River, where the boats are lined up, like in an old etching.

They each carry a leather suitcase; Arvid, careful as ever, also brought his umbrella, the same one he had with him when he met Harro in the Tiergarten. They walk along the riverbank. It is the same route that Germany's most famous philosopher, Immanuel Kant, took every day at midday two hundred years earlier, over the Grüne Brücke into the medieval Kneiphof, the island in the heart of Königsberg with its cathedral and city hall.

Mildred and Arvid desperately need this vacation, and plan to celebrate Mildred's fortieth birthday on September sixteenth on the coast. She is recovering from a terminated ectopic pregnancy that could have cost her her life. Their destination is Preil, a sleepy fishermen's village on the Curonian Spit, near Nidden, the artists' colony where Libertas was arrested in 1939. But first the Harnacks want to see Königsberg, this architectural gem, a city suffused with humanism. Kant's grave is on the side of the cathedral that faces the university: *That's* what they are striving for, the life of the mind, a sense of responsibility in everything one does.

Mildred and Arvid take the Krämer Bridge and walk toward the castle. Inside, the legendary Amber Room is on display, which the Wehrmacht stole from the Catherine Palace last fall during the storming of Leningrad. The couple enters, and gazes, fascinated, at the splendid, shimmering wonder. Two and a half years later, this very Amber Room will disappear without a trace.

Mildred and Arvid admire the mosaics and see their reflections in the panels, darkened over the years to a rich cognac color. They look around the seemingly enchanted room of artfully molded amber. But one of the other men present seems suspicious. And in fact since their arrival in the city they can't rid themselves of the feeling of having an extra shadow.

Mildred and Arvid leave the castle, trying not to walk faster than usual, and reach the tram stop. Should they take a streetcar over the Schmiede Bridge back to the Kneiphof, then down the Hauptgasse and back over the Krämer Bridge — would this shake off potential pursuers? Perfect Königsberg, where everything is orderly, suddenly transforms into a landscape of terror. The tram cars all around seem like moving cages. The couple takes the Holz Bridge, Arvid using his umbrella like a walking stick — then they stop in their tracks. Here, on the bank of the river, on Lindenstrasse, once stood the splendid Neue Synagogue, its architecture inspired by the cathedral in Aachen. After so-called Kristallnacht, Königsberg's Jewish community had to cart off the ruins of the charred building. Now there are wooden barracks here, dull and squat, in which Jewish forced laborers are quartered. Next door, the Jewish orphanage is still standing. Its windows are open, laundry is hanging out to dry in the courtyard, but only a few Jews are still living here. Königsberg was once home to a flourishing Jewish community of over 1,500 people. On June 24, 1942, 770 of them had been transported to the extermination camp at Maly Trostinets, in a pine forest near Minsk — a killing field with a rail connection, where the trains pulled up directly alongside the giant mass graves. On August 25, exactly a week before Arvid and Mildred's visit, a second train left with 763 Königsberg Jews, this time to Theresienstadt.

Mildred and Arvid spend a restless night at the hotel. The next day they are sitting in a tram to Adolf-Hitler-Platz and the North Station. Should they take the train to Cranz as planned, and from there the ferry to the Spit — even now, when they can sense that they are being observed? On the other hand, even if they're right, wouldn't calling off the vacation mean directing attention to themselves? Wouldn't it make them look suspicious? One hope remains: If the police in Berlin didn't arrest them, and they were able to escape this fate in Königsberg as well, why would the trap be sprung in remote Preil of all places? Wouldn't the wisest thing be to continue their vacation as if everything were normal and lead the Gestapo to believe that once their holiday was over, they would be heading back to Berlin as planned? It's possible that on the Spit there might be a chance to flee, with a boat to Sweden, maybe . . .

At the same kiosk where Libertas bought her ticket three years ago, Mildred and Arvid Harnack buy their passage to Cranz, one way, then walk out onto the platform and take their seats on the train. They have hit upon a strategy, deciding they will pretend to be the very thing they wish they were: harmless tourists. For this reason, during the thirty-three-minute trip to the coast, they write an inconspicuous-sounding postcard to their housekeeper — and assume that the Gestapo will also read it:

> Dear Frau Müller! Warm greetings from us both! Yesterday we visited the Amber Museum in Königsberg. Tomorrow we're heading out to the Curonian Spit. Our address is: at Kubillus, Preil.

In Cranz they drop the postcard into a mailbox. The card is stamped with a postmark showing the stylized likeness of an elk. The next morning — it is September 3, 1942, a Thursday — their steamer sails out over the glittering, deep blue waters of the lagoon. It all looks peaceful and quiet.

# 5

The interrogation room is on the top floor, an uncomfortable office with mismatched furniture that seems thrown together at random. The SS Untersturmführer Johannes Strübing, who leads the interrogations of Harro, is young, intelligent, a highly trained investigator with a keen sense of humor. He goes to work on his subject with psychological finesse, kindling hope, making promises, alternating between friendly gestures and threats. He knows how feared the Gestapo is, how frightened anyone who finds himself in their grips must be. Torture? It might not even be necessary. If Harro cooperates, let him have a cigarette or a decent meal or the promise that nothing will happen to Libertas. Let him be rewarded, like a good dog.

But this doesn't work with Harro. His Gestapo file no longer exists, but if the sources are to be believed, the typical lines — *you should go ahead and be honest with us, right at the outset, it's better for everybody that way* — have no effect on Harro. He disputes every accusation and denies involvement in any treasonous activity. In his work, he says, his sole purpose was to always do what was best for Germany. Even when they show him copies of the decrypted radio messages, he doesn't think of making a confession. All he did was meet with friends in private, sometimes they talked politics. There was nothing illegal about any of it. Strübing changes tack. He tries to win Harro's trust, engaging him in unpolitical, friendly chats about literature and the natural sciences — one colleague to another, almost — during walks together on the grounds of the Reich Main Security Office. Harro, who is still wearing his uniform, sees through the plan; he casually keeps the conversation going, but still refuses to talk.

And so it comes down to the so-called *verschärfte Vernehmung* approach after all, the *third-degree interrogation*. It is carried out in accordance with specific rules that were first laid out by Himmler, head of the SS, then refined by Heydrich, and finally written out by Müller. The bureaucratic guidelines for torture had been expanded just a few weeks ago, on June 12:

> Third-degree interrogation methods may . . . be used against Communists, Marxists, Jehovah's Witnesses, saboteurs, terrorists, members of resistance movements, enemy agents, anti-social persons, Polish or Soviet nationals who malinger or refuse to work . . . The third-degree can, depending on the particulars of the case, consist of e.g.: rudimentary provision (water and bread), harsh lodgings, dark-

ened cell, sleep deprivation, fatiguing exercise, and finally, administering blows with a cudgel (if more than twenty blows are administered a doctor must be called).

But does it stop with the practices described above? Harro is taken to the so-called Stalin room on the fifth floor of Gestapo headquarters. It almost looks like a normal office, but when he steps inside he immediately sees what is going on here. A strange contraption that resembles a bed dominates the room.

Harro is asked if he is prepared, in light of the circumstances, to make a full confession. He says no and is made to take a seat on a chair, his hands still bound behind his back. He doesn't see what happens next; he only feels it. A device is placed over his hands. It latches on to his wrists. To the left and right of this device are metal spikes. They are pressed into his skin by means of a screwing mechanism.

When the questioner doesn't get what he is hoping for — and he doesn't from Harro, who when he was forced to run the SS gauntlet was able to run an extra lap — they take the device away. He is now ordered to remove his boots and uniform pants. Two policemen tie him to the strange bed-like contraption with his head tilted down and wrap a blanket around his face. They bring out another device and attach it to his bare calves. On the inside are again metal spikes. Strübing asks a question. When the prisoner refuses to answer, the officer gestures with his hand and says: "One turn." With a vise, his colleagues screw the device tighter and the spikes bore into Harro's calves.

When he still won't talk, they take the calf clamp off and stretch the contraption apart, taking his bound hands and feet with it. They pull quickly and jerkily, then slowly, as prompted. When the procedure is over with, they bind his hands to his feet so that he is standing alone in a crouching position in the middle of the room. An officer with a club steps behind him and, when ordered, delivers a blow. Because of the way he's standing, Harro can't keep his balance. He falls forward with his full weight and hits the ground headfirst. The officers repeat this until Harro loses consciousness.

**6**

The doorbell rings at Altenburger Allee 19. When Libertas opens it, Horst Heilmann is standing there with the decrypted radio message in his hand.

They hold each other in a long embrace, then systematically search the apartment for bugs, but find nothing. They gather together everything that could somehow be incriminating. Much of it goes up in flames in the parlor fireplace, including, in all probability, Libertas's photo collection of the war crimes of the Wehrmacht. Heilmann packs the rest, including the scholarly work he had written with Harro, into a suitcase, which he later brings to his unsuspecting neighbor, the actress Reva Holsey, who lives in his parents' building on Hölderlinstrasse, for safekeeping. Next he heads out to Stahnsdorf and warns his friend John Graudenz.

The next day Graudenz's watchdog, Tasso, disappears.

At Gestapo headquarters in Prinz-Albrecht-Strasse 8 the members of the special commission are looking at a giant puzzle. Kopkow, Strübing; occasionally also Panzinger, Göpfert, Habecker: cigarettes lit, they look at the large board with all the names, photos, overlapping evidence. What is needed now is deductive reasoning, imagination. It is unclear what picture will emerge in the end. The rushed arrest of Harro, triggered by Horst Heilmann's attempt to warn him, has frustrated the Gestapo's plan to quietly observe the suspects until enough evidence was at hand. The investigators' work has gotten harder.

On September 5, Horst Heilmann is arrested. Around the same time, the Gestapo questions the head of the Kulturfilm-Zentrale, and after that Libertas starts to sense the mistrust of her colleagues in the hallways and in the cafeteria, and her boss is acting buttoned up around her. When she sends a telegram to Adam Kuckhoff, who is working on a film in Prague, and receives no answer, she starts to feel even more uneasy. During a tram ride with Alexander Spoerl, both believe they're being watched. At Potsdamer Platz they get off at the last minute, separate, meet up again at Westkreuz Station, then decide on his apartment in Wannsee because it seems more secure. When Libertas finally goes back home, the postal carrier takes her aside on the stairs at Altenburger Allee 19 and tells her that the Gestapo is inspecting her mail.

# 7

The calm in the village of Preil is eerie, the beauty of the place irresistible. The wind is perfectly still. Fishing boats lie on the shore in the rising sun, and as it climbs up toward the other side of the spit, toward the Baltic, it bathes the tall dunes in blue, green, and red light.

Arvid sits on the lagoon side and reads the *Memeler Dampfboot,* the local newspaper. It costs ten Reichspfennig and its name — the Memel Steamboat — is much too quaint not to leaf through it every now and then. One day the front-page headline references the Western Allies' convoys, which Harro, via his contact Melliand, had tried in vain to protect. "Thirty-Eight Ships and Large Amounts of War Materiel Sunk," the paper cheers. The subtitle reads, "How German Naval and Air Power Achieved a New Triumph in the North Sea: A Combination of Daring, Prudence, and Resolve." But in reality the determining factor is the Germans' ability to decrypt the Allies' radio communications, to know exactly when and where each convoy will set out. There is a photo taken from the cockpit of a German Condor long-range bomber. A black cloud of smoke rises into the sky from a sinking British freighter.

A few hours later Arvid sets out to pick up his friend Professor Egmont Zechlin, historian at the University of Berlin, and his wife at the ferry landing in Nidden. It's a good five kilometers away through the Elk Forest nature preserve. Arvid goes on foot, wearing shorts and a small rucksack. He walks among the tall pines with roots reaching deep into the sand dunes, passes a section of thin birch trees, then dusky rows of spruce standing as straight as soldiers. If, over the past few months, he has had the strength to remain inwardly calm, if he is able now to face whatever is to come with composure, then he believes he owes this above all to his communion with the good and beautiful things of this world, and to the sensitivity that he, like the American poet Walt Whitman whom he so admires, extends to the nature around him.

He passes over patches of bog, melancholy and acrid. This is where the elks live, "a mix of cow, horse, deer, camel, and buffalo, with very long legs and broad antlers," as Thomas Mann described them during a stay in Nidden. Arvid picks a bouquet for Mildred: violets, rockcress, thyme, and eyebright. Despite all the sorrows, he thinks, he can look back on his life up to this point with fondness. The light outweighed the dark. And the reason for this was, above all else, his marriage.

# 8

To get back from Nidden to Preil, Arvid and the Zechlins take a carriage with thick rubber tires. They sit between village girls with long skirts and baskets full of dried flounder.

In the garden at the home of Kubillus the fisherman, Mildred, Arvid, Anne, and Egmont have dinner. The blue of the windowpanes shines in the late light, a warm breeze tickles the skin, and the sun glows orange behind the sloping clouds reflected in the water of the lagoon. The fishermen climb into boats rigged with square rust brown sails and head out for the night to catch zander, or pike if need be. The world at this moment indeed looks like an expressionist painting by Max Pechstein.

Arvid proposes a short walk, and when they step out into the village, he asks the women to walk up ahead a bit. It seems to Egmont Zechlin that his friend has something on his mind, something he wants to confide in him.

For a while they wend their way in the twilight. Every now and again a horse passes on its way home, one of the many that run freely on the spit. The trees of the marsh rustle, the ocean roars, and the smell of smoked fish wafts over from the huts.

"How fine it is to be in nature, so free, finally removed from all the intrigues of the big city. How much I look forward to the next few days," says Arvid. Before he can say anything more, a heavy gust of wind announces a storm. Thunder rolls, and they have to hurry to reach the house before the rain.

Professor Zechlin never finds out what Arvid wanted to say.

# 9

Later that evening — it is still light out, and the sky has cleared — Mildred and Arvid walk to the beach, to the powerful Baltic Sea that Arvid, whose family comes from Dorpat in Estonia, feels so close to. They undress. The moon is narrow and waning, the sky is filled with stars.

As Mildred walks slowly out of the water and back on shore, she seems to Arvid like a goddess.

As they are making their way back to the village, an elk appears in their path. Its antlers look as though they were covered in velvet moss — an antenna for the moods of the primordial forest. Slowly, regally, the animal walks past them, and they watch it disappear in the distance.

*At twilight the elk step out from the dunes*
*And move from the moor to the sand*
*When night like a loving mother*
*Spreads her blanket o'er sea and land*

# 10

The Gestapo likes to come early in the morning. This way their victims are too sleepy to offer serious resistance. Early in the morning, a person isn't savvy enough to put up a fight, to run, to risk it all. Such a fateful occurrence at so early an hour, you simply don't believe it's happening, and this is your undoing. Morning is the time for breakfast, a cup of coffee, the newspaper — a peaceful time.

The fishermen come home from last night's run; their wives meet them, pulling little wooden wagons behind them for the catch. Arvid Harnack is standing in the courtyard in his shirtsleeves and speaking to a man who wears an ill-fitting suit. Close by, three more men are loitering by the garden fence, which is painted oxblood red. Two black cars are parked behind them.

Arvid hesitates a little before he speaks. In his calm way he says to Egmont Zechlin, who has stepped out into the courtyard: "The gentlemen have a breakfast date with a lady and can't remember which house is hers." Beneath his words is a faint note of scorn. One of the officers pulls out his badge: "We're from the border police. We're here to conduct a search of the village."

Zechlin still doesn't suspect anything and says, as Arvid and the officer go into the Harnacks' room: "Well, I guess I'll just go run and get our papers then."

One of the men accompanies Zechlin to his room at the back of the house, looks at the documents, and says, almost casually: "We've also been told to let Senior Councillor Harnack know that he is needed at the ministry. Did you actually plan to meet here?"

"Yes of course," Zechlin answers, taken aback, and runs out front through the garden and knocks on his friends' door. When no one answers, he opens it and sees Mildred and Arvid inside, packing, watched by the three officers. Arvid steps toward him: "We are going to accompany these gentlemen back to Berlin. I am needed in the ministry . . ." And after a short pause he adds with suppressed anger: "It is a disgrace what people in Germany have to . . ." Immediately one of the Gestapo men steps between them and cuts Arvid off.

"But they haven't even had time to have breakfast yet," Zechlin objects and tries to get close to his friend in case Arvid wants to whisper something to him. But the officers, moving almost nonchalantly, make sure to always place themselves between them. Even when Egmont tries to help

Mildred pack, one of them steps forward: "Oh please, let me do it!" The policeman offers Mildred a cigarette, and when she hesitates, he goads her on: "Take it, it'll do you good."

"I insist that we at least wait till we've all had coffee together," says Zechlin, playing along with the charade about the drive to the ministry. "Come along out here with me," he urges Arvid.

"The gentlemen are very friendly," Arvid replies. "They haven't had coffee either. You all go ahead, and we'll come join you after."

The professor leaves the room and hurries over to the inn. He and his wife get the coffeepot and cups together, and come back and place everything on the table while the Harnacks continue to pack. A horrible silence prevails in the room. Mildred covers her face with her hands: "What a disgrace, oh, what a disgrace."

"I'm sure it's a misunderstanding and will soon be cleared up," says Egmont to Arvid, trying to point out his friend's innocence. "If there's anything I can do to help, please let me know."

Mildred is finished packing the two leather suitcases. Arvid's umbrella lies on top. She strips the beds and makes sure everything is tidy so that their departure doesn't cause any unnecessary bother for anyone. As for the flowers that Arvid picked for her, she doesn't know what to do with them at first. She takes the pitcher by the washbasin, gives them fresh water, puts the vase back on the table, and plucks at the tablecloth, smoothing it out.

"Herr Professor," the leader of the Gestapo squad says to Egmont Zechlin, who has started to accompany Arvid and Mildred as they are being led outside: "You strike me as being too intelligent not to know what's going on here. I have orders to handle this matter and to draw as little attention as possible. Owing to your presence here, things didn't quite work out that way. But I must now inform you that you are not to speak of anything that you have seen or heard. Otherwise we will have to come back and see you again." To Egmont's wife he adds: "Gnädige Frau, the same goes for you."

"These are my colleagues," Zechlin responds: "You cannot prevent me from informing the faculty of the matter as soon as possible."

"You will do no such thing," says the officer, his tone suddenly harsh. "If you attempt to, by telephone or by telegraph, we will intercept it."

Egmont kisses Mildred's hand. As he says goodbye to Arvid he looks him in the eye. "Dear Egmont," says Arvid, who doesn't usually address his friend by his first name: "I thank you for everything, including for today." They shake hands. All the things that Egmont still wants to say he can only put into this gesture.

190

Separated from each other, Arvid and Mildred Harnack are driven off in the two Gestapo vehicles.

# 11

On September 8, 1942, it rains incessantly in Berlin. Libertas feels a constant urge to look over her shoulder. She tries to seem calm and show no sign of uneasiness. The hours drag on till the scheduled departure of the night train to Trier. She has reserved a berth in the sleeping car. She wants to visit friends in the Mosel Valley — and to continue on from there into the safety of Switzerland. Her former housemaid at Liebenberg, who now works for the Schulze-Boysens and other neighbors at Altenburger Allee 19, accompanies Libertas and her mother, Tora, to Anhalter Bahnhof. The platforms are full of men on leave from the front, a hospital train brings in the wounded, men everywhere in black or gray uniforms.

"I'm terribly afraid that I'm being followed," says Libertas to her mother.

"But, my child, what do you mean you're being followed?"

"I'm being shadowed."

*Shadowed?* Tora doesn't know what Libertas is talking about, but she senses that her daughter's desperation is real. Before they say goodbye on the platform, Tora takes off her gold necklace and puts it around her daughter's neck.

Libertas says goodbye and climbs on board with her suitcase.

No one stops her, and the train departs. She waves from the open window.

When she reaches Wannsee station, the last stop in Berlin, she is arrested by plainclothes officers and escorted off the train.

# 12

A few days later her mother receives a typed postcard in the mail:

Berlin, IX.9.42

Dear Mother!

I just wanted to write you very quickly so you wouldn't worry, since you've probably tried to call me. I was summoned back during my trip on account of an urgent matter and will likely be outside of Berlin for about a week.

Unfortunately I can't tell you anything more precise at the moment. It's to do with a project that I'm very interested in, so I don't mind the loss of a week's vacation.

I am healthy and doing well.

The rest when I see you in person!

A thousand greetings and thoughts

Ever yours,
Bieni

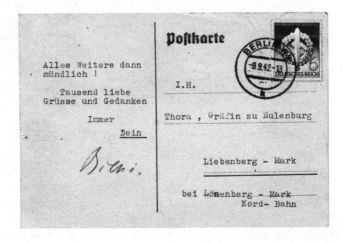

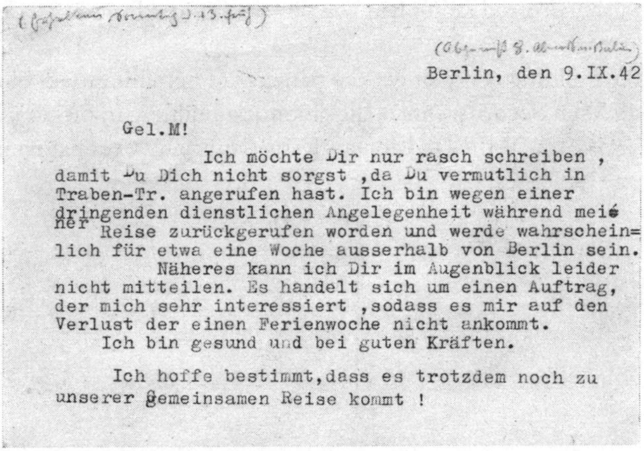

*(handwritten: (geschrieben Sonntag d. 13. Sept.))*

*(handwritten: (Absender: J. Alexander Berlin))*

Berlin, den 9.IX.42

Gel.M!

      Ich möchte Dir nur rasch schreiben ,
damit Du Dich nicht sorgst ,da Du vermutlich in
Traben-Tr. angerufen hast. Ich bin wegen einer
dringenden dienstlichen Angelegenheit während mei=
ner Reise zurückgerufen worden und werde wahrschein=
lich für etwa eine Woche ausserhalb von Berlin sein.
      Näheres kann ich Dir im Augenblick leider
nicht mitteilen. Es handelt sich um einen Auftrag,
der mich sehr interessiert ,sodass es mir auf den
Verlust der einen Ferienwoche nicht ankommt.
      Ich bin gesund und bei guten Kräften.

      Ich hoffe bestimmt,dass es trotzdem noch zu
unserer gemeinsamen Reise kommt !

Alles Weitere dann
mündlich !

    Tausend liebe
Grüsse und Gedanken

      Immer

        Dein

**Postkarte**

I.H.

Thora , Gräfin zu Eulenburg

Liebenberg - Mark

bei Löwenberg - Mark
Nord- Bahn

# 13

As a child, Libertas and her brother, Johannes, used to play in the wide corridors of Prinz-Albrecht-Strasse 8. At the time, the state School of Decorative Arts, where her father founded the fashion program, had its classrooms here. They are still the same familiar stone stairs, the same bright corridors with wooden benches under the large windows. Only back then there were no busts of Hitler, and also no swastika flags. Back then only one thing ruled in these halls: creativity. Back then her good-looking, always stylishly dressed father had been in charge, and fashion was created here.

But the building is no longer the paradise of her childhood. Now it is the Reich Main Security Office, the gloomiest building in the city, and its dark heart is Amt IV, the Division for Researching and Combating the Enemy, home to the secret state police — the Gestapo.

For Libertas the only hint of light in this dark hell is the attractive twenty-five-year old typist for Kommissar Alfred Göpfert, her lead interrogator. Gertrud Breiter is her name, and one late afternoon when Göpfert has left the room and the two women are alone, they get to chatting. Libs wants to know how a woman like her ends up in a job like this, and the typist replies that she couldn't find anything else and figured it was better than staying home. Besides, you didn't have to agree 100 percent with what went on where you worked. By now, though, she claims, she hates her job. Actually she admires what Libertas had done, and feels sorry for her for having ended up in this situation. It isn't the end of the world, though. See, Göpfert told her that in Libertas's case they didn't have anything serious. If she cooperates, Breiter goes on, she won't be looking at a harsh sentence. Thanks to her mother's connections with Göring, her life is safe. Still, she'd probably have to spend some time in prison. But Libertas could count on her support at any time.

Libs is relieved to have found a person she can talk to. A woman in this men's building in whom she can confide — maybe even vent her rage about Harro and Stella. She talks to Breiter more than two dozen times. Breiter visits her in her cell now and then and offers to be of help. Gradually the typist also tells her what she knows about the other prisoners, providing information about Harro or Horst Heilmann. She mentions the prospect of additional favors, like a typewriter — Libertas could use the time in the cell to write poems, to fulfill her childhood dream of becoming a poet. And Gertrud Breiter offers something else, too: She is prepared to warn others in the group to help them escape the Gestapo's clutches.

Meanwhile, the friends on the outside are at a loss for what to do, how to act. And above all, where to take the two radio transmitters. One of them, the battery-powered one, is in Hannelore Thiel's parents' apartment, behind a curtain in the bathroom. Here they keep the things they rarely ever need, like a sled, for example, or a swastika flag for April 20, Hitler's birthday.

When Fritz Thiel finds out about Harro's arrest, he hurries over to his in-laws' apartment. To avoid further endangering his mother- and father-in-law, he takes the suitcase himself. He wraps a length of steel wire around it with two loops at either end held together with a padlock and brings it to his apartment on Nürnberger Strasse. Around two-thirty in the afternoon on September 11, 1942, his seventeen-year-old wife Hannelore hides the dangerous cargo under her infant in its stroller and walks to nearby Lietzenburger Strasse 6, where she hands the device over to the dentist Helmut Himpel and Maria Terwiel at the front door. The vulcanized fiber case is meant for Helmut Roloff, who is already waiting inside the apartment. Himpel gives it to him with the remark that Roloff's house would probably be the least conspicuous place to keep it. When the concert pianist asks what's inside, the dentist replies that it's probably better not to know.

"One thing is certain, though," Helmut Roloff says: "If they find the case, then it's all of our necks."

"Right, which means we can't let them find it," Himpel replies dryly.

It's just a few minutes by tram from Lietzenburger Strasse 6 to Trautenaustrasse 10, the Roloffs' well-appointed apartment, where Helmut lives with his parents and sister. But time is relative, and it slows to a crawl when you're carrying something like a radio transmitter. Back home the musician hides the case behind the small music cabinet under his piano and resolves to keep playing Mozart till the Gestapo starts pounding on his door. His plan then is to tell the policemen he doesn't have a clue about any of it — he's just a mad musician who never stops playing Mozart.

Erika von Brockdorff, who lives in the same building as Greta Kuckhoff, also gets rid of the life-threatening device in her studio apartment. She puts it in a bag and hands it over to Hilde Coppi, Hans's heavily pregnant wife, on the corner of Leibniz Strasse and Berliner Strasse.

No one wants to be caught holding the bag. Fatally, they have no set plan for what to do now. The university teacher Werner Krauss and the psychotherapist John Rittmeister meet in a small restaurant next to the

S-Bahn to discuss over a glass of wine how they should act in case they are arrested. "Even if it's my neck," says John, the left-wing pacifist and fanatic for facts, whose exemplar is the Renaissance philosopher Giordano Bruno, burned at the stake as a heretic, "I will stick with the truth and tell them to their faces what I think of them."

Krauss disagrees. "The truth is the last thing we owe our enemies. Harro once said that in defending yourself against the Gestapo the only rule is that you don't harm a third party. *That* is how we fight for our lives. That is our duty."

# 14

On September 12, Adam Kuckhoff is arrested in Prague, Elisabeth Schumacher in her apartment in the Tempelhof neighborhood, her husband, Kurt, in his barracks in Posen, Hilde Coppi in her cottage near Tegel Prison, and Hans Coppi while with his unit in the Pomeranian village of Schrimm (present-day Śrem). Hans Coppi's parents also land in jail, as well as his brother Kurt. The Gestapo even locks up Hilde's mother: guilt by association. As the "radioman," Hans Coppi is a pivotal figure.

Greta Kuckhoff wakes up early on the twelfth, having slept in her rooftop garden. The weather is mild, the sun is climbing, the stars are fading; still quiet in the city. The only noise comes from the siskins making a racket in their cage, trying with their song to get the wild birds outside to come visit, as usual without success.

Greta had gotten breakfast ready the night before. She sits down on the red chintz couch in the studio, the largest room in the apartment. No one is bothering her now; she has time to read and cracks open *Resurrection*, Tolstoy's third and last novel. The story reads like a film script — Adam would like it. But she also enjoys the somewhat dry passages with direct reference to religion. A doorstop like this one takes commitment, but the book gives so much back to the reader.

Her gaze sweeps over the studio. It's not particularly tidy, but for once that doesn't bother her. She got the ironing board ready so she could start ironing first thing that morning; next to it is her suitcase, already half packed. As soon as Adam is back from Prague, they're going to the Alps — finally, a vacation.

It is six o'clock in the morning, and at six on the dot there is a knock at the door. Greta is seized with fright: *Now's the time! Take the sleeping child, run up onto the roof and down the other staircase.* Immediately the doubts start up: Wouldn't that be futile, even dangerous? If it is the Gestapo, then, thorough as they are, they'll have done their research on all the ways in and out of the building . . .

In this crucial moment, Greta falls prey to the legend of the Gestapo's impenetrable net of observation. She believes there's no chance left to escape — and for that very reason she doesn't try. Besides, where could she go? To her parents in Frankfurt? To innocent friends who know nothing of her activities? Desperately she tries to think — then there's the pounding again, even more impatient-sounding than the first time. She doesn't have a plan worked out — the realization hits her in a flash. The failure is unforgivable. After Harro was arrested she more or less stuck her head in the sand and hoped it would all pass over and leave her unscathed. Now there's no time left. With a knot in her stomach, she tiptoes down the narrow hallway to the door.

"Heil Hitler, Frau Kuckhoff. I'm Detective Henze. Geheime Staatspolizei." The officer shows her his badge, attached to the underside of his lapel. Two more officers stand on either side of him. "Is your husband of officer rank, and has he been in contact with First Lieutenant Harro Schulze-Boysen?"

Greta gives the policeman an aggressive look. His question suggests a surprisingly poor grasp of the facts. "If you're going to pay a visit this early in the morning, please take the trouble to be better informed," she says. "My husband is a writer and in contact with *Libertas* Schulze-Boysen; they both work on documentaries together. At the moment he is in Prague editing a film."

"You know very well what we're looking for," Henze replies, unfazed, and steps inside the apartment. "Will you help us find it? Please show us your study."

Greta knows that the radio isn't in her apartment, so she stays calm and leads the three men to the study. "Of course I'm prepared to help you," she says. "But you'll have to tell me what led you to the home of a writer and filmmaker — that is, not an officer."

In lieu of a reply, Henze lets his gaze wander over the bookshelf next to Greta's desk. "We're looking for something in particular."

"Is this about my Marxist books? I do own a few, it's true. You'll find that they're full of notecards. I needed them for the English translation of *Mein Kampf*. My translation of Hitler required a firm knowledge of socialism. But there are other titles here too, see?" She goes over to the shelf: "Alfred Rosenberg's *The Myth of the Twentieth Century*, Erich Gritzbach's *Hermann Göring: The Man and His Work*." She takes the lid off a jar painted with antique patterns and takes out three Party insignia. "Or might you be looking for these?"

Now the three officers laugh — exactly what Greta was going for. "The neighbors," Henze nods, grinning, "have already assured us that you were on the up and up."

By now little Ule is awake. Sleepily he walks into the room. "Mother, three uncles here for a visit this early in the morning?"

"These aren't your uncles," Greta answers a bit too sharply. "Your uncles are off fighting the war."

"We'd like to ask you to hand us the keys to all your drawers, Frau Kuckhoff. Including that one there." Henze points to an ornate baroque dresser decorated with a Chinese pattern in black lacquer and gold leaf. Suddenly the policeman has a hard twist to his mouth: "And please remove your clothes. We have to search you. After that you can get ready to go out."

Greta looks at him, stunned. Reluctantly she does what he says. Little Ule complies as well. He doesn't seem to have any problem with the strangers' presence. Greta has to stand naked in front of the officers, then get dressed again. In the meantime one of them has gone up to the roof and grabbed the cage with the siskins, along with the birdseed and sand; he walks down the building's staircase to leave the birds with neighbors, to whom he explains that Frau Kuckhoff has suffered a sudden bout of ill health: "Could you possibly be so kind as to assist her by taking care of her pets for a while?"

They do the same with the Kuckhoffs' turtle. Greta has to describe exactly how to feed and care for it.

"Will I be away for that long?"

"As we are leaving you may not under any circumstances let anyone know that you are being arrested," Henze replies, and his eyes wander over to Ule's toy train set. "If you meet any of your neighbors on the stairs, you will confirm that you have had a nervous breakdown. We are doctors and are taking you to a very good sanatorium."

"You're a doctor?"

"Yes," answers Henze. "I'm the head doctor. These two are orderlies at the nerve clinic."

"My nerves are in good order."

"Don't start boasting just yet, Frau Kuckhoff . . . or — Well, let's not talk about that."

"And my son?" Greta looks at Ule.

"If you give us the address of one of your friends, we'll take him there. But you can also take him with you. That might not be too bad, actually."

But Greta has another idea. Together with the Gestapo men she takes Ule down to the air raid shelter in the basement. Here there is a specially furnished room for children. The walls are painted with pictures from the fairy tales of the Brothers Grimm, there are light blue sheets for the boys' beds, pink for the girls. There's also a caregiver. "Be nice to Ule till my mother comes," Greta says to the surprised woman as she hands her the child. Despite the quick glance Greta gives toward the men with her, the nanny has no idea what is going on. "Do you mean — during the daytime, too?" she asks. "But he'll be all by himself."

"I hope it will only be for a short time," Greta replies. "The gentlemen say it won't be long." Again she glances at the three officers. And without any of them being able to stop her, she says calmly, "I'm being arrested."

"Sadly, Frau Kuckhoff has to go to a nerve clinic," Henze immediately steps in. "What she just said is typical for her condition. It is one of her delusions. She suffers from a persecution complex. You'd better just forget the nonsense that she just said. We are doctors and nurses and are here to pick Frau Kuckhoff up. Please remember this and disregard the rest."

Greta says goodbye to Ule, her four-year-old son. She doesn't know if she'll ever see him again.

Then she goes outside with Henze and his two companions. On the other side of the street, in front of a dairy, waits a black Mercedes. Henze tries to take hold of Greta as they cross the street, but then the postman comes walking toward them, beaming. He has good news and wants to hand her the long-awaited payment for the production of Adam's play *Ulenspiegel* at the Stadttheater in Posen, eight hundred Reichsmarks.

"Oh, never mind that. I owe it to my mother. Please send it to her." Quick thinking on Greta's part. If she were to take the money herself it would just be confiscated anyway, and her mother, with her meager pension of fifty Reichsmarks per month, could definitely use it — especially if she's going to have another mouth to feed, taking care of Ule for the foreseeable future. In the middle of the street, Greta writes down her mother's address to forward the letter, while Henze, whose orders are to avoid a scene at all costs, looks on calmly.

# 15

Karin, John Graudenz's sixteen-year-old daughter, is woken up at six in the morning by a loud noise. There's a commotion somewhere in the house, a harsh voice cries out: "Freeze! Stay where you are or I'll shoot!"

Never has the Graudenz family missed their German shepherd Tasso more than at this moment.

John Graudenz runs down to the cellar and out the door, then up the outside stairs to escape across the large garden, which borders a small wood. He can see daylight, it's the sun in the east between the leaves, their colors already starting to turn, and he takes off running — but a man in a long coat is waiting for him. John Graudenz, the former *New York Times* reporter, hesitates, then takes off in the other direction, heading west, but there's an officer positioned here as well. A woodpecker flies off in fright.

They are young, the men arresting them, and teenage Karin has the feeling that they don't enjoy doing it — that they would much rather be flirting with her and her sister. They're all sitting out on the terrace, John Graudenz's hands cuffed behind his back.

# 16

*Boom boom* goes the steam pile driver outside Aschinger's Restaurant on Alexanderplatz. Dusty air, September, the people don't quite know what to wear: Is it still summer or already fall? Definitely a hat, but a coat, too? The women still in thin stockings, even if it's a bit chilly: It looks nice. Bums spread *Der Stürmer* out on benches where Jews aren't allowed to sit. Ideologically sound sleep. They sip their booze, but man, what booze. You wouldn't want to be the corpse pickling in that stuff.

Located right on Alexanderplatz is one of the redbrick behemoths that give this part of the city its character: *Die Rote Burg*, it's called, *the Red Fortress,* police headquarters, with its own in-house lockup. The same building in which Marie Luise fought for her son Harro's freedom on May 1, 1933. Behind these walls, so-called discipline and order reign.

Thanks to the high volume of recent arrests connected to Harro and Libertas, however, the stolid machinery of the place has been thrown into disarray. On the sixth floor an extra unit for women has been set up. Upstairs, where the booking is done, a slate board shows new inmates and their cell numbers. Greta Kuckhoff reads the name of Hilde Coppi, seven months pregnant.

She has to hand over her valuables — scarf, belt, anything she could use to strangle herself. In Greta's purse are heirlooms from Adam's family and almost everything she has accumulated and held on to over the course of her nearly forty years of life: brooches, necklaces, bracelets, and rings. All of this is confiscated, and she hopes that the jewelry will find its way to her parents and to little Ule.

Now Greta sees sixteen-year-old Karin Graudenz with her mother, Antonie, and thinks: No way they've done anything serious. When the women get to talking, Greta tells them how she had to leave four-year-old Ule behind, and young Karin understands that there are others whose ordeal is even worse than hers.

# 17

On September 16, Erika von Brockdorff, Oda Schottmüller, Hannelore and Fritz Thiel, Maria Terwiel, Helmut Himpel, Cato Bontjes van Beek and Heinz Strelow, Elfriede Paul and Walter Küchenmeister, Heinrich Scheel, and still others are locked up.

On September 17, Helmut Roloff gets to stop playing Mozart. "Where's the suitcase?" is the first question from the policemen standing in his parlor.

"What suitcase?" He looks at the intruders with his gray eyes.

"Don't lie. Herr Himpel has already told us everything."

The officer has let slip two important pieces of information: Helmut Himpel has been arrested, and the Gestapo knows about the suitcase. Denying it doesn't make sense in this case. "Oh, you mean *this* suitcase," Helmut Roloff says, and pulls it out from behind his music cabinet like it's no big deal.

"What's inside?"

"That I couldn't tell you. I don't know."

"Do you have the key?"

"No."

With the pliers they've brought with them the officers cut through the cable and start going to work on the lock. The pianist watches them, tense. When they finally manage to open the case, he sees at first glance that it actually is the radio transmitter.

Twenty-nine-year-old Helmut Roloff is led off with an officer on either side of him. His well-proportioned face under his brown hair is redder than usual, even if he is trying to act as nonchalant as possible. He's intent on maintaining an air of normality in front of his mother and his aunt, who is visiting. Before he says goodbye to them, he urges them to go to the opera that evening as planned. He'll just be away for a little while; he has to straighten something out with these gentlemen.

Outside the door waits a small black car with a driver. Although there's hardly room in the back for three, his two escorts put him in the middle and sit down on either side of him, while the third officer sits up front with the case. "Today we finally got lucky and found the thing," one of them says to the driver.

When they stop in the inner courtyard of the Reich Main Security Office after a quarter of an hour and take the elevator upstairs, where two of the men disappear into a room with the suitcase, the third policeman says quietly: "That was all very good what you said back there. Now just stick to your story."

Without moving, Helmut Roloff looks him in the eye. Just like Harro said: There's resistance everywhere by now — even in the Gestapo. The officer puts handcuffs on him and takes him to his cell.

# 18

For hours Harro leans against the wall and watches the sun move across the sky. After the calf screws it took fourteen days before he was able to walk again. The Sundays are recurring ever more quickly, the acacias are starting to lose their leaves. What are two, four, six weeks? The windows in the basement cells are at ground level, what little bit of green you can see is a blessing. Every time he hears the roar of airplanes it kindles his hopes of a direct hit: In the chaos that followed, it would be possible to escape.

The only fresh air comes on his walk through the yard, which is always too brief. The wide, unbounded sky is wedged into a square between dark walls. Harro is accompanied by a Gestapo man, Strübing mainly, who makes conversation and sees to it that no one else talks to him, no information is exchanged. The outing is always orchestrated in such a way that he sees as little of his friends as possible.

Nevertheless, some of them see him. They tell the others that he was wearing a track suit, plus his blue sweater, and doing gymnastics to strengthen his injured legs, keep his menaced body in shape. That he was pale, true, but every sinew was taut and he had a look on his face like he had overcome everything.

The Reich Main Security Office is a carnival at this point. The flood of people doesn't let up — more than 120 in all, some with only the vaguest connection to the resistance. Almost daily, people are brought in as "*Schutzhäftlinge*" of the Gestapo, housed alone for their own "protection":

Günther Weisenborn and his wife, Joy; John and Eva Rittmeister; Marcel Melliand from Heidelberg; the dramaturge Wilhelm Schürmann-Horster, who knew the Brockdorffs. The system is so overburdened that the Gestapo has to commandeer part of the military prison in the western Berlin neighborhood of Spandau.

The thirty-eight individual cells in the basement on Prinz-Albrecht-Strasse have long been filled, one police records photo after another is taken of the new arrivals, the typewriters clack in chorus. The air is stuffy on the top floor, where the interrogations take place. The angled windows, which are set high up, at eye level — skylights that call to mind the old days of the School of Decorative Arts — always remain closed. They've put in partition walls to subdivide the once large rooms into a labyrinth of tiny chambers and cubbyholes. The doors keep opening and closing as the officers are constantly summoned elsewhere. The interrogations are always being interrupted. The prisoners have to wait their turn down in the basement, where there are two benches and a line of isolating walls, so that everyone has to sit alone in his niche.

Not that the exhausted, chain-smoking officers would complain about the workload. Being a member of the Sonderkommission Rote Kapelle is considered a privilege, and the pay is good. Kriminalkommissar Büchert says during a walk with one of the prisoners in the garden of Prinz-Albrecht-Palais "that he had never been on such an interesting case. It would make an amazing story if it weren't so illegal." The officer also finds the setting where the drama is unfolding, the former School of Decorative Arts, to be fitting, "since both artists and artists' studios play a big role in the proceedings."

All interrogations follow the same template. First the focus is on the background of the individual — trips taken abroad, acquaintances — until it moves to illegal activities. Since the loose network around Harro and Libertas has no hierarchy, and areas of responsibility aren't delegated to specific persons, in principle everyone is a suspect in every crime.

All of their lives are in extreme danger, which some of the prisoners don't realize at first. Inexperienced in dealing with the pros in the Gestapo, people like Cato Bontjes van Beek, the high school student Liane Berkowitz, the dancer Oda Schottmüller, the doctor Elfriede Paul, or Fritz Thiel and his frightened wife, Hannelore, try to prove how harmless they are by doing something they shouldn't do: they admit to small, seemingly trivial crimes that they don't think will be of any consequence. This turns out to be a mistake, because however harmless these admissions may seem at first glance, the Gestapo cultivates them: watering them carefully, letting them grow, if possible into something monstrous. "Great experts that they were," as Heinrich Scheel remembers, "the officers skillfully seized on these little details and turned them into something serious ... They live[d] off the mistakes that those arrested before us had made. And with those arrested after us they lived off the mistakes that we had made."

Anyone who speaks of seemingly unpolitical private meetings is already digging his grave, since in the paranoid world of the Gestapo nothing can be unobjectionable. Everything is part of a big conspiracy. Everything serves the enemy, in the worst case — as here — Bolshevism. Everything is considered treason against the Fatherland, plays into the hands of the Soviets, who right at that moment are putting a stranglehold on Paulus's Sixth Army in Stalingrad. Even the smallest activity is taken to be a cog in a much larger operation meant to destroy the German Reich and toss it into the jaws of the red hordes, who are out to extinguish European culture. The Gestapo tries everything to portray the behavior of every single person associated with Harro and Libertas as morally depraved — people without moral backbone, rotten characters willing to betray Western civilization.

It is the small missteps — divulging a name, a casual meeting — that fill out these preconceived patterns. The description of a camping trip — everyone naked by the water, Harro with a pipe in his mouth — grows in the transcripts into a conspiratorial meeting in which the lives of the brave Wehrmacht soldiers on the Eastern Front were put at risk. "They take even the most vacuous bit of chitchat and twist it around till they've turned it into a noose" — Oda Schottmüller writes in a secret message in prison, succinctly capturing the officers' methods.

The transcription methods used at Gestapo headquarters are also questionable. Secretary Erna Januszewski, for example, doesn't type up what Harro actually says, but rather those words with which Officer Strübing summarizes Harro's statements. Every choice of phrasing is directed toward a single goal: incrimination. It requires extreme stubbornness to exercise even the least amount of influence on the transcript. Werner Krauss, whose strategy it is to present himself as a solitary madman who was never really in contact with anyone in the network, is the only one to insist on writing his transcript in his own words, which, he tells the officers, he is perfectly within his rights to do. "All statements made by Prof. Krauss have *in large part* been recorded in his own words or were *influenced* in their wording by him and dictated for the typewriter," his interrogator notes with exasperation. But no one else has the chutzpah to keep something like that up, and the officers phrase the statements that will mean the difference between life and death in their own words. "They didn't allow for any nuance of language, even though afterwards the charges were *based* on these nuances," recalls Greta Kuckhoff. Even when an objection against a certain phrasing is considered, the original wording remains; the correction is merely written in the space above it, most of the time it only supplements it. *I knew that* becomes *I deny having known that* ... Already you've slipped one step further down, are that much more tangled in the giant spider's sticky web.

The best solution would be not to talk at all. But who can pull that off, to say nothing all this time and deny having known anyone? They are all asked about every person they know socially. In principle the entire population of Berlin is potentially suspect. In no time at all the daylong interrogations of so many prisoners produce a massive pool of data for the Gestapo men to manipulate and draw from. Then they come to you and hand you a statement made by a friend who has already gone on record saying this or that, and so now of course you are given the opportunity to confirm whether this is correct. And if not, how did it happen, exactly? They also work with surprise — or withheld — confrontations. It is a big game, the goal of which is to get information; every calendar and notebook, every confiscated diary is combed through from the first page to the last, every name mentioned inside put under the microscope.

Theoretically, for example, the interrogators should never have learned about the meeting in Fritz Thiel's apartment on May 17, 1942, at which the "Nazi Paradise" operation was discussed. There are no written records of this meeting; nevertheless the story is somehow put together. Hannelore Thiel, whose three-month-old baby has been taken away to be used as leverage against her, is the first to talk, then her husband, and so on — until piece by piece the mosaic starts to fit together. If they had all kept their mouths shut, the men investigating them would never have learned anything about that evening, never heard about Harro covering the kissing couples with his service weapon. But a person doesn't keep quiet — not always, in any case, not for days at a time and above all not when he isn't trained to do so.

It becomes clear what a disjointed network this was, a ragtag, idealistic crew. This is no elite Moscow-trained cadre sitting here, but rather perfectly normal Berliners, the majority of whom have no experience being interrogated. Free just days before, all of a sudden they are confronted with a Soviet radio message they didn't even know existed. All of a sudden there's a Gestapo officer screaming in their face, saying Moscow has sold them out.

# 19

Helmut Roloff sticks to his strategy of playing dumb. He stubbornly denies everything. What his interrogators don't know is that the person they're questioning isn't the mad musician he makes himself out to be. In fact, Roloff had studied law. He knows that the cardinal sin is to admit to something. In the Gestapo universe, lying is his only chance to save his life. Again and again his interrogators come back to the suitcase. He must have suspected its illegal contents. At some point the pianist admits that he actually did think Himpel had hidden something inside: namely apples that he had been given by grateful patients. But he really hadn't given any more thought to the matter; he had just gone on playing his piano. He hoped he wouldn't get too severe a punishment for not having reported the apples. Since neither Helmut Himpel nor his fiancée, Maria Terwiel, make statements that in anyway incriminate Roloff, a few days later his cell door is thrown open and he is sent home with the words "Well, go on, get out of here! Your mother just put the coffee on!"

Across the board, Harro's close confidantes prove their loyalty to each other. The women especially act bravely and show backbone. Maria Terwiel takes full responsibility for her actions in order to help Helmut Himpel, and he does the exact same for her. The trick is to say something that seems believable and doesn't betray anyone.

# 20

Preliminary results from the investigations are regularly sent to Hitler by special messenger. Every now and again the Gestapo boss, Müller, walks over to the RLM to keep Göring up to date.

On September 25, 1942, Göring, Himmler, and Müller meet to discuss what their next step should be in dealing with Harro and Libertas and the others. What astonishes the investigators is the variety of illegal activities gradually coming to light. Various pamphlets, the stickering operation "Nazi Paradise," support for Jewish refugees, meddling in the Spanish Civil War, wild parties to recruit more and more people, a multilingual newspaper for forced laborers — an outright conspiracy against National Socialism. There hasn't been anything like it before in Hitler's Reich — and there won't be anything like it again.

The resistance work of Harro, Libertas, and all the others in fact goes far beyond the narrow bounds of espionage that were first suspected, which means there is a decision to be made. Which line of attack should the regime take in prosecuting the merry band? Göring, Himmler, and Müller are all agreed: They'll stick to their guns. The whole network should stand before a judge on charges of espionage and treason. All resistance activities will be subsumed under this main accusation as a way of covering up what really took place in the heart of the Reich's capital.

Goebbels, too, has read the first reports from the special commission — and he sounds the same note. "In Berlin a cell was established for carrying out treasonous and high treasonous activity and was in contact with the Soviet Union by means of shortwave radio transmission," the propaganda minister writes in his diary, and the jab at Göring that follows says something about the scheming being done by those at the top of the Nazi hierarchy, who after the recent military defeats have been looking ever more frantically for a scapegoat for the Wehrmacht's difficulties. That what Goebbels writes isn't true is made even clearer by the small inaccuracies he makes. Thus, for example, he falsely describes Libertas's position in his own institution: "Sometimes even the most important military secrets were transmitted. It seems especially aggravating that a host of officers from the command headquarters of the Luftwaffe are tied up in this case. One of these officers was married to a secretary in our Kulturfilmzentrale, who was also involved in this enterprise and as a result has been arrested along with the officers. The whole matter is highly embarrassing and for the Luftwaffe especially compromising. It will be investigated with vigor and with care, and one hopes at least that a large number of the carriers of the Bolshevist disease will be brought to light... To show leniency or hesitation in fighting this sabotage would be a crime against the very war effort itself."

# 21

On the afternoon of September 28, Erich Edgar Schulze receives a telegram from his brother in Berlin. It includes a telephone number along with the request to call at once, "because bad news regarding son."

The next morning at seven o'clock E.E. arrives at Potsdamer Bahnhof in Berlin, takes a room at the Hotel Fürstenhof on Potsdamer Platz, and sets out for the Air Ministry. After asking for Harro's office he is sent to one of the upper floors: "But the rooms are empty," he later notes. The deserted spaces within the huge building issue an eerie quality as he walks past. Harro's division, the attaché group, has been transferred elsewhere, and Colonel Bartz, his superior, is in the hospital — so Erich Edgar is told by an officer who has stayed behind to complete the transition. Harro was ordered to a different post, he claims — but never got there.

His colleagues in the RLM had been informed that all further inquiries into this matter must cease. They suspected, however, says the transition officer, that Harro was in Gestapo custody. When Erich Edgar then announces that he is going to appeal to Admiral Canaris, the head of Military Intelligence and one of his old comrades from his navy days, the officer encourages him.

Erich Edgar calls the intelligence division of the Wehrmacht high command immediately, only to hear that Canaris is traveling. His deputy, however, Colonel von Bentivegni, is willing to meet Harro's father at two o'clock that very afternoon at Military Intelligence headquarters at Tirpitz-ufer 80.

Erich Edgar sets out in pouring rain. Bentivegni, who greets the highly cultivated field officer and nephew of Grand Admiral Tirpitz courteously, proves to be well informed. He candidly informs Erich Edgar that his son is being held at the Reich Main Security Office, and orders a car to take the father to Prinz-Albrecht-Strasse.

The head of the special commission, Senior Councillor Panzinger, receives E.E. at two-thirty p.m. in room 306 of Gestapo headquarters. "In consideration of your reputation as an officer of outstanding merit, we are prepared to make an exception and provide you with information," says Panzinger, proper and polite: "Your son's case is a serious one, indeed likely a hopeless one. In order to tell you more, I would like to call the man directly responsible for the investigation, Kriminalrat Kopkow." When Kopkow joins them, Erich Edgar is struck by how young the officer looks, how stiff, with his "piercing eyes," as he jots down later that evening.

"Your son has engaged in communist activity," says Panzinger. "Can you, who must surely know him well, explain to us how that could be possible?"

Erich Edgar thinks for a moment. "Harro grew up in a time of political upheaval, when young people were not able to rely on the leadership of the state and all belief in authority was shaken after the unfortunate end of the World War," he answers in his usual didactic way. "To a boy with such an agile mind, the guiding influence of the home was not able to provide a full counterweight." Then, he continues, in spring of 1933 came the order banning the *Gegner,* and with it Harro's arrest. Maybe those days had left their mark on him.

"Your son deserved the lesson he got back then!" Kopkow sharply interjects.

"Your son has admitted that for years he has been working with every means at his disposal against the Führer and the National Socialist government, primarily through all manner of incendiary texts that he wrote and distributed himself," says Panzinger. Now he comes to speak about something that is causing him concern. Namely that Harro claims to have smuggled highly important information abroad, to Sweden, around sixty classified documents, their content partly military, partly political, including accounts of atrocities. Panzinger tells E.E. that Harro has provided a list of these documents. They were still in Sweden in a safe place and had not yet been handed over or published, but Harro claims he had only to "press a button" and they would be delivered to the enemy. This would mean treason. The gravest crime of all, punishable by death.

When the surprised Erich Edgar answers that he doesn't know anything about it and can't imagine Harro doing such a thing, Panzinger offers to let him meet with his son the next day at five o'clock in the afternoon. Then they could talk about these stolen papers.

Back at the Fürstenhof, Erich Edgar picks up a pencil and writes down what happened during the last couple of hours. "Despite the deep distress that afflicted me as I write I have endeavored to reproduce exactly all my impressions and everything that was said." His hope is that these notes "will later help to shed light on what is now obscure."

That evening Erich Edgar is invited to dinner at the Engelsings' villa in Grunewald where Harro and Libertas once danced the night away on his thirtieth birthday, on the day World War II began. Dr. Hartenstein, the director of the Schering plant, is also a guest. He is friends with the attorney Count Goltz, whom he believes to be the best man for the case. But Erich Edgar doesn't think a normal defense is possible, not when the Gestapo has accused someone of treason.

The next afternoon Harro's father appears punctually on Prinz-Albrecht-Strasse. Again he is received by Panzinger and Kopkow, who now tell him that Harro intends to make sure that the controversial materials get to the British government in the event that he and his friends receive a death sentence. "Please ask your son if these documents really are in Sweden. We assume that he will tell you the truth. And please try to convince him to undo this treasonous act by providing a means of recovering the papers and bringing them back to Germany."

"I wish to speak to my son immediately and for him to tell me himself what he has been accused of and what he feels himself to be guilty of," says Erich Edgar in his quiet but firm manner.

"Then please go with Kriminalrat Kopkow. He will take you to him."

Kopkow leaves the office with Harro's father. He calls the elevator and they ride to the top floor. There he leads him into a room that seems little used. In the corner is an empty desk, on the long side of the wall a couch, two plain armchairs, a small table. Erich Edgar is left alone for two minutes. Suddenly another door opens and Harro comes inside, accompanied by Kopkow and Strübing, who introduces himself with the words "I am your son's minder." With a slow, somewhat heavy gait, as if he were unused to walking, Harro steps toward his father. He stands up straight, with both hands behind his back; at first Erich Edgar assumes his son is in handcuffs, but he isn't. Harro wears a gray civilian suit and a blue shirt. His face is ashen and gaunt. His already prominent features show even more starkly than before. Otherwise he seems well kempt, he is clean-shaven and his hair is combed, almost as if he had made himself presentable for this meeting. There are deep shadows under his bright blue eyes. He gives his father a warm and deep look and takes him by the hand. They sit in the two chairs. Erich Edgar moves close to Harro and reaches for his hands again. They hold each other tightly for several moments and look at each other without a word.

The officers sit in the corner by the desk and observe. Erich Edgar turns his chair so that the policemen can't see his face, which is overcome with emotion. "The reason I've come so late," he says to Harro, "is that I only learned of your arrest two days ago. I've come as your father, to help you and to intercede on your behalf. To hear how I can best do this and why you are in jail in the first place."

"It is impossible and hopeless to try to help me in any way," Harro answers calmly. "For years I have fought against the current regime wherever I could." The touch of the hands is like a silent, intense dialogue, taking place alongside the other. "I have acted in full knowledge of the danger," Harro continues, "and am now resolved to bear the consequences. For tactical reasons I have sometimes had to resort to methods and means that from the usual outlook were not always perfect." He takes his hands from his father's, holds them clasped above his knees, and stares straight ahead, unmoving, in order to better concentrate on his words, which Strübing is taking down. "*Landesverrat* [treason against the *land*, the country] I have not committed."

On hearing these words the two officers whisper something to each other. When Erich Edgar turns to them they shake their heads as if to say that they are of a different opinion.

"Is it true then," Erich Edgar asks his son, "that you had important documents, political secrets and the like, smuggled to Sweden to protect yourself?"

"Yes."

"Can you name the location of the documents and make a statement as to whether you would cooperate in getting them back?"

"I cannot and will not do this."

"Not even if I ask you to?"

"No, not even then. It would mean betraying my friends. These papers are the only thing protecting them. I'm not thinking of myself. I know it's over for me, and I am ready to stand by what I've done. But even still I wouldn't give up the documents; they are of the utmost political and military importance. Their publication would mean more for Hitler and the German government than just a lost battle. The consequences would be incalculable."

"I won't press you, and I won't try to make you do something against your convictions and against your conscience," says Erich Edgar. Up to now he has been able to maintain his outward composure, but he can feel his strength leaving him. "You have a hard road ahead. I don't want to make it any more difficult for you."

Harro and Erich Edgar stand up. In the presence of the two officers they struggle not to let their emotion show. Harro moves close to his father, looks at him, firm and proud. His eyes are teary. One tear, that much he allows. Erich Edgar can only say, "I had other hopes for you . . . I have always loved you."

"I know," Harro answers softly.

Erich Edgar holds both hands out to him. Harro grasps them tightly. His father goes to the door, turns around again, and nods to his son. Harro stands stiff and straight, like a proud Prussian officer, between the two slouching agents of the Geheime Staatspolizei.

# 22

Erich Edgar is asked to come back to the office of the head of the special commission. "It is regrettable that your son refuses to help recover the documents," says Panzinger. "Reich Marshal Göring has requested that all available means be used to ensure that this happens."

Erich Edgar looks at him gravely. "I strongly advise against any attempt to use violence against my son in order to compel him to make a statement. It will only have the opposite effect."

Panzinger says nothing to this.

That night at the hotel, Erich Edgar writes: "However mistaken he might have been in his intent and his actions, he was, standing there and speaking as he did, the embodiment of human greatness and dignity. I would have felt this even if I weren't his father. This is the completion of a tragic fate in the true sense of the word, and like all unfathomable things, it is to be borne with reverence."

Two days later, on October 2, 1942, the Reichsführer of the SS personally inserts himself into the investigation: Himmler takes part in an interrogation of Harro and afterward speaks with Müller about the documents in question, supposedly highly incriminating for the Nazi regime. Himmler is also present for an interrogation of Harro on October 8. On October 12, Erich Edgar is summoned back to Berlin: His son would like to speak with him again. Although his father now fears being jailed himself and used as leverage against Harro, he boards a train for the Reich's capital.

This time Panzinger receives him with the news that Harro has declared himself ready to provide information regarding the location of the documents on the condition that he be given assurance that his friends and fellow prisoners, assuming they receive a death sentence, will get a reprieve delaying execution until December 31, 1943, the end of the following year. After much deliberation, says Panzinger, those in authority have decided that it is in the state's ultimate political interest to accept this unusual agreement. Panzinger shows the surprised Erich Edgar the written declaration that Harro prepared himself and has already signed:

> I am prepared, in the presence of my father, Frigate Captain E.E. Schulze, to provide the information necessary regarding the location of the documents to prevent their dissemination and publication. I have also resolved to do so in order to demonstrate that I did not intend to commit high treason. I armed myself with the documents for the event that there was no intent to consider and to treat my friends and me as Germans because of our political stance and course of action.

There follows a list of persons who are to be entitled to the reprieve. The statement ends with the addition:

211

The same shall hold true for my wife, although she of course will not be eligible for a death sentence. This commitment shall, again, be made in the presence of my father and shall also be a commitment to my father.

"As you can see, what your son is asking for here is a reprieve for his friends only. Not for himself," comments Panzinger. "But we have extended this commitment to include him as well."

Harro's father is led to the same room on the top floor where he had met Harro once before. Kopkow is again present, as well as Strübing, who brings Harro inside.

Erich Edgar looks at his son carefully. Although still extremely pale, Harro seems in better shape than last time. His eyes show an expression of satisfaction and confidence. Can it really be that he managed, if not to overturn the balance of power, then at least to use it to his advantage? Father and son clasp hands for a long time. They again sit down at the small round table on one side of the room, Harro this time on the couch, Erich Edgar in one of the two chairs.

"Before I proceed," says Harro to the agents, "I would again like to receive assurance that the agreement will come into effect as soon as I have provided a credible declaration as to the location of the documents."

"I can assure you to that effect," says Kopkow.

Harro nods. "I had long been aware that my position was vulnerable, and I deliberated back and forth about ways I could smuggle information abroad as protection. Finally it became clear to me that I would achieve the same goal if I didn't actually get the documents to Sweden, but simply claimed that I had. I would then only have to remain 'hard' enough during the interrogations and despite all threats firmly maintain that the papers were out of the country. I remained hard enough, although the most extreme pressure was brought to bear against me. Herr Kopkow can attest to this. Now I can make my statement: I didn't send any documents abroad. Everything remains in its proper place among my files at the Air Ministry."

"Is this really true?" asks Erich Edgar, stunned.

"It is the whole truth. I wouldn't lie to you at a time like this." Harro gives his father a determined look, and in his eyes shines the old fighting spark. "You can vouch for me with confidence."

Erich Edgar turns to Kopkow: "Knowing my son, I am firmly and absolutely convinced that his statement is true."

"I wouldn't be inclined to believe it if your son had only said it to me," says Kopkow, who wasn't prepared for this outcome. "But since he has given assurance, to his father, in so solemn manner I intend to accept it as credible."

"And is the agreement now to be viewed as in effect?" asks Erich Edgar uncertainly. Kopkow says yes, without restriction.

The triumphant look on his son's face helps his father with the sorrow of the parting this time. Almost radiant, Harro looks at him, satisfied at the outcome of the meeting. "Yes, Papa, you can rest assured, I'm doing fine."

"It's strange," says Kopkow at the end, icily, before Erich Edgar leaves the Reich Main Security Office: "The way your son spoke of you so often in the past week. He asked for you. 'My father should come here again,' he kept saying."

# 23

The officer who interrogates Arvid and Mildred Harnack is named Walter Habecker. He trained to be a metal polisher and at forty-nine years old is merely a Kriminalinspektor without further chances for advancement: two ranks below Kopkow, his junior by seventeen years. Habecker is "small and squatly built, with a balding head and a Hitler mustache under his sweaty nose, the kind of face you find depicted as the typical criminal's visage." This is how Günther Weisenborn, who is also interrogated by Habecker, describes him. The writer goes on: "The gray, unclean color of his face, from which two filthy-colored sharpshooter's eyes stare out as if presaging disaster, extends to the brutal rigidity of his wide jaw. He cuts a cigarette in two halves and lights one of them; he pedantically organizes papers and pencils." When his victims are led into his office, he likes to start by "grabbing another pencil and sharpening it to a fine point, very slowly, almost with pleasure," without looking up. It takes a long time. A very long time. It is deathly quiet in the room.

Habecker isn't one of the young, trained investigators like Kopkow or Strübing. He is old school; he places his service weapon in plain sight on his desk and deals out blows without warning, sometimes making use of a Tibetan prayer wheel for the purpose. It is impossible for the prisoners, whose hands and feet are shackled, to defend themselves against these blows, which are often aimed at the face. Habecker also kicks his victims with his boots, and he is especially fond of using his sharpened pencils.

Mildred Harnack occupies cell 25 in Prinz-Albrecht-Strasse, and then is transferred to the police jail at Kaiserdamm 1, where she has no contact with other prisoners or her relatives. She is not permitted to write a letter to her family; nor is she allowed to receive mail or visitors. It is obvious that they are making her imprisonment particularly harsh because she is American. During the daily rec period, while the other prisoners walk along the wall of the square prison courtyard, Mildred is made to walk the diagonal. She wears a dark coat with a green hood that she has pulled low over her forehead to hide her suddenly graying hair. She looks scarily frail, and the other prisoners act reserved, keeping their distance. They don't want her to be suspected of violating the prohibition against speaking to someone. With long strides she walks from one corner to the other, day after day, including on her fortieth birthday, looking at no one and repeating like a mantra Goethe's poem "Testament," the English translation of which she is still working on:

*No thing on earth to nought can fall,*
*The eternal onward moves in all;*
*Rejoice, by being be sustained.*
*Being is deathless: living wealth,*
*With which the All adorns itself,*
*By laws abides and is maintained.*

# 24

On October 15, 1942, the first death occurs. John Sieg from Detroit, the man with an eye for detail and a sense for dialogue, who wrote the *Open Letter to the Eastern Front* with Adam Kuckhoff and edited *Innere Front,* the newspaper for forced laborers, hangs himself in his cell four days after his arrest. In doing so he is able to die on his own terms and avoid making unwanted confessions under torture.

In the second half of October Müller proposes a quick trial for Harro and his friends in the Volksgerichtshof, or People's Court, whose new president is the feared Roland Freisler. Himmler seizes on the idea and brings it to Hitler. But the Führer figures Göring made his bed by giving Harro a promotion at the Air Ministry, so now he must lie in it. He gives the Reich marshal orders to "burn out the cancer." With this decision he also gives Göring the chance to cover himself by organizing the trial in such a way that he isn't exposed in it. The deal Harro struck with the Gestapo concerning the alleged papers in Sweden is quickly forgotten.

Around this time Göring is also approached by someone who wants to speak of the matter from the opposite perspective. Tora zu Eulenburg, who once sang the "Rosenlieder" for him and who was his host when he came to Liebenberg for the hunt, asks him to intervene to spare her daughter's life. He brusquely throws her out: "To think I let myself be taken in by that creature, and then raised her husband to officer's rank on top of that — there is nothing I regret more. I wouldn't think of helping her in even the slightest way!" His reputation has suffered greatly because of the lost air war with England, and he doesn't want to sully it any further. He has to be dead certain that *this* matter will be taken care of. He orders that the case against his Luftwaffe officer be tried before the Reichskriegsgericht, or Reich Court-Martial — RKG for short. This goes for Harro's comrades, too, even if they are women or civilians who have nothing to do with the military. From the start, the charges of "aiding the enemy" and "treason" are to be at the forefront, because these crimes fall under the jurisdiction of Germany's highest military court.

This decision also carries risk for the regime. The RKG sees itself as a Prussian institution and is proud of its reputation for maintaining a fair judicial process. Nevertheless, Göring is confident that everything will go the way Hitler wants it to. There is a man who is meant to make sure of this, whom Göring meets on October 17, 1942, in the Ukrainian town of Kalynivka, near Hitler's provisional headquarters, code named *Werwolf*. It is Göring's special deputy for political cases, Colonel Dr. Manfred Roeder.

Merciless convictions, a willingness to stop at nothing, baby face: Oberstkriegsgerichtsrat Dr. Manfred Roeder.

At forty-two years old, Roeder is the same age as the century, though in his official Luftwaffe photo he looks much younger, with a baby face and a uniform cap that seems too big for his head. Merciless convictions, a willingness to stop at nothing, and a detective's instincts are the qualities that Göring esteems in him. Roeder's manners in society are impeccable, his vivacity is winning. He can bow to those above him just as easily as he can kick those below him. Since the beginning of his career he has always been recommended for sought-after promotions, even if he is no mental heavyweight — and not even a Party member, though he does belong to the German Association of National Socialist Attorneys. But no matter: In Roeder's eyes this case is about something more elementary than even the Party — that is, the defense of the *state*. Göring is kicking at an open door when he tells him, "Generally speaking, long prison sentences make little sense, because they do not carry the expectation that there will be any improvement on the part of the convicted. When dealing, then, with an enemy of the state, given the choice between a long prison sentence and elimination of the perpetrator, the latter option is to be preferred."

Hitler gives the Reich marshal's course of action his blessing. Although he doesn't fully trust the Reich Court-Martial, since to his mind the punishments it metes out are sometimes too mild, he relies on Göring's assurance that with "Roeder the bloodhound" the results will match the severity of the indictment. Either way, Hitler reserves the right to uphold or reject the court's decision.

Back in Berlin, Roeder is introduced to the officers on Prinz-Albrecht-Strasse. He walks around like the lord of the manor and drops allusions to his friendship with the Gestapo boss Müller and Göring at every opportunity, which earns him respect among the subservient detectives. Though he moves into an office in the building across the street, in room 4256 of the RLM, he really feels at home in Amt IV für Gegner-Erforschung und -Bekämpfung. Here Roeder is in his element, and doesn't hide his ambitions to be the most unscrupulous sleuth of all. Thus he sets the tone for how the case is to be handled from this point forward, a ruthless tone that sits well with the Gestapo officers, who now feel justified in having taken such a harsh approach.

The system Harro is fighting against now has a face. He couldn't have found a more dangerous antagonist than Roeder. The extremist attorney not only wants to make sure that everyone who showed even the least support for the resistance of Harro and Libertas dies, but also that the memory of the couple and their friends is erased for all time.

# 25

The morning of October 26, 1942, a mild Sunday despite the season, Arvid's younger brother appears at Prinz-Albrecht-Strasse 8. Dr. Falk Harnack is twenty-nine years old and works as a dramaturge at the National Theater in Weimar. He hands his valuables to a friend who has come with him and asks him to wait in a nearby restaurant, saying if he isn't back in two hours, he should sound the alarm. "When you stepped inside that building," Falk later writes about his visit, "I am not trying to exaggerate — you did it with the greatest worry, because you never knew if you would be coming out again."

"Your brother is lost," Panzinger tells him by way of greeting: "The evidence against him is overwhelming — he won't be able to deny anything." Falk is made to wait in the anteroom. After fifteen minutes he is summoned inside and is face to face with Arvid. They embrace. "There are certain things I've done," begins Arvid, who looks significantly older than before his arrest. "I've confessed to them."

Falk hands him the gifts he brought, which have been examined and approved by the guards: half a cake loaf; cigarettes and matches; twenty tablets of Cebion, a vitamin C pill made by the Merck company; the same amount of vitamin B.

When an agent comes into the room to deliver something and Panzinger is distracted for a moment, Falk asks his brother by means of hand gestures if he has been beaten. Arvid leans over the table and whispers: "They've tortured me." From the look on his face Falk sees that it must have been horrible.

"Up to now I have been something like a buttress for the family," says Arvid, suddenly composed again. "I can't be it anymore. You will have to be it now."

"I will, I promise you," Falk answers. After a silence he adds: "We've been moving heaven and earth trying to find a good lawyer."

"Talk to Klaus."

Falk looks at him. Arvid means their cousin, Dr. Klaus Bonhoeffer, the brother of the pastor and resistance fighter Dietrich Bonhoeffer. They know that the Bonhoeffers have connections among the officers of the Wehrmacht who are planning to assassinate Hitler. As Falk understands it, in this moment Arvid gives him full authority to open up contact with them in order to begin a rescue operation for him and his fellow inmates.

"I believe that in principle what I did was right," Arvid says in parting. "The war is lost, and our only hope is the path that we have chosen. I believe that we will still be needed."

# 26

A few days later, Pastor Dietrich Bonhoeffer is sitting across from Falk Harnack and smoking a cigarette, a few thin hairs combed over his egg-shaped bald head. He has just been in Sweden, where he spoke with the Anglican bishop George Kennedy Allen Bell, a friend of the British foreign secretary Anthony Eden. The latter, however, still isn't interested in hearing about the German resistance. As Bell explains it, the existence of such a thing does not lie in the United Kingdom's national interest. That is the extent of his reply to Bell, who was trying to establish contact between England and the Wehrmacht officers ready to initiate their putsch.

At this first meeting Falk proposes to the Bonhoeffer brothers that given the arrests of Arvid, Harro, and the others, the various groups in the resistance urgently need to band together. The fight against the dictatorship must be led jointly. What's more, the overt Western orientation of the conservative resistance, whether in the army or in the person of the former mayor of Leipzig Carl Friedrich Goerdeler, presented a political risk. They need the connection to the East that Arvid and Harro had established. Falk suggests that in carrying out their coup d'état the Wehrmacht officers could also free the prisoners on Prinz-Albrecht-Strasse. But the Bonhoeffers' reaction is reserved.

Next, Falk Harnack gets together with Hans Scholl and Alexander Schmorell, the two minds behind the student resistance movement in Munich, later named the White Rose. They meet in the Saxon city of Chemnitz, where Falk is stationed. Scholl and Schmorell put up at the Sächsischer Hof, and when the three of them get to talking they are immediately able to relate very openly, without the usual caution of those speaking of illegal activities.

"Up to this point our work has come out of a kind of intuitive and idealistic stance," says Alexander Schmorell, a twenty-five-year-old ethnic German born in Russia, with thick dark hair. He has brought the four White Rose pamphlets distributed in summer 1942. The texts show a strong philosophical influence; in the future they intend to develop a more realistic and politically clear approach, he says. Hans Scholl, "a dark, south German type, full of energy," as Falk writes, describes his goal as being "to build a broad anti-fascist front, beginning with the left wing and moving through the liberal groups all the way to the conservative military opposition." He is convinced that they can successfully mobilize against the Nazi dictatorship. A torch has to be lit, and then all the forces in the resistance that are free and unaligned will automatically band together and become active. To this end Hans Scholl wants to carry out his student resistance work on a wider scale; to build cells at every university and connect them, "in order to be able to coordinate pamphleteering operations with little to no delay."

These are nice words, but they don't produce any results. There is no banding together of the like-minded from Munich and Berlin. Falk soon receives a definitive refusal from Dietrich Bonhoeffer as well: He claims he is too exposed in his own group to risk anything further. Falk is frustrated: While on Prinz-Albrecht-Strasse the avalanche of interrogations rolls on, the fractured German resistance movement remains passive, is too politically divided and not courageous enough, and so misses the moment to attack the Nazi regime with combined forces. The various groups that could have fused together, as the circles around Libertas and Harro had, remain separate.

"The German resistance movement bled to death," a frustrated Falk Harnack summarizes after the war.

# 27

On November 19, 1942, Russia launches its counteroffensive at Stalingrad. As far as thirty kilometers away, the earth can be felt shaking from the impact of the Red Army's heavy artillery.

The Wehrmacht is fighting a losing battle; the search for scapegoats, supposed traitors, is in full swing, and there are many who think they can be found in the cells of Prinz-Albrecht-Strasse 8. But it's not Harro and Libertas and their friends — the writers, journalists, businessmen, doctors, office workers, students, blue-collar workers, artists, dancers, sculptors, graphic designers, actors, and pregnant mothers from Charlottenburg, Kreuzberg, or Mitte — who are to blame for the fact that the Wehrmacht "is now in a difficult position" per Stalin's cool analysis. The problem is rather that its "strategic plans were clearly not realistic."

Around this time another suspect is brought to Berlin, a supposed businessman from Uruguay arrested in Marseille on November 15, 1942, who goes by the name Vincente Sierra. After initial interrogations in the Belgian fortress of Breendonk, where his radioman Wenzel had also been tortured, Kent comes back to Berlin almost exactly a year after his visit with Harro and Libertas. This time he doesn't stop at the Excelsior, but rather languishes in a cell in the basement lockup of the Reich Main Security Office. On November 22, Strübing shows him various mug shots under the file name *Gestapa42Spt.178* that Kent recognizes right away, although she "had a different hair style at the time," as it says in the report. It's Libertas. For the investigators this is the key proof that she was actively involved in Harro's work.

Two days later Kent is again sitting across from Strübing. Did Harro send messages with the radio or not? "I cannot say with certainty," says Kent, "if telegrams were successfully transmitted. One can say with conviction, however, that up to that point in time telegrams had *not* been sent by the group *Choro,* since the leadership in Moscow had not heard anything about the group."

Long faces among the Gestapo. This is not what they had wanted to hear.

# 28

Hilde Coppi, heavily pregnant, the wife of the man who tried in vain to establish radio contact with Moscow, is transferred to the women's prison at Barnimstrasse 10 near Alexanderplatz. In Kaiser Wilhelm II's time, this was the jail for prostitutes and women who'd had abortions, as well as those who had advocated for equal pay or women's suffrage. Rosa Luxemburg was once locked up here. Countless Berliners had first seen the light of day in the prison's in-house delivery ward.

Another arrives on November 27, 1942, when Hilde Coppi gives birth to a healthy son. He is to be named after his father: Hans.

The two Hans Coppis meet a single time, on December 9, 1942. The infant is wrapped in a blanket and driven with his mother across the city. It is a gray, sunless day; rain falls off and on, and the temperature is forty-six degrees. The new father is standing in handcuffs behind a table in the Reich Main Security Office, guards to his left and right. He squints in order to see better as Hilde finally comes toward him. The police have taken his much-needed glasses from him — as if anything else were necessary to make clear how powerless he is. Now it is his own child that the state keeps from him. And now the regime wishes to murder his beloved wife.

Because now his Hilde is no longer protected by the law that shields pregnant women from execution. She has given birth, has done her duty, so to speak, and thus she can be beheaded.

Hilde asks the officers for permission to come closer to her husband so that he can see the baby clearly. She pulls the blanket back and shows him the child. Coppi, six foot one, bends forward and sways as the baby, looking at him with big blue-gray eyes, gradually comes into focus.

# 29

Dr. Manfred Roeder has put in overtime. He's been sleeping at most two to three hours a night on a couch in his office in the RLM. He has interrogated some of the inmates yet again; now he hands his several-hundred-page indictment to Dr. Alexander Kraell, the chairman of the Reich Court-Martial's Second Judicial Panel. What's at stake in these pages are the lives of Harro and Libertas Schulze-Boysen, Arvid and Mildred Harnack, Elisabeth and Kurt Schumacher, Horst Heilmann, John Graudenz, Hans Coppi, and others. They are to be the first wave to be tried. The trials against Adam and Greta Kuckhoff, Mimi Terwiel, Helmut Himpel, Fritz Thiel, Oda Schottmüller, Ursula Goetze, and Werner Krauss, Günther Weisenborn, and many more will follow in the coming year.

Libertas's Gestapo photo, from her police file.

By the end of November 1942 the ninety-page closing report from the Gestapo, written by Horst Kopkow, is also finished. Hitler, Himmler,

Göring, Goebbels, and other high-ranking Nazis each receive a sheaf of papers in a black binder. "Bolshevist *Hoch- und Landesverratsorganisation*" reads the title page, striking the key note. Graphics are included to make for a more vivid read: photos, organizational charts, even a "genealogical chart of the traitor Schulze-Boysen and Wife." The lines of this family tree run from Alfred von Tirpitz and the founder of sociology in Germany, Ferdinand Tönnies, through Marie Luise and Erich Edgar on the one side, from Prince Philipp zu Eulenburg on the other, down to those individuals who with their love of life dared to rebel against the Hitler regime. But there's nothing like *that* in the report, of course. It's not about the concepts of freedom, justice, and conscience, of responsibility and human dignity, but rather the unmasked ring of Soviet agents in Paris, Brussels, and Amsterdam — with Harro, Arvid, and the others mistakenly identified as the ring's Berlin cell.

About the parties that Harro and Libertas threw with their friends, the "picnic" soirées in their loft, the Gestapo is able to report the following: "Repeatedly held evenings of discussion, often involving sexual elements and taking place primarily in his apartment, were cleverly used by him and his wife Libertas to politically influence the participants and present a near-classic example of intelligence gathering with the goal of societal espionage."

The Kopkow report characterizes Libertas as "an impulsive woman with strong personal ambition," who worked "as her husband's deputy": "She acted in the role of courier, witnessed illegal meetings, wrote subversive texts and recruited suitable persons for the formation of partisan groups in Berlin."

With this summary of their investigations of the past three months, the Gestapo brings down the curtain on phase one. The mood on Prinz-Albrecht-Strasse is good, the work is considered a success — and handsomely rewarded. Göring taps in to a special fund and doles out 100,000 Reichsmarks in bonuses, "for special achievement in an extraordinarily important investigative case." The blood money is distributed to more than sixty-five officers, with Horst Kopkow receiving the largest chunk: a good 30,000 Reichsmarks, an enormous sum. Panzinger, Henze, Strübing, and Habecker are likewise rewarded — and Gertrud Breiter receives a cool 5,000 Reichsmarks, a personal note of commendation from Himmler, the War Merit Cross Second Class, and an "elevated salary tier." She managed to get Libertas to fall for her act. Everything Libertas confided in the typist landed fresh on the desk of her superior, Göpfert.

# 30

Handwritten letter to Marie Luise and Erich Edgar Schulze in Mülheim:

12.10.42

Dear Parents!

There isn't much of anything new to report from my cell. Here it's easy to lose one's self in one's thoughts and above all in one's memories, and it is strange to experience how much of what seemed important on the outside begins to pale in significance — and how other things, previously taken for granted, become central. It is a great process of finding my way back, and I wouldn't want to have gone without it in my life. To find my way home: above all to you! After so much restless living a great calm has come over me; and my heart grows heavy only at the fact that I am causing you so much suffering. I am happy to hear that Hartmut is doing a little better. How I like to think back on the days spent with you all in Freiburg: Mama, Helga and the cheerful kids! I draw strength from all of it, it is my daily bread. No, I really am not alone and "lonely and forsaken." Even in dreams, aspects of life are revealed that I never knew before! It is a strange thing about man — how much he is formed by his surroundings! It would of course be false to say that this is the true revelation about life. But it is nevertheless a very valuable corollary, for which one must be grateful. I am. Not that the metaphysical has made me forget everything else, but now I have at least felt and myself experienced what before now I at most partly understood.

Suddenly, and only at this late moment, it becomes clear to me what a writer friend of mine meant when he gave a novel of his the epigraph:

> "Sacrifice everything you have —
> and in the end sacrifice even that
> for which you sacrificed everything!"

Naturally the mind's instinct for self-preservation seeks for a while to fight against this, and honor forbids any move to recant in a time of need. But, "entre nous," things become incredibly simple and elementary when seen in the light of day, and in hindsight, fatefulness and the pure, naked instinct to live become the main components of the image.

Does it make a difference if one finds one's way ever closer to one's self? Certainly not: "So long as you do not have this, this dying and becoming..."

With profound love,<br>Your H

# 31

At midnight the night before the trial, Harro's cell door is thrown open. He is lying in handcuffs on the bunk. "Stay where you are! Are you Harro Schulze-Boysen? Tomorrow you will be led before the Second Judicial Panel of the Reich Court-Martial. You stand accused of the following crimes..." The voice rattles off a series of clauses with short summaries of their contents in legalese. "Did you get all of that? Good!" The procedure lasts less than a minute and is repeated for Arvid Harnack and Hans Coppi; for Libertas and Mildred Harnack in the prison at Kaiserdamm 1; in the lockup on Alexanderplatz for Elisabeth Schumacher and Erika von Brockdorff; and in the Spandau military prison, where Kurt Schumacher, John Graudenz, and, at the end of the hall, Horst Heilmann are all being held.

On the morning of December 15, 1942, soldiers with fixed bayonets are posted on every landing of the neo-baroque building that houses the Reich Court-Martial in Berlin. Every window is secured with an extra guard; the authorities want to be prepared for any attempt to free the prisoners. The regime is on its toes. Even in the *Wolfsschanze,* the "headquarters of the Führer" in the boggy, fly-ridden forest of East Prussia, the security protocols are strengthened at the start of the trial.

But the greatest fear of all is that some sense of the extent and the impact of these people's activities could get out. This explains the sign hanging on the door of the large courtroom: THE PUBLIC IS BARRED. No one is permitted to talk about the trial. The punishment for anyone who defies this prohibition is to be sent to a concentration camp. The relatives of the accused are not informed that the proceedings have begun. The court-appointed lawyers for the defense have never met their clients in person; they haven't even seen the indictment.

The latter move is calculated, because Chief Prosecutor Roeder has little to go on other than the statements made under torture. Will that be enough for him to succeed before the Reich Court-Martial? Dr. Alexander Kraell, the chairman of the Second Panel, is known to be a conservative military judge who works in the tense middle ground between Party membership and his own will to protect the Wehrmacht's judicial process from National Socialist abuses. He is no friend of Roeder; he turns up his nose at this upstart whose rudeness and coldness he, unlike the Gestapo agents, doesn't confuse with grit. For Chief Justice Kraell, here in the halls of the Reich Court-Martial, Roeder is an undistinguished rabble-rouser and careerist who was able to rise for reasons that don't accord with Kraell's idea of honor.

But Roeder is determined to show the Wehrmacht court what's what. The military situation plays into his hands: The Americans have landed in Morocco, Rommel is fighting a losing battle between Tripoli and Bengazi, and the Sixth Army in Stalingrad is surrounded. Hundreds of thousands of German soldiers find themselves in a hopeless situation with insufficient supplies and freezing cold weather. There is no worse time to appear before the Reich Court-Martial as a defendant accused of aiding the enemy army. No worse time to be seated on one of the chairs spaced a suitable distance apart from each other and facing the horseshoe-shaped judge's bench, with the raised platform for Oberstkriegsgerichtrat Roeder off to the right.

This morning, December 15, 1942, no one is in the room yet. At each of the five empty seats of the Second Panel — belonging to Kraell and another judge along with three high-ranking Wehrmacht officers — are a neat little stack of blank paper and three perfectly sharpened different-colored pencils, plus the officers' headgear: two general's caps and an admiral's hat with silver eagle. The seats for the court-assigned lawyers are off to either side and so far away from the defendants' chairs that consultations during the trial are impossible. Enthroned at the front of the room is a bust of Hitler, the "Supreme Army Commander and Supreme Head of the Judiciary." The bust dominates the room, staring lifelessly from dark, fist-size holes where the eyes should be. A second, smaller bust depicts Justice, her eyes blindfolded.

Shortly after nine a.m. the doors are opened for the few handpicked observers. Enter a few subaltern detectives from the Reich Main Security Office, looking like harmless civilians. Then the accused are led in: Harro, Libertas in a gray suit, Mildred and Arvid Harnack, Horst Heilmann, Elisabeth and Kurt Schumacher, Hans Coppi, Erika von Brockdorff, and finally John Graudenz. At nine-fifteen the judges enter the room. Everyone stands and jerks their right arm into the air, except for the accused. They were informed beforehand that they were not to make the Hitler salute. The head of the Second Panel and his fellow judges sit down, their backs ramrod straight. Kraell calls out the names and birthdates of the accused and confirms their identity. He turns his head to the side: "Herr Oberst-kriegsgerichtsrat, the indictment, please."

Unlike the judges, Roeder doesn't sit like a peg, but slouches on his seat as he reads out the text of the indictment. As the first of the "many flagrant occurrences" he speaks of the envelope that Gisela von Poellnitz dropped in the mailbox of the Soviet embassy in Paris. Then he describes the pamphlets *Der Stosstrupp, Napoleon Bonaparte,* and *Concern for Germany's Future Is Spreading Among the People.* Contained in these pamphlets was a "call to open revolt."

Next up is the support for the Allies. In a searing tone of voice Roeder announces that Luftwaffe First Lieutenant Harro Schulze-Boysen "learned that English radio transmissions announcing the departure of ship convoys bound for Russia could be decrypted by German Military Intelligence. He passed this knowledge on to the defendant Graudenz, who through friends in Heidelberg maintained connections with Swiss circles who supported England, with the comment that the English must be made aware of this information." He pauses for a moment and looks up. A murmur goes through the large room: treason.

Now it's Libertas's turn. Her lawyer wears a monocle, which he keeps having to screw into his right eye so it won't fall out on him. He looks at his client, who he is seeing for the first time this morning, with a faint air of fatherly pity. The other lawyers also eye the "Castle Girl" with curiosity. An almost sensuous pleasure plays on their features. So this is her, her husband's "most zealous co-conspirator," who lay under "the influence of his intellect," as it says in the Gestapo's closing report. She "provided technical help" for *Der Stosstrupp,* Roeder lectures eagerly; she likewise played a role in *Concern for Germany's Future.* She also took part in espionage activities. "She made suggestions to her husband regarding which apartments a transmitter could be placed in ... At least twice she took documents with notes intended for the enemy to Harnack, whom she knew would be encrypting them." She read at least one of these slips of paper, which contained production numbers for the German airplane industry.

Harro had been so confident that his wife would not be eligible for the death penalty. But for Libertas, sitting before the highest German military court, things are looking bad.

# 32

Then, on another level, a miracle happens. The isolation practices of the Gestapo don't hold for the Reich Court-Martial, and during the trial's first recess the defendants are all taken to the same waiting room. Their handcuffs are removed, even the men's. It is liberating to meet again after months of involuntary separation. But it's not easy, either. Libertas now learns from the others that Gertrud Breiter tricked her and that everything she told her made it to the Gestapo, with life-threatening consequences for some of them. The accusation hangs in the air: Libertas betrayed them all out of cowardice and to buy freedom for herself.

She is overcome by shame and feelings of guilt. How could she be so dumb as to trust the typist? What happened is exactly what she was most afraid of the whole time: She had lost her nerve. She was *naïve,* the one trait that you can never display around the Nazis. The same trait that Harro always tried to avoid after his days and nights in the SS basement. Libertas is crushed. *This* is much worse than the worst punishment that she could expect.

But then the miracle happens. The others have all gotten to know the Gestapo's tricks, their extreme violence. They have all learned how hard it is to resist the pressure, to *never* lose your nerve. Some of them were severely tortured: Kurt Schumacher, Hans Coppi, John Graudenz, Arvid Harnack, Harro. Now is not the time for accusations. Through imprisonment and extreme interrogation, they have all developed a keen sense for the difference between betrayal and exhaustion, *both* of which can have severe consequences. "There were no betrayals," Heinrich Scheel says after the war: "And anyone who might have stumbled under the burden and torment of interrogations was helped up by those who as a result had been put into even greater danger, even if this help meant only an encouraging look, a hastily whispered word. No one felt forsaken, no one felt that he had to walk a dark path alone." They forgive Libertas her weakness, her mistake.

What she experiences at this moment is "so great and wonderful that words can hardly describe it," as she writes a few days later in her farewell letter to her mother. Now they are all at peace with themselves, and "with a sense of togetherness that is only possible in the face of death, we go to face the end. *Without* sorrow, without bitterness."

The guards also sense that something uncommon has happened, and as the prisoners share the food they have brought, the staff donates a jug of beer.

Then all are taken back into the large courtroom.

# 33

The dancer and sculptor Oda Schottmüller, the woman with the slender, powerful figure, the elastic, determined gait, the calm, open face with large, frank eyes, who a few weeks later will have to appear before the same panel of judges, is unsparing in her criticism of the Reich Court-Martial. "The balance of power is completely skewed," she writes in a message smuggled out of jail: "The form of justice is basically: Whoever has the power is in the right. Every state must protect and defend itself. But what I have experienced in my case are the criminal actions of a tyrannical government that is desperately trying to defend itself."

Oda has nothing but scorn for Roeder. His performance seems so ridiculous to her that she finds it hard to remain serious: "He is an indescribably vain little peacock; unexpectedly enough, he seems much more human to me because of it . . . Suddenly something to laugh about again after all this time." Oda characterizes the defense lawyers as "Santa Clauses," "paid creatures," and "nothings in superlative," asking herself "what decent person could stoop to taking on such a pitiful role — a fig leaf, so to speak, for this mockery of justice." She hasn't many flattering things to say about the judges, either:

> The admiral with the perm was present, true — but already very much worse for the wear. At least he kept his eyes open, though, and sat up straight — albeit with great effort. Two other gentlemen were pretty indifferent — they did give occasional signs that they were paying attention though. One billiard ball with a suspiciously bright hooter was fully asleep. I didn't dare even look — it was so comical how his head kept almost hitting the desk, and it brought up so many associations for me. Unfortunately the chairman had to ask me twice to take the whole thing seriously. I tried my best, since for me it's of course damn serious — but the second time I was tempted to ask him either to wake his colleagues up or send them to bed already. Despite all the comedy, I just found it too shameless, like a scene from a period drama that they were all acting out.

Günther Weisenborn writes a similarly derisive critique of the highest German military court after his trial in 1943. The "five pale officers' faces" of the curly-haired, broad-shouldered judges gazed at him with the same mechanical lack of intelligence, the same look of stolid interest "that a tired group of card players has when staring out at a barren landscape from the window of a dining car."

# 34

After the evidence has been presented, Roeder makes his closing argument. It is December 19, 1942, and this is his big moment. Now he drops his strategy of objectively presenting the facts. He wants to denounce the accused in moral terms, attack their legacy. The goal is to establish a link between the reprehensibility of their actions and their moral depravity, to lump together the loathed notions of freethinking intellectualism, artistic activism, and left-wing politics into a single, all-encompassing slur — *champagne Bolshevism* — that is supposed to express their lack of "decent character." Their free sex lives and extramarital relationships, which some spoke about during the interrogations in order to underscore the political harmlessness of their social interactions, are twisted to mean the exact opposite and presented as incriminating. Something as small as a "soiree with dancing at the Schulze-Boysen home" at which a "free atmosphere" reigned is for Roeder traitorous and deserving of the severest punishment.

Erika von Brockdorff, the sensual woman who doesn't hide her charms, is a particular thorn in his side. He describes this fun-loving mother of five-year-old Saskia as having "a less than active mind"; her activities up in her "studio apartment" are for the prosecutor a combination of weakness of character and Bolshevist industriousness. Only a woman with "limited [intelligence] and personal indifference" could, while her child slept peacefully, "carry on for this and other reasons" an "intimate relationship" with the radio operator Hans Coppi, who possessed a key to her apartment and therefore "constant access." Erika stands up, and in lieu of a retort she bursts out laughing. "Soon enough you won't have much to laugh about!" Roeder cries angrily. But Erika is apparently not as mentally handicapped as he tries to present her. She nimbly fires back: "I will as long as I'm looking at you!"

# 35

In the name of the German people!

In order to make it easier to hand down the verdict, the judges have developed a modular system. The individual components are high treason (*Hochverrat*), wartime treason (*Kriegsverrat*), treason against the country (*Landesverrat*), subverting the Wehrmacht, aiding the enemy, espionage, or a combination of all of these. It is a house of cards of legalese, with a guillotine in its inner courtyard. A shaky edifice, but one that in the moment has a deathly legal force.

> For the crimes, jointly committed, of conspiring to commit *Hochverrat*, subverting the Wehrmacht, and aiding the enemy, according to the legal provisions outlined in Section 83 Paragraph 1.3 Subparagraphs 1, 2, 3, 73 and 91b of the Reich Penal Code; Section 57 of the Military Penal Code; and Section 5 Paragraph 1 Subparagraphs 1 and 2 of the Wartime Special Penal Code, no form of punishment other than that of execution can be considered.

So goes the verdict for Harro. Next it's Libertas, Mildred and Arvid, John Graudenz, Hans Coppi, Horst Heilmann, Erika von Brockdorff, and Elisabeth and Kurt Schumacher's turns.

# 36

In the jails the mood has changed. The prisoners are now *Todeskandidaten* — death candidates — or *TKs* for short. Before going to sleep they must put all their clothes on a stool outside the cell door, so that they are left with nothing they could use to take their own lives. They have to sleep shackled and naked.

Only for Mildred Harnack and Erika von Brockdorff do things look different. To Roeder's great disappointment, they get off with prison sentences, because according to the court they were not actively involved in the crimes: six years for Mildred, ten years for Erika.

Jesko von Puttkamer, the officer responsible for passing information between the Reich Court-Martial and headquarters, flies to the *Wolfs-*

*schanze,* where he presents the sentences to Hitler. On Monday, December 21, the "Supreme Head of the Judiciary and Supreme Army Commander," who despite having taken strong barbiturates barely slept the night before, dictates the following:

### I.

I uphold the verdict of the Reich Court-Martial on December 19, 1942 against First Lieutenant Harro Schulze-Boysen and others . . .

### II.

I decline to issue a pardon.

### III.

The sentences are to be administered, and in the case of . . . Harro Schulze-Boysen, Arwid [*sic*] Harnack, Kurt Schumacher and Johannes Graudenz, are to be carried out by means of hanging. The other death sentences by means of beheading . . .

### IV.

I nullify the verdict of the Reich Court-Martial on December 19, 1942 against the wife Mildred Harnack and Erika Gräfin von Brockdorff. The trial is to be reassigned to another judicial panel of the Reich Court-Martial.

Sgd. Adolf Hitler.

The Führer will show no mercy. Because even the memory of the group is to be wiped away, no one can be allowed to survive to tell the true story. And that goes for Mildred and Erika, too.

# 37

Hanging has all but ceased to be practiced as a means of execution in Germany since the seventeenth century. It is considered by the Nazis the cruelest and, for the victim, most shameful method of execution. Normally, death sentences under the National Socialist regime are carried out by beheading. Members of the military are shot — supposedly the most honorable method — as is for example Stauffenberg on July 20, 1944, after his failed assassination attempt. A notice from the Reich Ministry of Justice shows that Hitler's decision to further punish some of the resistance fighters from bohemian Berlin with hanging wasn't spontaneous. It concerns the construction of a gallows in the Berlin-Plötzensee prison:

It is to be expected that in the near future several death sentences . . .
will need to be administered . . . The Führer will likely order hanging, and the legal authorities shall be asked to immediately comply.

The memo — termed "essential to the war effort" and "priority" —
calls for procuring a "means of hanging eight persons simultaneously."
Thus, at the direction of Justice Minister Thierack, a T-beam is installed
on the ceiling of the execution shed at Plötzensee, with eight movable
meat hooks that slide on rollers.

The notice is dated December 12, 1942. Three days prior to the trial before the Reich Court-Martial, the verdict was already fixed.

# 38

In these last days before Christmas 1942, Günther Weisenborn is on his
way from an interrogation on the fifth floor of the Reich Main Security
Office back to the basement, where his cell is. He steps off the elevator after the detective accompanying him has opened the grate. There, another
detective is waiting to ride up. He also has a prisoner with him. It's Harro.

"There he stood, tall and thin and his face very pale," Weisenborn describes the last meeting with his friend: "His hair shone blond under the
lamp. In his face was a kind of iron cheerfulness that made you cheerful
to see it. He winked at me on the sly, and I winked back. He wore his blue
sweater under his jacket, and he was in handcuffs. Here he was in the Gestapo basement, young, talented, clean, a tortured messenger of the world
to come, he had everything behind him now, struggle and torment. These
were his last hours in the basement, here stood the Germans' hope, bold,
pure and young . . . In those days in which human lives were as cheap as
blackberries, in those days I understood the greatness and strength of the
human race."

The former Prussian minister of culture, Adolf Grimme, who is swept
up in the wave of arrests on account of his friendship with Adam Kuckhoff,
also sees Harro one last time, in the elevator of Prinz-Albrecht-Strasse
8. They aren't permitted to speak to each other. Grimme doesn't know
Harro and only later finds out from the detective who this man was with
whom he shared the brief span of an elevator ride. Grimme will remain
in prison for two and a half years and during this time he will encounter all manner of people, among whom, as he later recalls, "there were so
many who maintained an unbelievable heroic poise, right up to the end.

But still I must say that the image of Harro from this fleeting encounter was indelibly stamped upon my memory. The way he looked at me, there was in his eyes something so human, so devout and compellingly motivating, that I immediately said to the detective accompanying me: If I had met Herr Schulze-Boysen as a free man, I would have [followed] the call of his humanity and the conviction that shines in his eyes — no matter what."

## 39

His mind races all night long, thinking of his friends in the neighboring cells. The hours until dawn drag on endlessly, and his overwrought brain tries not to think of the execution. The yearlong reprieve that the Gestapo had guaranteed him in his father's presence for securing the documents believed to be in Sweden is a distant memory. In this, his last night, Harro pulls a poem from a crack in the floorboards that he composed back in November and hid. It bears the title "Gestapa Zelle 2" — Gestapo Cell No. 2.

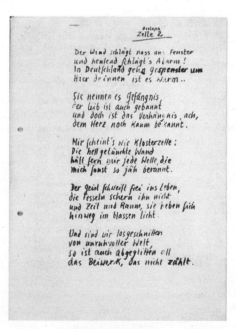

Harro's farewell poem . . .

Now that Harro knows that Hitler has ordered him killed by hanging, he has to change a word in the last stanza:

~~Bullet~~ Hangman's rope and guillotine
Won't have the final say.
The <u>world</u> will be our judges,
Not the judges of <u>today</u>.

Es gilt nur letzte Wahrheit
dem überscharfen Blick
und ungetrübte [crossed out] wird
hier stolz zum Daseinsglück.

Der Stunde Ernst will fragen:
Hat es sich auch gelohnt?
An Dir ist's nun zu sagen: Doch!
's war die rechte Front.

Das Sterben an der Kehle
hast Du das Leben lieb ...
und doch ist Deine Seele satt,
von dem, was vorwärtstrieb.

Wenn wir auch sterben sollen,
so wissen wir: Die Saat
geht auf. Wenn Köpfe rollen, dann
zwingt doch der Geist den Staat.

Die letzten Argumente
sind ~~Schuss~~ [strang] und Fallbeil nicht,
und uns're <u>heut'gen</u> Richter sind
noch nicht das <u>Weltgericht</u>.

Schulze-Boysen
Nov. 42.

...discovered after the war in his Gestapo cell.

# 40

The next day is a cold, gloomy Wednesday with wind from the east. Lunch has yet to be served after the walk in the oval of the prison yard in Spandau, and the nervousness is tangible in the large brick building that resembles a medieval fortress. The prison guards order the *TKs* out of their cells even more loudly and vigorously than usual, and lead them off in shackles.

Around eleven-thirty a.m. a police van trundles through the iron gate, which closes with a dull bang. It turns right onto Heerstrasse, and from there drives toward the city center. Kurt Schumacher, John Graudenz, and Horst Heilmann sit on two wooden benches against the wall. At the end of the car are two alcoves that are so cramped that one can only just stand up inside them. They are reserved for Arvid and Harro.

If it were possible to look out, Kurt, John, and Horst would see to their right through bare trees the black glittering water of the Scharfe Lanke, the bend in the Havel River where the Blau-Rot boathouse stands, half on land, half in the water — where the *Duschinka* is still docked and also the *Haizuru*, the sailboat that belonged first to Ricci von Raffay, then to Harro and Libertas, and finally to Günther Weisenborn. It is also the place where Gisela von Poellnitz was arrested in 1938. Next the transport passes Adolf-Hitler-Platz, where on neighboring Reichsstrasse Oda Schottmüller's masks stare out expressively from the walls of a frigid, deserted studio on the top floor, and if they were to turn left and then immediately right, they would arrive at Altenburger Allee 19 — but there wouldn't be anyone at Harro and Libertas's home.

They head for the prison at Kaiserdamm 1. The car stops, the gate opens with a screech, the car drives into the yard, the shackled Libertas is brought to join them.

Now they go down the East-West Axis, lined by the two-armed streetlamps that Albert Speer designed, past the Great Star with the Victory Column at its center, and through the Brandenburg Gate, past the Hotel Adlon and the shuttered Soviet embassy to Alexanderplatz, where Elisabeth Schumacher gets in.

Prinz-Albrecht-Strasse is the next stop. The door opens, a guard steps out, then a prisoner: It's Hans Coppi. Another guard, another prisoner: Arvid Harnack. Harro, thin, walking upright like an officer, is escorted in the same way.

# 41

Past the Reichstag, which burned nine years earlier, when the *Gegner* was still being published, the police van turns off toward the Invaliden cemetery. Buried here are "notable and meritorious officers of the Prussian-German army." To the right is the Moabit freight depot. Eight days earlier, on December 14, the third deportation train to Auschwitz departed, with 815 Berlin Jews, also on their way to their deaths.

Another kilometer and a half. Now they cross the Hohenzollernkanal, where Henry Erlanger is meant to have committed suicide. But Harro didn't go along with that lie.

Libertas wears a silver bracelet, her beloved silver ring, and a silver cross with her gray suit. "The ring is from my father," she says to Harro, and raises her right hand slightly. Out of his alcove he bends toward her and kisses the ring, reaffirms the oath that he swore to her on Kristallnacht. They are together now — until the end.

# 42

Upon arrival in Plötzensee the car door is thrown open: "Out!" They have to line up. Two guards per prisoner bring each separately to their cells on death row. There are broad red strips of fabric on the doors, fifteen centimeters long and two centimeters wide. They are the only touches of color aside from the bright blue of Harro's sweater. The cells are cold; the radiators were removed to prevent suicide. So close to the end, the state won't be robbed of its valuable prizes.

The lamp in the ventilation hole above the cell door only scantly illuminates the small room; the switch is outside, as usual. No one speaks loudly, and all activities are muted: a consideration that is even more horrifying than the rough tone on Prinz-Albrecht-Strasse, in the Spandau jail, or in the *Rote Burg* on Alexanderplatz.

Harro's handcuffs are removed so that he can write his farewell letter. The Plötzensee prison chaplain is with him, Harald Poelchau. By chance he witnessed the arrival of the transport around one o'clock; no one had informed him of the upcoming execution, as they normally would have. In answer to his questions he was told the matter was secret. Hearing this, he took it upon himself to visit the cells on death row. Now he is bringing Harro ink and a pen. "My impression was that he, unlike the others, had not come to terms with the sentence to be carried out," the clergyman describes the meeting: "True he was outwardly composed, but inside passionately embittered over his fate and the fate of his movement. Such an attitude is of course not determined by logical and rational reflection, but rather is a matter of temperament and of passion. And Schulze-Boysen had a strong temperament."

At two p.m. the clergyman visits Arvid, who makes the calmest impression on him of all of them. He has been brought a piece of chocolate, a few cakes, two rolls, and grain coffee. He eats it all except for the bread. The pastor has cigarettes with him and a little wine.

"This morning I kept repeating the 'Prologue in Heaven' to myself: 'The sun contends in age-old fashion . . . ,'" Arvid says, and wraps a second blanket around himself. "I think a lot about the enormity of nature. I feel so connected to it." He asks the pastor if he knows Goethe's "Primal Words — Orphic" by heart, and Poelchau, who has never been so happy for the fruits of his education, recites for him:

*As stood the sun to the salute of planets*
*Upon the day that gave you to the earth,*
*You grew forthwith, and prospered, in your growing*
*Heeded the law presiding at your birth.*
*Sibyls and prophets told it: You must be*
*None but yourself, from self you cannot flee.*
*No time there is, no power, can decompose*
*The minted form that lives and living grows.*

Arvid voices his wish to read the Christmas story from the Gospel of Luke together later that evening, a small before-Christmas celebration in memory of his childhood and his father, who died in 1914. The hanging, he comments, was a "personal slap in the face from Hitler." Then he adds that the soul of the German people under the National Socialist dictatorship was "leached out."

Arvid calmly writes his farewell letter. "But above all I think that humanity is on the ascendant," he writes.

# 43

It gets dark early this afternoon. The electric light pops on in cell after cell, and Block III seems like "a primordial beast with countless eyes" lying curled up, restless and half asleep. An old cobbler comes by and brings clogs for Harro. He must finally take off his blue sweater and exchange it for the beige prison uniform. The cobbler cuts Harro's hair short and handcuffs his hands behind his back. Next, one of the executioner's assistants comes to visit Harro to look in his mouth and see if there are any gold teeth.

## 44

Around six o'clock the pastor comes back to Arvid. They read from the Bible together:

> And it came to pass in those days, that there went out a decree from Caesar Augustus, that all the world should be taxed.
>
> (*And* this taxing was first made when Cyrenius was governor of Syria.)
>
> And all went to be taxed, every one into his own city.
>
> And Joseph also went up from Galilee, out of the city of Nazareth, into Judæa, unto the city of David, which is called Bethlehem; (because he was of the house and lineage of David:)
>
> To be taxed with Mary his espoused wife, being great with child.
>
> And so it was, that, while they were there, the days were accomplished that she should be delivered.
>
> And she brought forth her firstborn son, and wrapped him in swaddling clothes, and laid him in a manger; because there was no room for them in the inn.

By now Hans Coppi Jr. is three and a half weeks old.

## 45

The dark corridor of Block III has a door that leads out into the yard. It is only a few steps to the shed that stands in the middle of the complex, a windowless brick building with a cement floor, eight by ten meters. There's one door leading inside and another leading out to the morgue, where the wooden coffins are stacked and where each executed prisoner can be taken before the next comes through the front door.

A black curtain that can be opened and closed with a rope-and-pulley mechanism divides the shed. It moves gently in the faint draft that blows in when the door is opened and the hangman enters his place of work. Wilhelm Röttger lives on Waldstrasse in Moabit and runs a large carting business on the side. Usually executioners tend to come from the butchery trade, just as their assistants are often butcher's apprentices, but Röttger carries himself like a "finer gentleman." He wears a black tux, black top hat, and white gloves. He receives three thousand Reichsmarks a year for his work, plus sixty per execution, "a worthy remuneration for highly personalized services." He has to work hard for his money this time; he even had to pore over books and reports about the method of execution, which has been ordered for the first time and is new to him.

"*Heil Hitler!*" In the harsh light he raises his right arm with its white-gloved hand and takes his place with his three assistants in immediate proximity to the scaffold.

The black T-beam with its eight movable hooks spans the ceiling from one wall to the other. Five hooks are in position, the other three are pushed to the side. Sheets of black paper are hung between each hook to separate the condemned from one another. Every man dies alone.

In front of the T-beam, on the right side of the room, stands the guillotine and a willow basket.

A platform with four steps screens the back part of the room. Röttger plants himself on the top step. In his hands he holds a rope that ends in a loop on both ends.

# 46

At precisely seven o'clock Harro is led by two prison captains to the place of execution. A representative from the state prosecutor's office looks at him, confirms with his signature that he and the condemned are one and the same person. Then he decrees that the sentence of the Reich Court-Martial on December 19, 1942, be administered: "Executioner, perform your office."

The executioners' assistants take the place of the two prison captains. With a hard jerk on the pulley mechanism Röttger pulls open the black curtain. It makes a gnashing sound. Even those who have heard it before are chilled to the marrow.

Dear parents!
The time has now come. In a few hours I will leave this self be-

hind. I am completely calm and beg you also to take it with composure. There is so much at stake in the world today, one life coming to
an end isn't very much ... Everything I did, I did in accordance with
my mind, my heart, and my convictions, and within those bounds,
you, as my parents, must assume the best. This I beg of you! This
death is fitting for me. Somehow I always knew of it. It is "my own
death," as Rilke once wrote!

My heart grows heavy only when I think of you who are so dear
to me. (Libertas is close to me and shares my fate at the same hour!)
In what I demanded and what I wanted, however unclearly at times,
I was merely a forerunner. Believe, with me, that time is just, and will
bring everything to fruition!

To the last I think of the final look Father gave me. I think of my
dear sweet mother's tears at Christmas. These past months were necessary for me to grow so close to you. I, your lost son, have found
my way home to you, completely, after so much storm and stress, after going down so many paths that seemed foreign to you ... If you
were here, if you were invisible: You would see me laugh in the face
of death. I have long since overcome it. It is simply the normal thing
in Europe that thought should be sown with blood. It may be that we
were just a bunch of fools; but now, at the eleventh hour, I think one
has the right to a few private historical illusions.

Yes, and now I reach my hands out to you both and place here one
(a single) tear as seal and pledge of my love.

Your Harro

# 47

We are always searching, fatally, for the perfect person, in love as well as
in our writing of history. The saint who has no flaws, the ideal hero who is
faced with a challenge, is cleansed of his faults and transformed, and then,
when the time is right, enters into the struggle against evil for the common good, risking his life for the collective. But human reality is usually
more fragmentary.

"Use only the lines! Do not write in the margins!" Thus admonishes
the paper template for Libertas's farewell letter. Now the cobbler comes
by her cell too. He cuts her hair short too. Her hands too he binds behind
her back.

Everything she did she did not out of rational conviction but from a gut
feeling. This was what drove her, but the gut isn't as stable as the head; it

mulls, it seethes, it churns and sleeps. She vacillated; she was full of contradictions and weaknesses and never set down a clear written statement against National Socialism. This she left to others. She was a follower, first in the system, the exclusionary politics of which she benefited from, then in the resistance. But she changed her initially positive opinion of the regime and became active, proved that it was possible to take another stance, that it would be possible for anyone. And thus she found her freedom. She is Libertas.

> All the currents of my scattered life flow together, and all my wishes are fulfilled: I remain young in your memory. I no longer need to be apart from my Harro. I no longer need to suffer. I am permitted to die as Christ died: for the people! Whatever a person can experience in a lifetime, I was able to experience all of it and more. And — since no one ever dies before their task is fulfilled — so was I able, only in death, to arrive at this grand achievement that proceeds from the divide in my nature.
>
> For my final request I have asked that my "remains" be left to you. Bury them, if possible, in a beautiful place surrounded by sunny nature; I would ask for Liebenberg, but as I don't want to be separated from Horst and Harro, you parents will have to figure it out together.
>
> So, my dear, the hour tolls: Harro goes first, and I will be thinking of him. Then goes Horst, and I will be thinking of him. And Elisabetchen will be thinking of me, and love . . .
>
> In unending affection and joy — all strength and all light . . .

# 48

Then, at the very last, Libertas writes to Harro. They are lines that Pastor Poelchau brings to him, from her cell to his, and that she also — and this is why they have survived — encloses in a second letter to her mother with the note: "Harro's last sight of me."

> *You are more dear to me than life*
> *I pay the highest price*
> *I have nothing else to give, you see —*
> *And now you have the proof.*
> *We never need part again,*

*How beautiful this is, and grand!*
*Let us proudly call it freedom —*
*The spirit will live on.*

# 49

Tora zu Eulenburg, the daughter of Fürst Philipp, stays up late into the night at Castle Liebenberg putting together Christmas presents and a small Christmas tree for her daughter. The next morning, December 23, 1942, a cold, stormy winter's day without a single minute of sunshine, she sets out for Berlin. She was told there was a place where she could drop off Christmas presents for the prisoners. But when she arrives there isn't anyone there, just an officer who doesn't have a clue about anything. She heads to the jail at Kaiserdamm 1, where Libertas was held, and is again sent away with little explanation. Now she sets out for Prinz-Albrecht-Strasse, although on the phone she had been told that all those in charge were on Christmas vacation. But she manages to make it to the third floor, where Kommissar Alfred Göpfert and Gertrud Breiter are sitting in their office. They look at Tora zu Eulenburg, feeling uncomfortable and displeased. Göpfert says he no longer has anything to do with the case. The Oberstkriegsgerichtsrat was alone responsible for everything. But he wasn't there anymore.

In the phone book Tora looks up the private number for Dr. Manfred Roeder. The name indeed is listed — and he even picks up. But the Oberstkriegsgerichtsrat states coldly: "I will not tell you anything about the matter. No information whatsoever."

"Is there any way that I can get in touch with my daughter? It's Christmas."

"That isn't possible," he answers coldly.

"Is there no way for me to find out where my daughter is?"

"You'll hear something eventually," Roeder answers in a voice that cuts through her heart, and hangs up.

On Christmas Eve the fifty-six-year-old Tora takes the train back to Löwenberg, where a car picks her up at the train station and takes her to Liebenberg. She is broken. She can barely speak, and takes to her bed.

On December 26, Marie Luise Schulze looks up the Oberstkriegsgerichtsrat. After he has informed the horrified mother, without warning, of the death of her son Harro and her daughter-in-law Libertas, he forces her to sign a piece of paper compelling her to maintain complete silence about everything that has happened. Otherwise she and her husband, her daughter, Helga, and her son Hartmut are subject to the severest consequences.

Roeder refuses to release the remains or even the smallest token of remembrance. "The name of your son is to be expunged from human memory for all time," he says in conclusion. "This is an additional punishment."

# 50

Harro had reached an agreement with Heinrich Starck, the kapo for his cell block, a bricklayer by trade. Starck promised to secretly hide Harro's poem in a suitable place in the wall and seal it up so he could recover it after the war and hand it over to Harro's parents. And that's exactly what he does.

Thus Harro's poem survives, walled up in the Reich Main Security Office, along with the word that he changed on his last night. In summer 1945, after the National Socialist regime has fallen, it is recovered from the ruins of the former Gestapo headquarters and delivered to his parents.

> ~~Bullet~~ Hangman's rope and guillotine
> Won't have the final say.
> The _world_ will be our judges,
> Not the judges of _today_.

# EPILOGUE:
# RESTITUTIO MEMORIAE

There are times, it is true, when madness reigns.
And days when the best heads are those that hang.

— ALBRECHT HAUSHOFER, EXECUTED ON APRIL 23, 1945

# 1

An assistant from the University of Berlin's Anatomical Institute was present at the executions on December 22, 1942. He placed the bodies in wooden coffins and transported them in a specially outfitted truck to Charité, the largest hospital in Berlin and one of the largest university clinics in Europe.

Hermann Stieve, for many years the head of the Anatomical Institute, sought out primarily the younger women, from whom, late that night or early the morning after the executions, he removed tissue samples and examined them for his research. The men's bodies were used as cadavers for students to perform autopsies on.

Libertas's final wish to be laid to rest in Liebenberg was not fulfilled. The relatives were prohibited from burying the bodies of their loved ones. There was to be nothing left to preserve their memory; they were not even granted their right to peace in death. After the removal of tissue samples and the autopsies, the mortal remains were taken to the Zehlendorf crematorium. Where the ashes were taken has yet to be determined.

In 2019, seventy-six years after the executions, Stieve's descendants found artifacts from his research in the attic of the family home. These preserved tissue remains were handed over to the relatives of the victims. Among them was Hans Coppi, who was able to have these remains buried in Berlin's Dorotheenstädtischer Cemetery, in a ceremony presided over by a Catholic priest, a Protestant pastor, and a Jewish rabbi. Thus, finally, some of the victims — and their relatives — were able to find some peace.

## 2

I do not know the endpoint of the path you chose to follow, maybe it was still unclear even to you; maybe you would have found it if you had wandered longer and more patiently. But you followed it bravely and fearlessly to the bitter end. Some fire that burned within you consumed you quickly. No one, now that you are dead, shall slander or speak ill of you in my presence. No one shall tear my love for you out of my heart. For you the words were spoken: "In the world ye shall have tribulation: but be of good cheer; I have overcome the world."

I meanwhile call out to you in your unknown grave to say something that once, perhaps, you wouldn't have understood, but that in the end you felt most deeply: "Love never faileth!"

E.E.

## 3

In June 1943 the sailing club Blau-Rot receives a visit from men in ill-fitting suits. The *Duschinka*, Harro and Libertas's sailboat, is inspected, but judged worthless by the Gestapo. Their reason: "Hull completely rotten." The following inventory is taken: "1 sail with mast (sail severely tattered), 1 rudder, and the floor boards." The head of the Charlottenburg-West financial office places his stamp on the document and it is sent to the estate assessor's office, a division of the Ministry of Finance created in 1941 with the main purpose of appraising and selling off the possessions of dispossessed Jews.

For twenty Reichsmarks Horst Kopkow makes off with the crockery from Altenburger Allee 19. Harro's officer's pants, his topcoat, his peaked cap, and the short dagger with holster as well as his sword knot go to the army attire office. Over the course of this war that will last another two and a half years, they will be used by other men. The twenty-four-horsepower "Fiat-Cabrio-Limousine" is also confiscated; the estate assessor's office for

246

Berlin-Brandenburg is free to dispose of Caesar, which once drove to Venice and then back to Kristallnacht in Berlin.

A police officer, Kriminalrat and SS-Hauptsturmführer Dr. Werner Gornickel, moves into the apartment at Altenburger Allee 19. He is responsible for a monthly rent of 123 Reichsmarks. He keeps some of the furniture, sits at the desk where Harro once sat. Harro's typewriter, a 1925 Remington Portable, is bought by a man from Berlin-Wilmersdorf.

# 4

The execution victims of December 22, 1942, are just the beginning. On February 16, after being retried, Mildred Harnack climbs the scaffold. Pastor Poelchau records the American's last words: "And I loved Germany so much." This is what she says, the once radiant blond woman, whose hair is now white and who in her cell on death row translated the last lines from Goethe's "Testament" into English. Among her registered effects is a ticket for ship's passage to the United States, valid for any date, a present from Arvid. A gift she never got to use.

Erika von Brockdorff's case is also retried, with the same result.

On May 13, 1943, the dentist Helmut Himpel, the toolmakers Walter Husemann and Karl Behrens, the gifted linguist Wilhelm Guddorf, the psychologist Dr. John Rittmeister, the soldier and aspiring poet Heinz Strelow, the anarchist substitute teacher Friedrich Rehmer, the precision engineer Fritz Thiel, the writer Walter Küchenmeister, the sinologist Dr. Philipp Schaeffer, and Erika von Brockdorff are beheaded.

On July 21 of the same year, Hitler refuses fifteen requests for stays of execution, thirteen of them for women.

On August 5 the guillotine claims the writer Dr. Adam Kuckhoff, the philologist Ursula Goetze, the musically gifted lawyer Maria Terwiel, the dancer and sculptor Oda Schottmüller, the secretary Rose Schlösinger, the young mother Hilde Coppi, the student Eva-Maria Buch, the fortuneteller Annie Krauss, the ceramicist Cato Bontjes van Beek, the high school student Liane Berkowitz, the milling-machine operator Stanislaus Werolek, the eighty-one-year-old furniture dealer Emil Hübner, and the stenographer Klara Schnabel. On September 9, the actor Wilhelm Schürmann-Horster is also murdered in Plötzensee.

The physician Dr. Elfriede Paul, the writer Günther Weisenborn, the librarian Lotte Schleif, the university teacher Werner Krauss, the historian Heinrich Scheel, the Heidelberg publisher Marcel Melliand, the actor

Marta Husemann, and Greta Kuckhoff receive prison sentences and live to see the end of the Nazi dictatorship.

Marie Luise and Erich Edgar Schulze celebrate their sixtieth wedding anniversary in 1968. Harro's mother dies in 1973, his father in 1974.

# 5

What happened in the past is constantly evading attempts to pin it down. The transcript of the trial of Harro and Libertas was destroyed, likewise their Gestapo interrogation transcripts. One of the defense attorneys assigned to the proceedings, Dr. Behse, testifies after the war that all records of the trial before the Reich Court-Martial were shamefully destroyed by officials. In this way the Nazi regime meant to perpetuate the "Secret Reich Matter" designation. The hail of bombs in which so many files burned took care of the rest.

After the war both East and West seized hold of the legend of a cell of Soviet agents in the heart of Berlin — a legend created by Horst Kopkow for thirty thousand Reichsmarks — and bent it to fit their own respective ideologies. In the Ministry for State Security — home of the Stasi — and at KGB headquarters a heroic tale was cobbled together, centered around a so-called scout unit that fought the imperial evil from the heart of the Nazi capital in the name of world peace and socialism, guided of course by the canny headquarters in Moscow. In the East the loose network was known until 1966 as the Schulze-Boysen-Harnack Resistance Group, and after 1966 as the Schulze-Boysen-Harnack Resistance Organization. Harro was celebrated as a hero; he, along with Arvid Harnack, Adam Kuckhoff, and John Graudenz, was posthumously awarded the Order of the Red Banner by the Soviet government — the highest medal in the "Great Patriotic War." Harro had streets named after him, Berlin-Lichtenberg is still home to the Mildred Harnack Secondary School, and Berlin-Karlshorst to the Hans and Hilde Coppi High School. A torpedo boat of the East German navy, the *Arvid Harnack,* once sped over the torpid waves of the Baltic Sea — maybe all the way to the Curonian Spit.

In the West there wasn't any interest in a genuine investigation either. When Harro's brother, Hartmut Schulze-Boysen, who pursued a diplomatic career and worked in the West German embassies in Tokyo, Bucharest, and the United States, appealed to Chancellor Helmut Kohl in the 1980s with the question of whether Harro shouldn't finally be included in Germany's culture of collective memory, the chancellor's office wrote back with a snide reply saying that all resistance fighters "deserve our respect. When we ask however what it is we must build on . . . then the idea of a state founded on the rule of law must be reckoned as the legacy of the resistance." As if Harro, the proud Prussian, would have had any objection to this. Only in 2006 did Hartmut Schulze-Boysen manage to have the verdict of the trial before the Reich Court-Martial on December 19, 1942, nullified.

Thus the nuanced reality of the group that never gave itself a name — a group that didn't fail as a result of its own actions, but rather as a result of a mistake made by the supposed pros in Moscow — was distorted even as its memory was handed down. Professor Johannes Tuchel, head of the German Resistance Memorial Center in Berlin, speaks of a "baffling similarity" in the reception on both sides of the Iron Curtain. The memory of the very people who advocated for a reconciliation between East and West was ground up between the two blocks on either side of the Cold War.

After 1945, Dr. Manfred Roeder, the "bloodhound," worked with the U.S. Army Counterintelligence Corps, a precursor to the CIA. He told the intelligence-hungry Americans that the "Red Orchestra" still existed and was working for Moscow. Under the code name *Othello,* the Counterintelligence Corps mined Roeder for stories, trying to learn as much from him as possible about the Soviets' intelligence agency. A trial brought against the retired Oberstkriegsgerichtsrat by Greta Kuckhoff, Adolf Grimme, Günther Weisenborn, and others in the years right after the war was dismissed in 1951: here he was saved by an old boys' network of former Nazis like himself, who still had a lot of say in the young Federal Republic.

Horst Kopkow, until May 1945 responsible for the torture and death of countless allied agents and German resistance fighters, likewise suffered few consequences for his actions. He was questioned about his methods for combating Soviet espionage by MI6, the British intelligence agency, given immunity from potential prosecution, and in June 1948 was even declared dead so that shortly thereafter he could return to the Federal Republic of Germany with falsified papers. There he called himself Peter Cordes and continued to work for MI6.

Friedrich Panzinger, former head of the special commission *Rote Kapelle,* was arrested in October 1946 by the Austrian authorities in Linz, handed over to the Soviet Union, and sentenced there to twenty-five years of hard labor. In 1955 he was released to the Federal Republic of Germany in connection with Chancellor Konrad Adenauer's efforts to secure the release of German prisoners of war. Afterward he served in the newly founded German intelligence agency, the Bundesnachrichtendienst.

Johannes Strübing, Kopkow's deputy and Harro's interrogator, was also an in-demand source for Western spy agencies and found a job in the 1950s with the newly founded Verfassungsschutz — Germany's domestic intelligence agency — as an expert on the "Red Orchestra."

The trail of the other protagonists gets lost in the fog. What became of Stella Mahlberg? Could she have been something more than a minor character? Her arrest and release from Gestapo custody were undated, unlike every other person arrested, more than 150 in all. She remains the phantom with the raven-black hair. She goes to Stuttgart and keeps a low profile until in 1947 she is interrogated there by the Counterintelligence Corps — and in the course of these interrogations dies. My request for information from the FBI under the Freedom of Information Act brought no further details to light. The National Archives in Washington couldn't help either: "We were unable to locate a file pertaining to Stella Mahlberg . . . It is possible that you are seeking a file that no longer exists." For some things the explanation is simply lost.

# 6

In Plötzensee, a few minutes by car on the way to Tegel Airport from Kurfürstendamm, Berlin's major boulevard, a somewhat hard-to-find memorial is located today. The iron beam hangs, unchanged, from the ceiling of the spare execution shed. A drain in the floor, around which the cement is still lightly discolored, shows where the blood flowed.

It is a lonely room, but still it is never completely silent. As if from a great distance comes the clatter of typewriters: the black ones the Gestapo used, with a special key for the SS rune insignia; the dark green Soviet models with Cyrillic letters; but also the beloved American Remingtons that belonged to Harro and Libertas, to Adam Kuckhoff, Mildred and Arvid Harnack, Dr. John Rittmeister, Werner Krauss, Günther Weisenborn, John Graudenz, and all the others, who wrote constantly, feverishly, and together composed this story of the German resistance, a story that has been fought over like few others.

# ACKNOWLEDGMENTS

I thank Hans Coppi, who attended this project with great trust and helped me to find my way around the complex subject. I express my heartfelt gratitude for all his research and inspiration and all his time and patience in answering my questions. It is to all of those who, because their closest relatives were a part of it, have the most direct connection to this story, that I owe the most thanks: Karin Reetz, the daughter of John Graudenz, who provided me with homemade cherry pie and relevant information; Eva Schulze-Boysen, who visited me in my writer's tower, bearing such a resemblance to her uncle Harro that it was as if he himself were in the room; Regina Schulze-Boysen, who crucially helped supplement her sister's information at a meeting in Goa; Stefan Roloff, who showed me the briefcase in which his father, Helmut, the concert pianist who was so fond of playing Mozart, carried *Concern for Germany's Future Is Spreading Among the People*. Christian Weisenborn was also incalculably helpful, allowing me access to the unpublished private diary of his father, which no historian has yet been able to draw on. My heartfelt thanks for your trust!

I especially thank Dr. Geertje Andresen, whose help with the research was incalculable. The discovery of details about Gisela von Poellnitz in the German Federal Archives is entirely the result of her efforts. I also wish to give kudos to the German Resistance Memorial Center, where I found an ideal place for researching and working, and which supported me with the use of photographic material. I would like to thank Professor Leiserowitz, who was able to tell me a great deal about Jewish refugees on the Curonian Spit. In this connection kudos as well to Silke Kettelhake for her book about Libertas.

As for my loyal test readers, I am in this case particularly indebted to Roland Zag, who helped set me on the right course at a crucial time. I don't want to forget the literary team without whom this book would not exist: my agents Andrew Nurnberg and Robin Straus, my editor Alex Littlefield, and my translators Tim Mohr and Marshall Yarbrough, who handled this rather monumental task in stride.

I would also like to thank Nuri and Demian from the bottom of my heart — simply for being there. And finally, I thank my late grandfather for the story he told me in the garden of the Morgensonne house. Maybe that was the start of everything.

# NOTES

## PROLOGUE

page

xxi  *"Concerning your request"*: Erich Edgar Schulze Papers, Red Orchestra Collection
(hereafter RK), German Resistance Memorial Center (hereafter GDW).
*Sir Neville Henderson*: Cf. Henderson, *Failure of a Mission — Berlin 1937–1939*, 288.

xxiii  *"Now more than ever!"*: Ingeborg Engelsing-Kohler, "Erinnerungen an Harro und Libertas Schulze-Boysen" (Memories of Harro and Libertas Schulze-Boysen), RK, GDW.

xxiv  *"I don't wish to destroy"*: Ibid.
*Initially, the dictatorship*: Malek-Kohler, *Im Windschatten des Dritten Reiches. Begegnun-
gen mit Künstlern und Widerstandskämpfern*, 181.
*She's revised her opinion*: Ingeborg Engelsing-Kohler, "Erinnerungen an Harro und
Libertas Schulze-Boysen" (Memories of Harro and Libertas Schulze-Boysen), RK,
GDW, 5.

## 1. ADVERSARIES

3  *"ready at any moment"*: Arnold Bauer, "Erinnerungen an Harro Schulze-Boysen"
(Memories of Harro Schulze-Boysen), RK 37/67, GDW, 1.

4  *no longer seem to represent*: Harro Schulze-Boysen, "Randbemerkungen," *Gegner* vol.
9, December 1932, 2: "The style of their meetings, their symbols, their structure and
their historical development — everything places them on the side of the dying."
*"Europe was the clock"*: Schulze-Boysen, "Gegner von heute — Kampfgenossen von
morgen," 7.
*"The communist party"*: Harro Schulze-Boysen to Marie Luise Schulze, February 25,
1932, ED 335/1, Institute for Contemporary History (hereafter IfZ), Munich.

5  *"big city disease"*: A. Bomhoff, "Begegnungen mit Harro Schulze-Boysen" (Encounters
with Harro Schulze-Boysen), RK, GDW, 3.
*Harro knows the crowd*: Cf. Hans Coppi, "Besuch bei Helga Mulachie, Schwester von
Harro Schulze-Boysen" (Visit with Helga Mulachie, sister of Harro Schulze-Boysen),
Venice, end of June 1989, RK, GDW, 18.
*shake hands*: Bauer, "Erinnerungen" (Recollections), RK 37/67, GDW.

6  *"ardent German"*: Hans Coppi, conversation with Werner Dissel, 1 July 1987, 22.
*"the German cause"*: Harro Schulze-Boysen to Alfred von Tirpitz, 12 August 1929, ED
335/1, IfZ Munich.

7  *"public contradictory debate nights"*: *Gegner*, March 1932, Berlin, 2: "In the future, *Der
Gegner* will host a meeting on the 20th of every month (at 8:30 p.m.) in order to

give those readers interested in participating the opportunity to debate and further develop the lines of thought dealt with here in-person (occasionally with the authors themselves). These are meant to become public contradictory debate nights."

*The meetings quickly:* For example, in Frankfurt am Main, Darmstadt, Wiesbaden, Offenbach, Heidelberg, Mannheim, Homburg, Stuttgart, Karlsruhe, Saarbrücken, Innsbruck, and Leipzig.

*"Young people who"*: "Ptx ruft Moskau," *Der Spiegel,* June 17, 1968, 103.

*"invisible alliance"*: Harro Schulze-Boysen, "Der neue Gegner," *Gegner,* vol. 4, March 5, 1932.

*"A people divided"*: Harro Schulze-Boysen, "Die Saboteure der Revolution," *Gegner,* February 2, 1933. He continues: "People will come and ask which party we serve, which agenda we are pushing. We serve no party . . . We have no agenda. We know no rigid truths. The only thing that is sacred to us is life, the only thing we consider valuable is movement."

*"The crust"*: Salomon, *Der Fragebogen,* 357.

8    *From the hall:* Klaus Jedzek, "Einer ist tot. Für Harro Schulze-Boysen" (One of us is dead. For Harro Schulze-Boysen), RK, GDW, 3.

    *"fairly crazy piece"*: Harro to his parents, (early February 1932), ED 335/1, IfZ Munich.

    *"Every person feels inspired"*: Harro to his mother, 23 May 1932, ED 335/1, IfZ Munich.

    *"the discussions between fish and roast"*: Salomon, *Der Fragebogen,* 182.

    *"never more alive"*: Harro to his parents, 8 June 1932, ED 335/1, IfZ Munich.

    *"The Gegner is gaining"*: Harro to his parents, 26 August 1932, ED 335/1, IfZ Munich.

9    *"It must be shattered in pieces"*: Fröhlich, *Die Tagebücher von Joseph Goebbels.,* vols. 2 and 3.

10   *"O, you, my Liebenberg"*: Eulenburg, *Libertas Schulze-Boysen.*

12   *"Hitler is chancellor!"*: Turel, *Bilanz eines erfolglosen Lebens,* 266.

13   *"For goodness sake"*: Ibid.

    *"I'll lead the battle"*: Hans Coppi, "Nachdenken über Libertas Schulze-Boysen" (Thoughts on Libertas Schulze-Boysen). Speech given at the memorial celebration for the 100th birthday of Libertas Schulze-Boysen, Liebenberg, November 17, 2003.

    *"an abundance of brilliant ideas"*: Fürst Eulenburg-Hertefeld, notes and letter, Militärarchiv N 239/83, Bundesarchiv; also printed in Kurt Gossweiler and Alfred Schlicht, "Junker und NSDAP 1931/32," *Zeitschrift fur Geschichtswissenschaft* 15, no. 4 (1967): 644–62.

14   *"Completely convinced"*: Harro to his parents, 17 February 1933, ED 335/1, IfZ Munich.

    *"The first two weeks"*: *Gegner,* 15 February 1933, 2.

16   *"because those who"*: Hans Coppi, conversation with Werner Dissel, 28.

    *"interrogated by subordinate"*: Ibid.

    *"If I end up in prison"*: Harro to his mother, February/March 1933, ED 335/1, IfZ Munich.

    *"deliberate appraisal"*: Police report AD II 4 on the structure and activities of the group *Gegner*: "Zeitschrift für neue Einheit," 16 March 1933, St 22/165, Bundesarchiv, Potsdam branch.

    *"friendly, well-informed, engaged"*: Hans Coppi, conversation with Werner Dissel, 21.

    *"An officer stood up:* Ibid.

17   *"but he missed"*: Harro to his brother Hartmut, February 1933, ED 335/1, IfZ Munich.

    *"The association isn't composed"*: Police report AD II 4.

18   *On one of the last:* Werner Dissel, "Bericht über Harro Schulze-Boysen" (Report on Harro Schulze-Boysen), RK, GDW, 21.

"One night": Ibid.

"Just released": Harro to his parents, 4 March 1933, ED 335/1, IfZ Munich.

19 It takes them hours: Coppi, Harro Schulze-Boysen — Wege in den Widerstand, 122.

20 This is SS-District III: Cf. SS-Abschnitt III, Abtlg. Hilfspolizeikommando to Harro Schulze-Boysen, 19 May 1933, ED 335/2, IfZ Munich.

"the eternal assistant director": Hans Coppi, conversation with Werner Dissel, 1 July 1987, RK, GDW, 4. Cf. Klaus Jedzek, "Einer ist tot. Für Harro Schulze-Boysen" (One of us is dead. For Harro Schulze-Boysen), RK, GDW, 5.

21 "shut up": Turel, Bilanz eines erfolglosen Lebens, 259, 264–65.

"Is there a Turel here?": Elsa Schulze-Boysen, Harro Schulze-Boysen — Das Bild eines Freiheitskämpfers, 6.

22 "We saw it": Regine Schütt, "50 years later. The way I saw it," RK, GDW.

She's convinced: Ibid.

23 is attending: Marie Luise Schulze, "Warum ich 1933 in die NSDAP eingetreten bin" (Why I joined the Nazi Party in 1933), 14 February 1966, RK, GDW, 3. Subsequent quotes in this passage all ibid.

"between Potsdamer Platz": Marie Luise and Erich Edgar Schulze to the Betreuungsstelle für politisch Geschädigte (care center for political victims), Mülheim, 13 December 1946, RK, GDW.

24 "it wouldn't be": Hans Coppi, conversation with Hartmut Schulze-Boysen, August 1989, RK, GDW, 2.

25 But Harro is: Werner Dissel, "Bericht über Harro Schulze-Boysen" (Report on Harro Schulze-Boysen), RK, GDW, 26.

26 "report this crime": Marie Luise Schulze, 3.

"We've heard": Ibid., 4.

28 "Erlanger's barbarous murderers": Ibid., 6.

"We have terrific income in Germany": Ben Urwand, The Collaboration: Hollywood's Pact with Hitler (Cambridge: Belknap Press, 2013), 74. The beginnings of Hollywood's submitting to the swastika lie in the Weimar Republic, with the film adaptation of All Quiet on the Western Front, the international bestseller by Erich Maria Remarque. The film appeared in theaters shortly before Christmas 1930 and was later awarded an Oscar; it shows the horrors of World War I, taking as its subject the senselessness of death at the front. For the first large screening in Berlin, the Nazis bought three hundred tickets and started booing the screen when French troops were shown fighting successfully against the German army. "German soldiers were brave!" someone in the crowd screamed: "An outrage, that such a film could be made in America!" When the interruptions didn't stop, the projectionist stopped the projector and turned on the lights. Goebbels, already head of propaganda for the Nazis, stood up from his seat in the balcony and gave a speech in which he claimed that the film had only been made to ruin Germany's reputation in the world. Once he was finished, his men threw stink bombs in the aisles and set loose white mice they had brought with them in cages. Six days later, when the furor against this "unpatriotic film" still hadn't ceased, the distributor pulled it. Carl Laemmle, head of Universal, ordered that the film be recut, and in summer 1931 a sanitized version of the film went to theaters. Satisfied, Goebbels commented, "We brought them to their knees!"

29 "we have terrific income in Germany": Ibid.

31 "He stopped me": Salomon, Der Fragbogen.

They set the chairs: Werner Dissel, "Bericht über Harro Schulze-Boysen" (Report on Harro Schulze-Boysen), RK, GDW, 27.

"explosive aimed": Ibid., 28.
"the long march": Ibid., 2.

# 2. WORK AND MARRIAGE

36    are a bunch of aspiring: Cf. Herbert Schidlowsky to Günther Weisenborn, RK 1/4, GDW.
      "cowardice rules": Harro to his parents, 31 May 1933, ED 335/1, IfZ Munich.
      "You can do": Harro to his sister Helga, 9 October 1933, ED 335/1, IfZ Munich.
37    "Already 50% of": Harro to his mother, 25 July, 1933, ED 335/1, IfZ Munich.
      "not top-class": Harro to his mother, 21 September, 1933, ED 335/1, IfZ Munich.
38    "Yes, the last": Harro to his father, 3 September 1933, ED 335/1, IfZ Munich.
      "I'm appalled": Ibid.
      "intellectual matters": Harro to his mother, 25 July 1933, ED 335/1, IfZ Munich.
      "The hair on top": Ibid.
      "I sit here": Harro to his father, 5 August, 1933, ED 335/1, IfZ Munich.
39    "All in all": Harro to his father, 15 September 1933, ED 335/1, IfZ Munich.
      "To fly is a pure": Harro to his sister, 9 October 1933, ED 335/1, IfZ Munich.
      "I have the vague": Harro to his father, 15 September 1933, ED 335/1, IfZ Munich.
40    "sea of hypocrisy": Harro to his sister, 9 October 1933, ED 335/1, IfZ Munich.
41    "grandest and largest": Harro to his father, 3 September 1933, ED 335/1, IfZ Munich.
      "I'm convinced": Harro to Adrien Turel, early November 1933, ED 335/1, IfZ Munich.
43    Leaded-glass windows: Roloff, Die Rote Kapelle, 74.
      he's being watched: Cf. Falk Harnack, "1. Besuch bei Arvid Harnack am 26.10.1942" (First visit with Arvid Harnack on 26 October 1942), RK 32/55, GDW.
      "The relevant Commissar": Harro to his parents, 6 December 1933, ED 335/1, IfZ Munich.
44    "I could have": Harro to his parents, Easter 1934, ED 335/1, IfZ Munich.
      always lift his right arm: "Fragebogen betr. Einstellung von Angestellten und Arbeitern im R.L.M." (Form re: hiring of employees and workers in the RLM), Reichsgesetzblatt I, RK, GDW, 679.
      "downright touching effort": Harro to his parents, 4 April 1934 and 19 July 1934, ED 335/1, IfZ Munich.
      And his job: Harro to his parents, Easter 1934, ED 335/1, IfZ Munich.
      the poor wages: Harro to his parents, 15 May 1934, ED 335/1, IfZ Munich.
      "earthly goods": Harro to his sister, 9 October 1933, ED 335/1, IfZ Munich.
      having virtually no life: Harro to his parents, 15 May 1934 and 7 August 1934, ED 335/1, IfZ Munich.
45    this valuable time: Cf. Coppi, Harro Schulze-Boysen: Wege in den Widerstand, 146.
      "One is hired": Harro to his parents, 15 May 1934, ED 335/1, IfZ Munich. The following two quotes ibid.
      "shoved together": Harro to his sister, 1 May 1934, ED 335/1, IfZ Munich.
46    "Hitler's speech": Ibid.
      "The political atmosphere": Harro to his father, (Summer 1934), ED 335/1, IfZ Munich.
48    "Röhm, you're under arrest": "Röhm Putsch," Wikipedia, http://de.wikipedia.org/wiki/Röhm-Putsch.
      "calm and always funny": Harro to his parents, 19 July 1934, ED 335/1, IfZ Munich.
51    "the warm July night": Poem by Libertas, 1 August 1934, GDW, RK.

"eat real Chinese": Harro to his parents, 11 September 1937, ED 335/1, IfZ Munich.

"She can't do": Harro to his parents, 19 July 1934, ED 335/1, IfZ Munich.

52   "I have to hang": Ibid.

54   "The same people": Harro to his parents, 16 July 1935, ED 335/1, IfZ Munich.

also drums, a giant gong: Regina Schulze-Boysen, conversation with author, 1 February 2019, Goa, India. This conversation also provided countless additional details from the lives of Marie Luise and Erich Edgar.

55   "family home": Harro to his parents, January 1936, ED 335/1, IfZ Munich.

Harro's parents: Eva Schulze-Boysen, conversation with author, 17 November 2018, Berlin; Regina Schulze-Boysen, conversation with author, 1 February 2019.

56   the nation would benefit: Hans Coppi, "Besuch bei Helga Mulachie, Schwester von Harro Schulze-Boysen" (Visit with Helga Mulachie, sister of Harro Schulze-Boysen), Venice, end of June 1989, RK, GDW, 12. The rug story ibid.

"Jewish mouth": Ibid., 20.

"As long as": Harro to his mother, 27 July 1935, ED 335/1, IfZ Munich. The following quote also ibid.

"If Libs spends": Harro to his parents, 26 January 1936, ED 335/1, IfZ Munich.

57   "On Sunday morning": Harro to his parents, 10 July 1936, ED 335/1, IfZ Munich; also published in Coppi and Andresen, Dieser Tod passt zu mir — Harro Schulze-Boysen, 220.

"nice and atmospheric": Harro to his mother, 16 June 1936, ED 335/1, IfZ Munich.

the Liebenberg cellar: Cf. Tora von Eulenburg to Marie Luise Schulze, 17 August 1936, GDW, RK.

59   "The women wear": Salomon, Der Fragebogen, 397.

The display cases: Ibid., 376.

60   the five-meter-high: Nakagawa, "Das Reichsluftfahrtministerium — Bauliche Modifikationen und politische Systeme," 18.

61   Harro urges his friend: Werner Dissel, "Bericht über Harro Schulze-Boysen" (Report on Harro Schulze-Boysen), RK, GDW, 27.

62   He's a distant: Harro to his mother, 21 August 1936, ED 335/1, IfZ Munich.

63   "As the son": Werner Bartz to the Wehrbezirkskommando Berlin IX, 5 August 1937, GDW, RK.

64   After the Reich Minister: Hans Coppi, conversation with Frau von Schönebeck, 15 April 1989, GDW, RK, 8.

65   Göring nods: Coppi, Wege in den Widerstand, 147.

"Wonderful, even enchanting": Libertas to Marie Luise Schulze, 23 April 1936, ED 335/1, IfZ Munich.

Especially promising: Ibid.

"scared of the style": Libertas to Marie Luise Schulze, 29 April 1936; Libertas to Marie Luise Schulze, 23 April 1936, ED 335/1, IfZ Munich.

"We are both": Libertas to Marie Luise Schulze, 29 April 1936, ED 335/1, IfZ Munich.

66   "The little crystals": Harro to his brother Hartmut, undated, RK, GDW. The following two quotes ibid.

"not as fiery": Ibid. Cf. Hans Coppi, "Bericht über die Reise in die BRD vom 28.9.-3.10.1989," first conversation with Hartmut Schulze-Boysen, RK, GDW, 3.

"A bit of": Ibid.

"It goes without saying": Libertas to the Reichsleitung der NSDAP München, 12 January 1937, RK, GDW.

67   "bohemian in a truly": Salomon, Der Fragebogen, 398.

"A nice picnic": Harro to his parents, 24 February 1937, ED 335/1, IfZ Munich.

"overcome the negative": Harro to his parents, 9 December 1937, ED 335/1, IfZ Munich.

Some of the guests: Hans Coppi, conversation with Vera and Wolfgang Rittmeister, 1990, RK, GDW, 2.

68    "At the same time": Werner Dissel, "Jour Fixe 1936," GDW, RK, 1.

During the interrogation: "Zur Sache," R/3017, Archivnr. 5574, Bundesarchiv, 14.

"gothic verse": Ibid., 24, 30.

"Granting her a license": Berlin Chief of Police, 6 April 1937, R/30171, Archivnr. 5574, Bundesarchiv, 2.

Gisela von Poellnitz: "Zur Sache," 13.

usually does so alone: Her brother's testimony, 18 February 1938, Bundesarchiv.

She's been to Scotland: Ibid.

traveled frequently to London: Cf. Paul, Ein Sprechzimmer der Roten Kapelle, 107–8.

69    She's a mysterious: Fechter, An der Wende der Zeit: Menschen und Begegnungen, 288.

Klaus Mann describes Oda as "grotesque and highly talented, with a curiously short, Mongolian face, [who] loves to perch on dressers or windowsills, picturesquely folded into herself. She could perform fantastic and wild dances; she could draw and paint just as fantastically and wildly. On her canvases, phantoms rose out of bottles, snakes wound around gnarled trees . . . Often [she had a] silent sadness, often she was bouncing up and down, wanting to dance." (Mann, Kind dieser Zeit, 147; quoted in Andresen, Oda Schottmüller — Die Tänzerin, Bildhauerin und Nazigegnerin, 50.)

the Grand State Prize: Werner Dissel, "Bericht über Harro Schulze-Boysen" (Report on Harro Schulze-Boysen), RK, GDW, 29.

a commission for the door carvings: Ibid., 37.

Harro gives a Karneval: Herbert Dahl, "Bericht über meine Beziehungen zu Harro Schulze-Boysen" (Report on my connections with Harro Schulze-Boysen), RK, GDW. Cf. Coppi, Wege in den Widerstand, 184.

70    normal social contact: Hans Coppi, Wege in den Widerstand, 276; Werner Dissel, "Bericht über Harro Schulze-Boysen" (Report on Harro Schulze-Boysen), RK, GDW, 29.

normal social contact: Werner Dissel, "Bericht über Harro Schulze-Boysen" (Report on Harro Schulze-Boysen), RK, GDW, 29.

"cleverly disguised communist": Personal Staff Reichsführer-SS to the Main Office of the Sicherheitspolizei, 3 June 1937. Cf. Hans Coppi, Wege in den Widerstand, 185.

"cultural Bolshevist activities": Ibid.

"reconnaissance about military": Werner Dissel, "Erinnerung an Begegnung mit Harro Schulze-Boysen im RLM" (Recollection of a meeting with Harro Schulze-Boysen at the RLM), 24 November 1988, RK, GDW, 3.

71    He knows how: Ibid., along with the quotes to follow here.

"Yeah, I should have": Ibid.

72    "the personal wish": Brief biography of Harro Schulze-Boysen, late fall, 1936, ED 335/1, IfZ Munich.

detailed reports: Harro to his parents, 12 September 1936, ED 335/1, IfZ Munich.

"The Spanish atrocities": Harro to his parents, 6 September 1936, ED 335/1, IfZ Munich.

73    "in Moscow": Harro to his parents, 12 September 1935, ED 335/1, IfZ Munich.

74    the postbox of: "Akte Korsikanez" (Korsikanez file), Archive of the Foreign Intelligence Service, Moscow, No. 34118, vol. 1, RK, GDW, 220. Hans Coppi, the son of the identically named friend of Harro's, traveled in the early 1990s, during the perestroika era, to Moscow. There, after several attempts, he managed to get ahold of a volume of documents that had been previously made available to historians. With it he was able

to look at materials from the Soviet intelligence services — sensitive files that in the Putin era have once again been sealed.

"*The young lad*": Libertas to Harro, 11 November 1937, RK, GDW.

75 "*Later it might*": Harro to his parents, 23 October 1937, ED 335/1, IfZ Munich.

"*the current just brings*": Harro to his mother, 13 October 1937, ED 335/1, IfZ Munich. The previous quote also.

76 *Often she thinks*: Libertas to Harro, 21 October 1937, RK, GDW.

"*When it comes to*": Ibid.

"*How I sense*": Libertas to Harro, 1 November 1937, RK, GDW.

77 "*If you're opposed*": Weisenborn, *Memorial*, 15–16, for the whole sequence.

*Accompanied by her mother*: Libertas to Marie Luise and Erich Edgar Schulze, 21 December 1937, GDW, RK.

"*The decrees of the Secretary*": Harro to his parents, 27 December 1937, ED 335/1, IfZ Munich.

78 *Libertas takes him*: Ibid.

"*that there is but one thing*": Ibid.

"*a little run*": Ibid., the following three quotes as well.

"*I read in front*": Günther Weisenborn, 20 January 1938, private diaries, vol. 13, Christian Weisenborn private collection.

79 "*for a very long and wonderful time*": Ibid., 27 January 1938.

"*Rented two rooms*": Ibid., 10 January and 2 February 1938.

*At ten-thirty in the morning*: "Zur Sache," R/3017, Archive no. 5574, Bundesarchiv, 16.

80 *they've secured documents*: In all, seventeen documents are seized, for example "The Aeroplane, Der technische Stand der britischen Luftwaffe" (The Aeroplane, the technological state of the British air force), 12 May 1937, or "United Services Review," 18 March 1937: "Luftkrieg über Spanien" (Air war over Spain). Cf. "Nachweisung der sichergestellten Gegenstände" (Proof of confiscated items), Durchsuchungsbericht Geheimes Staatspolizeiamt (Search report, Secret State Police Headquarters), 17 February 1938, R/3017, Archive no. 5574, Bundesarchiv.

"*I followed Harro's car*": Weisenborn, *Memorial*, 15.

"*The translation materials found*": "Zur Sache," Bundesarchiv, 31.

"*I can't cross the border*": "Akten des Oberreichskriegsanwaltes in der Strafsache gegen den Professor Gefr Dr. Werner Krauss wg Landesverrats" (Files of the Oberreichskriegsanwalt in Criminal Proceedings Against Professor Dr. Werner Krauss for the Charge of Treason), "Vernehmungsprotokoll der Gestapo von Fritz Thiel" (Gestapo interrogation transcript for Fritz Thiel), 23 September 1942, 29/39 GDW, RK, 3. Cf. Stefan Roloff, *Die Rote Kapelle*, 170, and Günther Weisenborn, private diaries, 3 March 1938.

81 "*Lately I've seen*": Harro to his parents, 27/28 January 1938, ED 335/1, IfZ Munich.

"*dance and laugh happily*": Günther Weisenborn, private diaries, 3 March 1938.

82 *shaken by her cousin's appearance*: Libertas to Marie Luise Schulze, 12 January 1939, GDW, RK.

*Torn between the two men*: Günther Weisenborn, private diaries, 27 March 1938. In mid-May the two lovers also go on a short vacation to the island of Hiddensee (cf. the entries on 17 and 18 May 1938): "All day long we lay naked in the dunes, ran, played, loved, burning hot, animalistic, climbed, swam, Libs and I, tan . . . Have a wonderful bedroom: full moon, nightingale, May, Baltic outside the balcony, love!"

"*immediately arrested*": "A-Kartei," 17 October 1938, RK 15/17–15/20, GDW.

"*She was scared*": Silone, *Gratulatio für Joseph Caspar Witsch zum 60*, 272.

83    *"Ate and drank, chatty"*: Mann, *Tagebücher 1937–1939*, 267.
      *"overtures to Thomas Mann"*: Gestapo-Abschlussbericht (Gestapo closing report), RK,
      GDW, 51. 214.1 Hans Coppi, conversation with Hartmut Schulze-Boysen, August 1989,
      RK, GDW.
      *Libertas introduces Hartmut to sex:* Stefan Roloff, interview with Hartmut Schulze-
      Boysen.
      *"He needs to ask Göring"*: Libertas to Marie Luise Schulze, 21 August 1938, GDW,
      RK. She continues: "Weisenborn wants me to go along with him to direction, stag-
      ing, everywhere; of course you learn a lot there and I'm looking forward to it. The
      monologues are much argued over. I'm almost afraid we might have to do without
      them, because people haven't much understanding for them. The decision is totally
      mine . . . I admit, in my mind I was picturing a film, but it also lends itself to being
      produced on the stage. By the way, we have received various offers to make a film of it.
      Then Weisenborn and I would also write the screenplay, which would bring in a lot of
      money."
      *"But it is a claim"*: "Wir wollen gar keine Tschechen" (We don't want any Czechs at
      all), NS-Archive, Dokumente zum Nationalsozialismus (https://www.ns-archiv.de/
      krieg/1938/tschechoslowakei/wollen-keine-tschechen.php).
84    *"materiel and psychological 'machinery' of world politics"*: Harro to his father, 1 October
      1938, ED 335/1, IfZ Munich.
      *"Not seeing her"*: Günther Weisenborn, private diaries, 30 September and 1 October
      1938.
      *"Whether it breaks out"*: Harro to his father, 1 October 1938, ED 335/1, IfZ Munich.
85    *task of making fifty copies:* Coppi, *Wege in den Widerstand*, 187.
      *Then Dr. Elfriede Paul:* Handakte in der Strafsache gegen Elfriede Paul, Anklagever-
      fügung, Reichskriegsgericht (Reference file from the trial of Elfriede Paul, sentence
      decree, Reich Court-Martial), 16 January 1943, RK 2/7, GDW, 2.
      *"man of truly superior character"*: Karl Bartz to Wehrbezirkskommando Berlin IX, 5
      August 1937, GDW, RK.
      *"at the most beautiful time"*: Harro to his parents, 11 November 1938, ED 335/1, IfZ
      Munich. Libertas sold her old car, Spengler, to Günther Weisenborn.
86    *"Before we started haggling"*: Ibid.
87    *"far more composure than the Italians"*: Ibid.
      *"a Christian without a church"*: Silone, *Gratulatio für Joseph Caspar Witsch zum 60*,
      272–73.
88    *"What a person!"*: Ibid.
      *"victoriously conquered all the customs problems"*: Harro to his parents, 11 November
      1938, ED 335/2, IfZ Munich.
      *a huge festival:* Cf. Günther Weisenborn, *Memorial*, 191.
      *"They shouldn't have pushed"*: Greta Kuckhoff, *Vom Rosenkranz zur Roten Kapelle*, 236.
89    *"This is the new"*: Libertas to Harro's parents, 21 November 1938, ED 335/2, IfZ Mu-
      nich.
      *"What can I write"*: Libertas to Erich Edgar Schulze, 1 October 1939, ED 335/2, IfZ Mu-
      nich.

# 3. RESISTANCE AND LOVE

93    *It's a free plane ticket:* Harro to his parents and his brother Hartmut, early July 1939, ED
      335/2, IfZ Munich.

*"a very nice evening flight"*: Harro to his parents, 7 August 1939, ED 335/1, IfZ Munich.
*"bathing is not limited"*: Hotel brochure: "Herm. Blode, Nidden (Kurische Nehrung) Memelgebiet," Museum Blode, Nida, Lithuania.
*a ship called* Memel: Advertisement by the Memeler Dampfschiffahrts-Gesellschaft (Memel Ferry Company), "Nehrungs-Bäderdienst," Museum Blode, Nida, Lithuania.

95    *"Valley of the Dead"*: Cf. Mann, "Mein Sommerhaus."

96    *Libertas gets out her camera*: Johannes Haas-Heye, interview by Silke Kettelhake. Cf. Kettelhake, *Erzähl allen, allen von mir!*, 248.

97    *a new, four-engine Condor*: Cf. Harro to his father, 4 August 1939, ED 335/1, IfZ Munich.

98    *Dressed in a blue prison uniform*: Files of the Oberreichskriegsanwalt in the trial of Lotte Schleif, Gestapo interrogation transcript, 25 September 1942, RK 1/5, GDW, 5.
*On August 15, 1939*: Ibid., 1.

99    *"stupidity," pure and simple*: Elfriede Paul to Walter Küchenmeister, 13 November 1939, NY 4229/21, Bundesarchiv.

100   *"slim, handsome, and neat"*: Weisenborn, *Memorial*, 19.
*thirty-two straight hours of work*: Cf. Harro to his father, 30 August 1939, ED 335/1, IfZ Munich.
*"Up to this point, Hitler"*: Weisenborn, *Memorial*, 19, including the following quotes and descriptions in this passage.
*Driving cars is restricted*: Ibid., 2.

101   *boulevards of fragrant greenery all around*: Cf. Harro to his father, 1 May 1939, ED 335/1, IfZ Munich.
*They sit separately*: Cf. Harro to his parents, 16 September 1939, ED 335/1, IfZ Munich.
*"working on this or that"*: Libertas to Marie Luise Schulze, 12 January 1939, RK, GDW.
*"had as an outlet"*: Libertas to Erich Edgar Schulze, 1 October 1939, RK, GDW.
*"And he's full of hope"*: Libertas to her father, Otto Haas-Hee, 16 August 1939, LA-1.23.
*As a result*: Libertas to Erich Edgar Schulze, 1 October 1939, RK, GDW.
*"Otherwise it won't be bearable"*: Ibid.

103   *"Behold, ye are of nothing"*: Isaiah 41:24, King James Version.
*"But that's how"*: Stefan Roloff, *Rote Kapelle*, 48. The following quote as well.
*"How would a concert pianist"*: Thus for example Helmut and Mimi help to distribute a sermon by Bishop Clemens August Graf von Galen, who describes so-called euthanasia, the ending of "lives unworthy of living," as what it really is: murder. The bishop's actions are successful: Operation T4, as it is called, is no longer pursued.

104   *the women wear hula costumes*: Günther Weisenborn, private diaries, 8 May 1940.
*"Among the latter"*: Harro to his parents, 9 August 1940, ED 335/1, IfZ Munich.

105   *another difficulty*: Libertas to Erich Edgar Schulze, 13 December 1940, RK, GDW.
*As for the few films*: Harro also helps her out: He writes two movie reviews himself, "letting rip" to such an extent that he jokes: "Hopefully they don't lock Libs up for it." Harro to his parents, 21 August 1940, ED 335/1, IfZ Munich.
*"Only in an authoritarian state"*: Wegner, *Libertas Schulze-Boysen — Filmpublizistin*, 107. It's worth pointing out, for example, Libertas's review of the film *Das Mädchen von Fanö*, based on a novel by Günther Weisenborn. The *Zeitschriften-Dienst* demands that "in discussing this film" she "concentrate on the *images*." But for Libertas what is crucial is something else: the screenplay's divergence from the original. She isn't happy with the cinematic presentation of the two female protagonists, because in her view they have lost their contemporary and realistic aspect and are meant to show how female heroism is based on forbearance and not on independence: "In the end,

261

the main character, the passionate and capricious 'Mädchen von Fanö,' has become a good fisherman's wife, and Angens, her rival, whose bloodless angelic nature, so brilliantly described in the novel, drives Ipke the fisherman into the arms of the other woman, has become a heroically strong forbearing woman, who makes out grandly in the end." (Ibid., 119).

106 *They manage to skate by:* Carsten Würmann, "Zwischen Unterhaltung und Propaganda: Das Krimigenre im Dritten Reich" (Diss., Freie Universität, Berlin, 2013), 256.

108 *"An interesting example":* George Messersmith to Herbert Feis, 4 June 1938, State Department Documents RG 59, H 353/214, National Archives, Washington, D.C. Cited in Shareen Blair Brysac, *Resisting Hitler — Mildred Harnack and the Red Orchestra,* 225. Cf. Ferdinand Mayer, chargé d'affaires, to Secretary of State Cordell Hull, State Department cable, 13 August 1937. State Department Documents, RG 59, 862–50, National Archives; Attaché's report on espionage, 16 September 1937.

109 *learns during this fall:* "Akte Korsikanez" (Korsikanez file), Archive of the Foreign Intelligence Service, Moscow, No. 34118, vol. 1, RK, GDW, 63.

110 *all Russian literature:* Ibid., entry on 2 October 1940, 23.
*There the general staff:* Harro to his parents, 23 January 1941, ED 335/1, IfZ Munich.
*Harro no longer:* Harro to his parents, 3 February 1941, ED 335/1, IfZ Munich.

112 *opposition circles as far away:* Gestapo reports 1939–1943, vol. 2, Berlin, 1989, RK, GDW, 184.
*"Dear Mama — Papa and you":* Harro to his mother, 11 March 1941, ED 335/1, IfZ Munich.
*"advisable to keep up the appearance":* "Akte Korsikanez" (Korsikanez file), Archive of the Foreign Intelligence Service, Moscow, No. 34118, vol. 1, RK, GDW, 206.

113 *railway main lines:* Ibid., 243, the previous and following quote as well.

114 *"It is essential to activate":* Ibid., 225, the following quote as well.

115 *"The German team advances":* "WW2: Schweiz: 1941: Schweizer- gegen Hakenkreuz: Die Schweiz besiegt Deutschland 2 : 1," video posted by ww2schweiz (https://www .youtube.com/watch?v=2_u8iwRIRes; from 2:00 on).
*"with obligatory fecklessness":* Libertas to Marie Luise Schulze, 28 May 1941, RK, GDW.

116 *"new fulfilling activity":* Ibid.
*"Send your 'informant'":* Cf. Coppi et al., *Die Rote Kapelle im Widerstand gegen den Nationalsozialismus,* 136.

117 *"Marriage problems":* Weisenborn, private diaries, 17 June 1941.
*She decides to consult:* Kuckhoff, *Vom Rosenkranz zur Roten Kapelle,* 284–85.
*"that on the one hand":* Libertas to Marie Luise Schulze, 13 June 1941, RK, GDW.

118 *"I once again insist":* Quoted in Richard Sakwa, *The Rise and Fall of the Soviet Union* (New York: Routledge, 1999), 253.

119 *Meanwhile, on Unter den Linden:* Kuckhoff, *Vom Rosenkranz zur Roten Kapelle,* 287.
*After the hatches:* According to Greta Kuckhoff's account, Korotkov gave her the first.

121 *"Believe me, we are robust":* Greta Kuckhoff, RK 34/62, GDW, 389.
*vulcanized fiber case:* "Akte Korsikanez" (Korsikanez file), Archive of the Foreign Intelligence Service, Moscow, No. 34118, vol. 1, RK, GDW, 346–47.
*notorious for their complicated codes:* Cf. Höhne, *Kennwort: Direktor,* 117.

122 *And sure enough:* "Akte Korsikanez" (Korsikanez file), Archive of the Foreign Intelligence Service, Moscow, No. 34118, vol. 1, RK, GDW, 347; Coppi et al., *Die Rote Kapelle im Widerstand,* 137.

123 *"clear up the situation":* "Akte Korsikanez" (Korsikanez file), Archive of the Foreign Intelligence Service, Moscow, No. 34118, vol. 1, RK, GDW, 50.

124 *"In Berlin find Adam Kuckhoff"*: Coppi et al., *Die Rote Kapelle im Widerstand*, 138.

125 *On August 28, 1941*: For more on Kent's trip to Berlin, see "Protokoll der Vernehmung des Verhafteten Gurewitsch Anatolij Markowitsch" (Interrogation transcript for prisoner Gurewitsch Anatolij Markowitsch), 13 May 1946, GDW, RK.

*a room at Hotel Skroubec*: Ibid., along with the rest of the passage. "I went to Prague because I had received orders from the director in Moscow to look up a collection of paintings. There, by mentioning a portrait of a saint, I was supposed to arrange a meeting with a man I didn't know who also was active in our organization," as Kent puts it in an interrogation.

127 *They begin their conversation*: Transcript of Kent's interrogation by the Gestapo on 23 November 1942, RK, GDW, 12.

129 *"central manager of production"*: Bock and Töteberg, *Das Ufa-Buch*, 438–43. Neumann: "It is necessary to establish regular and close contact with those who make *Kulturfilme*, in order to be able to truly lead and guide them and inform them of the desires of the state. At the same time they must not be made to feel as though they were under censorship."

*an excellent eight hundred Reichsmarks per month*: In today's money about 3,200 Euros. Libertas writes one last article for the *National-Zeitung*. It is published on 13 November 1941 and introduces her friend Oda Schottmüller. "Auferstehung der Maske im Kunsttanz" ("Resurrection of the Mask in Dance").

*"hanging out to dry"*: Bock and Töteberg, *Das Ufa-Buch*, 438–43.

130 *music from Japan, India, Bali*: Andresen, *Oda Schottmüller — Die Tänzerin, Bildhauerin, und Nazigegnerin*, 295.

135 *"Much of the time"*: Libertas to Marie Luise Schulze, 6 January 1942, RK, GDW.

*"The infamously stupid state bureaucracy"*: "Die Sorge um Deutschlands Zukunft geht durch das Volk," RK, GDW.

136 *"It's rotten luck of course if a bomb"*: Harro to his parents, 29 October 1940, ED 335/1, IfZ Munich.

*"The risks of bombardment"*: Ibid.

137 *"Germany, because of its raw material"*: Harro to his father, 3 May 1942, ED 335/1, IfZ Munich.

*The two met at the fair in Leipzig*: Flügge, *Meine Sehnsucht ist das Leben*, 116ff.

139 *"This neighborhood! This apartment!"*: Cf. Heinrich Scheel, *Vor den Schranken*, 214.

140 *inborn sense of camaraderie*: Hildebrandt, *Wir sind die Letzten*, 138.

*determines the intellectual direction*: Scheel, *Vor den Schranken*, 214. The following quote as well.

*the practice of Dr. Elfriede Paul*: Cf. Poelchau, *Die letzten Stunden, Erinnerungen eines Gefängnispfarrers, aufgezeichnet von Graf Alexander Stenbock-Fermor*, 69.

*helping Jewish acquaintances*: Roloff, *Die Rote Kapelle*, 63.

141 *It is no longer enough to "gripe" or make stupid jokes*: "Die Sorge," RK, GDW. The following quotes as well.

*they distribute the load*: Helmut Roloff, "Bericht — Über die Arbeit in einem Teil der Gruppe Schulze-Boysen" (Report — on the work in one part of the Schulze-Boysen group), RK, GDW, 1.

142 *"Send this letter"*: "Offener Brief an die Ostfront," RK, GDW.

*"The pamphlets, produced"*: Stefan Roloff, *Die Rote Kapelle*, 63.

*"The enclosed pamphlet"*: Ibid.

*"single-drum device, probably an older model"*: Ibid., 65–66.

143 *"A review of the recipients"*: Ibid., 67.

144 *born in 1903 in Detroit:* Schmidt, *John Sieg, einer von Millionen spricht.*
*Open Letter to the Eastern Front:* "Offener Brief an die Ostfront," RK, GDW.
147 *made it on into Russia:* Cf. "Feldurteil gegen Harro Schulze-Boysen u.a." (Sentence against Harro Schulze-Boysen et al.), 19 December 1942, RK 1/2, 15–16, GDW, 21.
148 *"I have to tell you":* Account of Alexander Spoerl, RK 11/14, GDW, 1.
149 *"I still tremble deep in my soul":* Harro to Stella Mahlberg, 6 April 1942, RK 9/13, GDW.
150 *"I am too close to you to face you":* Ibid.
*the walls that have grown up around him:* Harro to Stella Mahlberg, 12 April 1942, RK 9/13, GDW.
*a Tibetologist trained:* Antonia Tosca Grill, "Philipp Schaeffer — mein Vater" (lecture at the Philipp-Schaeffer-Bibliothek, Berlin, 17 June 2003).
151 *"to use the air raid rope":* Coppi, "Philipp Schaeffer, Orientalist, Bibliothekar, Widerstandskämpfer," 366–68, 383–84.
*"The longer the German people":* Eden, *Freedom and Order: Selected Speeches 1939–1946,* 159.
152 *"wait to win his biggest victory":* Harro to his parents, 25 July 1942, ED 335/1, IfZ Munich.
153 *the most successful propaganda exhibition:* Harro and his comrades aren't the only ones who do something against the propaganda show in the heart of the capital. Herbert Baum and some of his Jewish friends enter the exhibition on May 18, 1942. They have a bag with them in which a canister of explosives is hidden, and they wait for a moment when they aren't being watched to place it in a cottage, where a desolate-looking "Russian bed" is on display. When the bag starts to burn and a guard appears, they quickly leave the exhibition. They aren't able to use the *Brandplättchen* — "calling cards" — they bring to fuel the fire, and so little damage is done. Baum dies in Gestapo custody; twenty-eight members of his group are murdered by the Nazi regime.
*"Minsk, the City of Lies":* A poster for the same exhibition that ran in Vienna from December 13, 1941, to February 1, 1942: "In countless letters from soldiers, reports and first-hand accounts, it has been demonstrated again and again that the most vivid imagination, even with the aid of the printed or spoken word, or even the image, is not sufficient if one is to understand the actual, abysmal depravity and misery of the Bolshevist slave state."
*"This promises to be a first class achievement":* Fröhlich, *Die Tagebücher von Joseph Goebbels.*
154 *In* The Soviet Paradise: "By destroying this enemy, we remove a threat to the German Reich and to all of Europe, a threat more horrible than any that has loomed over the continent since the times of the Mongolian hordes." This text stood in large type at the entrance to *The Soviet Paradise.*
*Using these ship convoys:* Joseph Schmid, "Entstehung, Aufgaben und Wesen des Generalstabes der deutschen Luftwaffe," RK, GDW, 47.
155 *Johnny Graudenz knows:* Diethart Kerbs, "John Graudenz (1884–1942) Bildjournalist und Widerstandskämpfer" (John Graudenz [1884–1942] photojournalist and resistance fighter), RK, GDW, 7.
*in such "poor" conditions:* Harro to his sister, brother, and mother, 19 May 1942, ED 335/1, IfZ Munich.
156 *"certain fanaticism in organizing things":* Harro to his mother, 8 January 1934, ED 335/1, IfZ Munich.
158 *"There's no way":* Cf. "Akten des Oberreichskriegsanwaltes in der Strafsache gegen den

264

Professor Gefr Dr. Werner Krauss wg Landesverrats," RK 29/39, GDW 40; also RK
28/38, 38, 302–3, 374.

*"Fritz offered me a pistol"*: During his Gestapo interrogation, Werner Krauss says that
he knowingly put his uniform on in order to put a time limit on the operation. Cf.
"Akten des Oberreichskriegsanwaltes in der Strafsache gegen den Professor Gefr Dr.
Werner Krauss wg Landesverrats," RK 29/39, GDW, 40.

160   *hears suspicious noises*: Ingeborg Engelsing-Kohler, "Erinnerungen an Harro und Libertas Schulze-Boysen" (Memories of Harro and Libertas Schulze-Boysen), RK, GDW,
4. Cf. Hans Coppi, "Gespräch mit Frau von Schönebeck am 15.4.1989," RK, GDW, 13.

  *"No deception where Libs is concerned"*: Harro to Stella Mahlberg, undated letter, RK
9/13, GDW.

161   *Around his mother*: Elsa Schulze-Boysen, *Harro Schulze-Boysen*, 9.

  *A calm lies over everything*: Harro to his parents, 22 June 1942, ED 335/1, IfZ Munich.

162   *"rediscover a little of what I am"*: Harro to Stella Mahlberg, 20 June 1942, RK 9/13,
GDW. The following quote as well.

163   *Horst Heilmann is again*: Harro to Horst Heilmann, 18 June 1942, RK, GDW.

  *"see him in a condition fit for a human being"*: Harro to his parents, 22 June 1942, ED
335/1, IfZ Munich.

  *On June 30, 1942*: "Protokoll über die Befragung des Genossen Johann Wenzel vom
19.10.1967" (Transcript of the questioning of Comrade Johann Wenzel, 19 October
1967), RK 43/112, GDW, 60–61.

164   *"I will never confess"*: "11 Gebote für das Verhalten Verhafteter," RK 39/84, GDW, 8.

  *It starts with an orgy*: "Protokoll über die Befragung des Genossen Johann Wenzel," 61.

165   *"all sorts of things cooking"*: Harro to his parents and brother, 6 July 1942, ED 335/1, IfZ
Munich.

167   *"I intend not to"*: Harro to Stella Mahlberg, 5 August 1942, RK 9/13, GDW.

  *"tan nice and brown and jump"*: Harro to his parents and brother, 6 July 1942, ED 335/1,
IfZ Munich.

  *"The people"*: Ibid.

  *"One really is hungry"*: Ibid.

  *"the kind of food that could keep a person"*: Libertas to Marie Luise Schulze, 6 January
1942, RK, GDW.

168   *"overreaching capitalist system of government"*: [Arvid Harnack,] *Das nationalsozialistische Stadium des Monopolkapitalismus*, pamphlet circulated in spring 1942. The author
is not attributed. RK, GDW.

  *"where it costs a whole pile of money"*: Harro to his father, 24 December 1941, ED 335/1,
IfZ Munich.

  *"a heavy burden for everyone"*: Harro to his parents, 6 February 1942, ED 335/1, IfZ
Munich.

  *"in every respect"*: Harro to his parents, 25 July 1942, ED 335/1, IfZ Munich.

169   *"synthetic tomato soup"*: Harro to his parents, 6 July 1942, ED 335/1, IfZ Munich.

  *"Here we're all starved'"*: Harro to his parents, 23 August 1942, ED 335/1, IfZ Munich.

171   *"With exemplary composure and rare nerve"*: Schattenfroh and Tuchel, *Zentrale des Terrors — Prinz-Albrecht-Strasse 8: Hauptquartier der Gestapo*, 378.

173   *"How is one supposed to lead a resistance movement"*: "Falk Harnack: Über Arvid und
Mildred Harnack" (Falk Harnack: On Arvid and Mildred Harnack), RK 32/55, GDW,
10.

  *an ever more active resistance network*: For the historian Hans Mommsen, the Kreisau
circle represents a "comprehensive vision for the future, whose boldness and rigor was

unsurpassed by any other political reform concept in the German resistance against Hitler."

176     Heilmann thinks: Trepper, Die Wahrheit — Autobiographie des "Grand Chef" der Roten Kapelle (Munich: Ahriman, 1975), 134.

# 4. THE BLACK CURTAIN

179     Horst Heilmann's phone finally rings: Trepper, Die Wahrheit, 134. This version of events is to be regarded with caution, as Trepper doesn't name his sources.

180     At four o'clock the guard: Weisenborn, Memorial, 66. Thus will Günther Weisenborn describe his own experiences a few days later. His descriptions are here attributed to Harro.

181     There's a yellowed light brown stool: Roloff, Die Rote Kapelle, 36–37.
        A day earlier, on September 1, 1942: "Falk Harnack: Über Arvid und Mildred Harnack," RK 32/55, GDW.

183     the trains pulled up directly: A few gas trucks are parked there as well, but most of the Königsberg Jews are shot by eighty policemen and members of the Waffen-SS: the same special units and police captains to whom Adam Kuckhoff's Open Letter to the Eastern Front is addressed.
        "Dear Frau Müller!": Mildred and Arvid Harnack to Gertrud Müller (housekeeper), 2 September 1942, RK 13/15, GDW.

184     you should go ahead and be honest: Cf. for example the interview with Heinrich Scheel in Coburger, Griebel, and Scheel, Erfasst? Das Gestapo-Album zur Roten Kapelle — Eine Foto-Dokumentation, 300.
        He disputes every accusation: Höhne, Kennwort: Direktor, 189; Heinrich Scheel to Ricarda Huch, 23 June 1946, RK 8/13, GDW, 4.
        "Third-degree interrogation methods may": Schattenfroh and Tuchel, Zentrale des Terrors, 381. Cf. "Auszüge von einer Vernehmung M. Roeders durch Kempner" (Excerpts from an interrogation of M. Roeder's by Kempner), RK 8/13, GDW, 45. Roeder: "Verschärfte Vernehmungen were used with Schulze-Boysen . . ."

185     Stalin room: Bergander, "Das Ermittlungsverfahren gegen Dr. Jr. et rer. Pol. Manfred Roeder, einen 'Generalrichter' Hitlers," 13.
        A strange contraption: "Gestapo: Um Geständnisse zu erlangen" (http://www.spiegel .de/spiegel/print/d-29193277.html). The description of what Harro might have experienced in the "Stalin room" is based on the assumption that the procedure resembles methods of torture used in this time period at Prinz-Albrecht-Strasse 8. There is no extant source describing the actual torture of Harro, only sources according to which such torture took place.

187     A few hours later: Egmont Zechlin, "Arvid und Mildred Harnack zum Gedächtnis — Aus der Geschichte der deutschen Widerstandsbewegungen" (In memoriam, Arvid and Mildred Harnack — from the history of the German resistance movements), RK 13/15, GDW, 22.
        "a mix of cow, horse, deer, camel, and buffalo": Mann, "Mein Sommerhaus."
        Despite all the sorrows: Arvid Harnack to Mildred Harnack, 14 December 1942, RK 32/55, GDW, 123ff.

188     a horse passes on its way home: Zechlin, 22. Likewise the following quote.

189     pulling little wooden wagons: Thomas Mann, "Mein Sommerhaus."

"The gentlemen have a breakfast date": Zechlin, 22ff. All quotes and descriptions in this passage.

191    Libertas feels a constant urge: "Aufzeichnung von Johannes Haas-Heye, Bruder von Libertas" (Chronicle of Johannes Haas-Heye, brother of Libertas), RK 37/67, GDW.

        "I'm terribly afraid": Magda Linke, "Meine Erinnerungen an Libertas Schulze-Boysen" (My memories of Libertas Schulze-Boysen), RK 37/67, GDW, 3.

193    they get to chatting: Coppi et al., Die Rote Kapelle im Widerstand, 148.

194    One of them, the battery-powered: Cf. Roloff, Die Rote Kapelle, 166–67.

        The vulcanized fiber case: Ibid., 45.

        "One thing is certain": Ibid.

        The university teacher Werner Krauss: "Werner Krauss: Über meine Beteiligung an der Aktion Schulze-Boysen mit Anmerkungen von Greta Kuckhoff" (Werner Krauss: On my participation in the Schulze-Boysen operation, with remarks by Greta Kuckhoff), RK 33/58, GDW.

195    Greta Kuckhoff wakes up early: Kuckhoff, Vom Rosenkranz zur Roten Kapelle, 326–33. Cf. RK 35/64, 119.

199    They sip their booze: Cf. Döblin, Berlin Alexanderplatz, 155.

200    "Where's the suitcase?": Roloff, Die Rote Kapelle, 35.

201    That was all very good: Ibid., 36.

        before he was able to walk again: Heinrich Scheel to Ricarda Huch, 23 June 1946, RK 8/13, GDW, 3.

        he was wearing a track suit: Arnold Bauer, "Erinnerungen an Harro Schulze-Boysen" (Memories of Harro Schulze-Boysen), RK 37/67, GDW, 8. Cf. Bauer in RK 11, 105–6 and 194ff.

202    They've put in partition walls: "Protokoll über die Befragung des Genossen Prof. Dr. Heinrich Scheel vom März 1968" (Transcript of the questioning of Comrade Prof. Dr. Heinrich Scheel in March 1968), RK 42/102, GDW, 1.

        "since both artists": Wolfgang Havemann, "Arbeitsmaterial zur Widerstandsorganisation Rote Kapelle, Juni 1968" (Working material on the Red Orchestra resistance organization), RK 42/102, GDW, 1.

203    "Great experts that they were": Scheel, Vor den Schranken, 201; Roloff, Die Rote Kapelle, 162.

        They take even the most vacuous bit: Andresen, Oda Schottmüller, 283.

        "All statements made by Prof. Krauss": Roloff, Die Rote Kapelle, 180.

204    "They didn't allow for any nuance": "Bericht Greta Kuckhoff, 6. Februar 1947" (Greta Kuckhoff, report, 6 February 1947), RK 11/14, GDW.

205    "Well go on, get out of here!": Roloff, Die Rote Kapelle, 275.

        Maria Terwiel takes full responsibility: Ibid., 176.

        The trick is to say something: Ibid., 185, 191, and 193. Ursula Goetze stubbornly denies that her boyfriend Werner Krauss was involved in the stickering operation: "I went to post the stickers completely by myself and without anyone accompanying me," she goes on record as saying: "Krauss scolded me for it and described my participation in the stickering operation as wrong and told me that I mustn't do such things." This statement supports his own testimony; his strategy is to deny everything: "Even the words stickering operation are completely unfamiliar to me." Only when Ursula Goetze admits — it is no longer possible to reconstruct why she does this — that her boyfriend did in fact come along with her on Sachsendamm on the night of May 17, 1942, does he change his version and claims he had run after her, not knowing anything about it, of course. In the Gestapo transcript his testimony reads as follows: "On the night in question I myself did not know that Ursula Goetze was going to post subversive notes. In the neighborhood around Sachsendamm I followed her at a distance of about 30 meters in order to remain close to her. If Goetze posted any stickers, I didn't see it. I was only able to see the outline of her from afar and followed her down the different streets. When I am told that after eleven p.m. the outline of Goetze was visible even from very far away and that it therefore does not seem credible when I claim not to have seen Goetze post several stickers on bus stops, lampposts, stop signs and building façades, my explanation here is that I had no interest in seeing what she was doing and only wanted to maintain contact with her." As strange as this version is, it is kept on record, since the Gestapo has no proof that things were otherwise.

206    *"Sometimes even the most important military secret":* Joseph Goebbels, war diary, 23 September 1942, FB 5849, Bundesarchiv, Koblenz.

      *"because bad news regarding son":* Erich Edgar Schulze, "Zum Gedächtnis meines Sohnes Harro" (In memory of my son Harro), handwritten, RK, GDW. Cf. Erich Edgar Schulze's testimony before state prosecutor Dr. Finck on 13 February 1950 in the trial against Manfred Roeder. All quotes and descriptions in this passage.

211    *Two days later:* Coppi and Andresen, *Dieser Tod passt zu mir — Harro Schulze-Boysen,* 372.

213    *"small and squatly built":* Cf. Weisenborn, *Memorial,* 47. The previous quote as well.

      *It is impossible for the prisoners:* "Gestapo: Um Geständnisse zu erlangen," *Der Spiegel.* "Leg shackles were on each ankle, a chain between them. . . The shackles were so tight that you couldn't walk."

      *Habecker also kicks:* "Walter Habecker: German. A Gestapo Officer in Berlin," KV 2/2752, British National Archives.

      *She is not permitted:* Ingrid Kamlah, "Abschrift 14.2.1947," 1–3. Cf. Heinrich Scheel to Ricarda Huch, 23 June 1946, RK 8/13, GDW, 7.

214    *"No thing on earth to nought can fall":* Goethe, "Testament," *Selected Poems.*

      *"burn out the cancer":* Gilles Perrault, *Auf den Spuren der Roten Kapelle,* 279.

215    *"To think I let myself be taken":* Alexander Spoerl, "Bericht," RK 11/14, GDW.

216    *At forty-two years old:* "Ausführungen zu Roeder," RK 35/63, GDW, 4. Greta Kuckhoff writes: "Dr. Roeder feared the danger for National Socialism — not for Germany — especially because what was achieved was not a one-sided political orientation but rather a broad project with support from all classes. The arrests took place at a point in time when he, as a high-ranking officer, could survey Germany's military situation and was duty-bound to recognize the necessity of doing away with National Socialism for the good of Germany and the world. Out of personal vanity, which was apparent in every single word he spoke, and out of a personal lust for power and thirst for revenge, he made sure that the sentences handed down by the Second Judicial Panel of the Reich Court-Martial were more severe than they would otherwise have been. He condoned the methods of the initial Gestapo investigation, about which he was informed — if, that is, he didn't give the orders for the methods in the first place."

      *"Generally speaking, long prison sentences":* "Vortrag des Senatspräsidenten Kraell bei Göring über die ergangenen Urteile in der Strafsache Rote Kapelle" (Presentation by panel chairman Kraell to Göring on the sentences passed down in the Red Orchestra criminal case) located among the "Akten des Oberreichskriegsanwaltes in der Strafsache gegen den Uffz. Heinz Strehlow u acht andere" (Files of the Oberreichskriegsanwalt in the criminal case against Uffz. Heinz Strehlow and eight others), vols. 1 and 2, RK 27/38, GDW, 465ff.

"Roeder the bloodhound": "Kennwort: Direktor," *Der Spiegel*, vol 21., 20 May 1968, 80. *Back in Berlin:* Bergander, "Das Ermittlungsverfahren gegen Dr. jur. Et rer. Pol. Manfred Roeder, einen 'Generalrichter' Hitlers," 18.

217    *"When you stepped inside that building":* Falk Harnack, "1. Besuch bei Arvid Harnack am 26.10.1942" (1st visit with Arvid Harnack on 26 October 1942), RK 32/55, GDW. *"The evidence against him":* Falk Harnack, "2. Besuch bei Arvid Harnack am 15.11.1942" (2nd visit with Arvid Harnack on 15 November 1942), RK 32/55, GDW. For narrative purposes, the two visits Falk pays his brother have been condensed into one.

218    *"I believe that in principle":* Ibid., 16. *Scholl and Schmorell put up:* "Zusammentreffen von Scholl und Schmorell mit Falk Harnack" (Meeting between Scholl and Schmorell and Falk Harnack), RK 23/37, GDW, 19. Likewise all quotes and descriptions in this passage.

219    *"is now in a difficult position":* Der Spiegel, vol. 9, 2005, 77.

220    *"I cannot say with certainty":* Transcript of Kent's interrogation by the Gestapo on 23 November 1942, RK, GDW, 11. The previous quote as well.

221    *Dr. Manfred Roeder has put in overtime:* Bergander, "Das Ermittlungsverfahren gegen Dr. jur. Et rer. Pol. Manfred Roeder, einen 'Generalrichter' Hitlers," 20.

222    *"Repeatedly held evenings of discussion":* Gestapo-Abschlussbericht, RK, GDW, 54. *"an impulsive woman":* Ibid., 55. *"for special achievement":* Tuchel and Schattenfroh, *Zentrale des Terrors*, 385.

223    *"Dear Parents!":* Harro to his parents, 10 December 1942, ED 335/1, IfZ Munich.

224    *At midnight the night before:* Heinrich Scheel to Ricarda Huch, 23 June 1946, RK 8/13, GDW, 6. *and in the Spandau military prison:* Heinrich Scheel, "Horst Heilmann — Hitlerjunge und Widerstandskämpfer" (lecture, Universität Rostock, February 1988), 8. *But the greatest fear of all:* Heinrich Scheel to Ricarda Huch, 23 June 1946, 6.

225    *Then the accused are led in:* The other defendants that day are Herbert Gollnow, thirty-one years old, a confidant of Arvid and Mildred Harnack, who also worked with Harro, and Kurt Schulze, forty-seven, who worked with Soviet reconnaissance and instructed Hans Coppi in how to operate the radio. *At nine-fifteen the judges enter the room:* Senatspräsident Dr. Kraell as presiding judge, Reichskriegsgerichtrat Dr. Schmitt, and, filling out the panel, General Musshoff, Vizeadmiral Arps, and Genralmajor Stutzer.

226    *Unlike the judges:* Scheel, *Vor den Schranken*, 8. *"many flagrant occurrences":* Cf. Gestapo-Abschlussbericht: "The cunning manner in which Schulze-Boysen went about aspects of his subversive work is evident in the political treatise on Napoleon Bonaparte that he wrote and sent to a large number of intellectuals, among them officers and officials of officer rank." *Next up is the support for the Allies:* "Feldurteil des Reichskriegsgerichts gegen Harro Schulze-Boysen u.a. vom 19.12.1942," RK 1/2, GDW, 55. *"most zealous co-conspirator":* Gestapo-Abschlussbericht, RK, GDW, 5. *"She made suggestions":* "Feldurteil des Reichskriegsgerichts gegen Harro Schulze-Boysen u.a."

227    *"There were no betrayals":* Heinrich Scheel to Ricarda Huch, 23 June 1946, RK 8/13, GDW, 4. *"so great and wonderful":* Libertas to her mother, Tora, second farewell letter, 22 December 1942, RK, GDW, 2.

228    *"The balance of power is completely skewed":* Andresen, *Oda Schottmüller*, 280. Likewise the other quotes by Oda Schottmüller here.

229 *"five pale officers' faces"*: Weisenborn, *Memorial*, 95.
*"decent character"*: "Feldurteil des Reichskriegsgerichts gegen Harro Schulze-Boysen u.a.," 12.
*"a less than active mind"*: Ibid., 20.
*"limited [intelligence] and personal indifference"*: Ibid.
*"I will as long as"*: Heinrich Scheel to Ricarda Huch, 23 June 1946, RK 8/13, GDW, 7.
230 *"For the crimes, jointly committed"*: "Feldurteil des Reichskriegsgerichts gegen Harro Schulze-Boysen u.a."
231 *strong barbiturates:* "Eintrag Morell," 21 December 1942, N1348, Bundesarchiv Koblenz. "Two tablespoons of *Brom-Nervacit* and a *Phanodorm.*"
*"I uphold the verdict"*: Wehrmacht high command to the Chairman of the Reich Court-Martial, 23 December 1942, RK 29/43, GDW, 165.
232 *"It is to be expected"*: Reich Justice Ministry memo re: the construction of a gallows in Plötzensee, 12 December 1942.
*"There he stood"*: Weisenborn, *Memorial*, 8.
*"there were so many"*: Erich Edgar Schulze, "Harro Schulze-Boysen," 16.
233 *"Gestapa Zelle 2"*: Harro Schulze-Boysen, found summer 1945 in cell 2 of the basement prison of the Reich Main Security Office. The full poem reads as follows:

> Gestapo Cell No. 2
> The wind-blown rain hits the window
> And howling sounds the alarm!
> In Germany ghosts are on the prowl
> Here inside it is warm . . .
>
> They like to call it prison,
> The body too is bound
> But of this fate, despite it all
> The heart still scarcely knows
>
> To me it's a monastic cell:
> The wall all bathed in light.
> It shields me from the crashing waves,
> Protects me in my plight.
>
> The spirit roams out in the world,
> Shackles don't concern it,
> And time and space, arise and leave,
> Dissolving in the pale light.
>
> And if we've been cut loose
> From this unrestful world,
> Then all the dross has been sloughed off
> Like sand washed from a pearl.
>
> To the keen and sharpened gaze
> Only the final truth has meaning
> And the unclouded [illegible] [illegible] becomes
> Here proudly joy in being.

> The grave hour begs the question:
> Did any of it matter?
> And my reply to you is: Yes —
> It was the right battle.
>
> Death has got you by the throat,
> Life to you is dear . . .
> And yet your soul is surfeited
> On that which drove it on.
>
> And though we all should die, still
> We know the seed is planted.
> Though heads may roll, the state
> will by the spirit by <u>supplanted</u>.
>
> ~~Bullet~~ Hangman's rope and guillotine
> Won't have the final say.
> The <u>world</u> will be our judges,
> Not the judges of <u>today</u>.

236   *"notable and meritorious officers"*: Cf. Website of the Invalids' Cemetery Association (http://www.foerderverein-invalidenfriedhof.de).
*"The ring is from my father"*: Libertas to her mother, Tora, first farewell letter, 22 December 1942, RK, GDW.
*The cells are cold*: Cf. Poelchau, *Die letzten Stunden*, 40–41.
*No one speaks loudly*: Poelchau, "Die Lichter erloschen — Weihnachtserinnerungen 1941–1944." Likewise the following quote and descriptions in this passage.

237   *"True he was outwardly composed"*: Ibid.
*"This morning I kept repeating the 'Prologue in Heaven'"*: Ibid. The "Prologue in Heaven" quote: Goethe, *Faust*, TK 467.1 Goethe, "Primal Words — Orphic (1817–18)," *Selected Poems*.
*"As stood the sun"*: Ibid.
*"personal slap in the face"*: Poelchau, "Die Lichter erloschen — Weihnachtserinnerungen 1941–1944," 61.
*"But above all I think that humanity"*: Arvid Harnack, farewell letter, RK, GDW.
*"a primordial beast with countless eyes"*: Poelchau, "Die Lichter erloschen — Weihnachtserinnerungen 1941–1944," 81.

238   *An old cobbler comes by*: Ibid., 29.
*"And it came to pass"*: Luke 2:1–7, King James Version.
*The dark corridor of Block III*: Ibid., 28ff.

239   *"finer gentleman"*: Ibid., 25.
*"a worthy remuneration"*: From the ruling of the Magdeburg District Court on 27 November 1933, quoted in Poelchau, *Die letzten Stunden*, 25.
*In the harsh light*: Bergander, "Das Ermittlungsverfahren gegen Dr. jur. Et rer. Pol. Manfred Roeder, einen 'Generalrichter' Hitlers," 21.
*"Dear parents!"*: Harro to his parents, 22 December 1942, RK, GDW.

241   *"All the currents of my scattered life"*: Libertas to her mother, Tora, first farewell letter, 22 December 1942, RK, GDW.

"You are more dear to me": Libertas to her mother Tora, second farewell letter, 22 December 1942, RK, GDW.

242  *Tora zu Eulenburg:* Harald Poelchau, 69ff. Likewise the following quotes and descriptions in this passage.

243  *"The name of your son is to be expunged":* Elsa Schulze-Boysen, *Harro Schulze-Boysen*, 14.

# EPILOGUE

245  *"There are times":* Albrecht Haushofer, *Moabiter Sonette*, 31.

246  *"I do not know the endpoint":* Erich Edgar Schulze, "Zum Gedächtnis meines Sohnes Harro" (In memory of my son Harro), handwritten, RK, GDW.
*For twenty Reichsmarks:* Proceedings on 26 March 1943, Az. O 5205 a/483, Bestand Oberfinanzpräsident, Landesarchiv Berlin.

247  *A police officer:* Ibid., RA Siebert, official letter, 27 March 1943; property manager Alfred Schrobsdorff, official letter, 7 October 1943.

248  *Harro had streets named:* Also worth mentioning here is an elaborately produced DEFA film, the most expensive film ever produced in the German Democratic Republic, shot on 70mm (!) and released under the clunky title *KLK an PTX* (KLK to PTX). All the important characters in Harro and Libertas's story appear in this ill-advised flick, with its cookie-cutter dialogue and bad haircuts — plus a nameless figure who is worked into the story and is meant to represent the leading role the Berlin branch of the German Communist Party was supposed to have played in the resistance network.

249  *"deserve our respect":* Head of the Chancellor's office to Hartmut Schulze-Boysen, 2 August 1994, Schulze-Boysen private collection, Bad Godesberg.
*Only in 2006:* In 1988, efforts to place a memorial plaque on the court building for the victims of the Reich Court-Martial failed. In 1989 a judge ordered a provisional plaque made of wood removed and destroyed.

250  *Johannes Strübing:* Goschler and Wala, *"Keine neue Gestapo." Bundesamt für Verfassungsschutz und die NS-Vergangenheit.*
*"We were unable to locate":* Email to author, 24 August 2018, National Archives, Washington, D.C.

# BIBLIOGRAPHY

The most important sources for this book were unpublished documents from the Red Orchestra Collection (Sammlung Rote Kapelle — RK) at the German Resistance Memorial Center (Gedenkstätte Deutscher Widerstand — GDW) in Berlin. These were supplemented with archival material from the Institute for Contemporary History (Institut für Zeitgeschichte — IfZ) in Munich made available specifically for this research, other previously unpublished materials, as well as reports and files from the German, British, Russian, and United States national archives.

## Works Cited

Andresen, Geertje. *Oda Schottmüller — Die Tänzerin, Bildhauerin und Nazigegnerin*. Berlin: Lukas Verlag, 2005.

Andresen, Geertje, and Hans Coppi, eds. *Dieser Tod passt zu mir — Harro Schulze-Boysen. Grenzgänger im Widerstand*. Berlin: Aufbau Verlag, 1999.

Bergander, Hiska. "Das Ermittlungsverfahren gegen Dr. jur. Et rer. Pol. Manfred Roeder, einen 'Generalrichter' Hitlers." PhD diss., University of Bremen, 2006.

Bock, Michael, and Michael Töteberg. *Das Ufa-Buch. Kunst und Krisen, Stars und Regisseure, Wirtschaft und Politik*. Frankfurt am Main: Zweitausendeins, 1992.

Borchardt, Rudolf. *Weltpuff, Berlin*. Reinbek: Rowohlt, 2018.

Brysac, Shareen Blair. *Resisting Hitler: Mildred Harnack and the Red Orchestra*. New York: Oxford University Press, 2000.

Coburger, Marlies, Regina Griebel, and Heinrich Scheel, eds. *Erfasst? Das Gestapo-Album zur Roten Kapelle — Eine Foto-Dokumentation*. Berlin: Audioscop, 1992.

Coppi, Hans. *Harro Schulze-Boysen — Wege in den Widerstand, eine biographische Studie*. Koblenz: Fölbach, 1995.

———. "Philipp Schaeffer, Orientalist, Bibliothekar, Widerstandskämpfer." *IWK Internationale wissenschaftliche Korrespondenz zur Geschichte der deutschen Arbeiterbewegung* 41, no. 3 (September 2005): 366–86.

Coppi, Hans, Jürgen Danyel, and Johannes Tuchel. *Die Rote Kapelle im Widerstand gegen den Nationalsozialismus*. Berlin: Edition Hentrich, 1994.

Döblin, Alfred. *Berlin Alexanderplatz*. Trans. Michael Hoffman. New York: New York Review of Books, 2018.

Domeier, Norman. *Der Eulenburg-Skandal — eine politische Kulturgeschichte des Kaiserreiches*. Frankfurt am Main: Campus Verlag, 2010.

Eden, Anthony. *Freedom and Order: Selected Speeches 1939–1946*. Boston: Houghton Mifflin, 1948.

Eulenburg, Tora zu, ed. *Libertas Schulze-Boysen: Gedichte und Briefe*. 1952.

Fallada, Hans. *Jeder stirbt für sich allein*. Berlin: Aufbau, 2011.

Fechter, Paul. *An der Wende der Zeit: Menschen und Begegnungen*. Berlin: Bertelsmann, 1950.

Flügge, Manfred. *Meine Sehnsucht ist Das Leben*. Berlin: Aufbau Verlag, 1998.

Fröhlich, Elke, ed. *Die Tagebücher von Joseph Goebbels. Teil 1, Aufzeichnungen 1923–1941*. Vols. 2 and 3, October 1932–March 1934. Munich: De Gruyter Saur, 2006.

———, ed. *Die Tagebücher von Joseph Goebbels. Teil 2, Diktate 1941–1945*. Vol. 6, October–December 1942. Munich: De Gruyter Saur, 2006.

"Gestapo: Um Geständnisse zu erlangen." Der Spiegel. Vol. 8, 1951. http://www.spiegel.de/spiegel/print/d-29193277.html.

Goethe, Johann Wolfgang von. *Faust*. Edited by Cyrus Hamlin and translated by Walter Arndt. New York: W. W. Norton, 2001.

———. *Selected Poems*. Edited by Christopher Middleton and translated by David Michael Hamburger, Christopher Luke, John Middleton, Frederick Nims, and Vernon Watkins. Princeton, N.J.: Princeton University Press, 1994.

Goschler, Constantin, and Michael Wala. *"Keine neue Gestapo." Bundesamt für Verfassungsschutz und die NS-Vergangenheit*. Hamburg: Rowohlt, 2015.

Haase, Norbert. *Das Reichskriegsgericht und der Widerstand gegen die nationalsozialistische Herrschaft*. Berlin: Gedenkstätte Deutscher Widerstand, 1993.

Haushofer, Albrecht. *Moabiter Sonette*. Munich: Beck-Verlag, 2012.

Henderson, Neville. *Failure of a Mission: Berlin 1937–1939*. London: Putnam, 1940.

Hildebrandt, Rainer. *Wir sind die Letzten: Aus dem Leben des Widerstandskämpfers Albrecht Haushofer und seiner Freunde*. Neuwied: Michael-Verlag, 1949.

Höhne, Heinz. *Kennwort: Direktor. Die Geschichte der Rote Kapelle*. Frankfurt am Main: Fischer, 1970.

Knopf, Volker, and Stefan Martens. *Görings Reich — Selbstinzenierungen in Carinhall*. Berlin: Christoph Links Verlag, 1999.

Kuckhoff, Greta. *Vom Rosenkranz zur Roten Kapelle*. Berlin: Neues Leben, 1972.

Malek-Kohler, Ingeborg. *Im Windschatten des Dritten Reichs. Begegnungen mit Filmkünstlern und Widerstandskämpfern*. Freiburg: Verlag Herder, 1986.

Mann, Klaus. *Kind dieser Zeit*. Reinbek: Rowohlt, 1987.

Mann, Thomas. "Mein Sommerhaus." Notes for weekly lecture IV/22 given at the Rotary Club, Munich, December 1931.

———. *Tagebücher 1937–1939*. Frankfurt am Main: Fischer, 1980.

Mazzetti, Elisabetta. *Thomas Mann und die Italiener — Mass und Wert, Düsseldorfer Schriften zur deutschen Literatur*. Frankfurt: Peter Lang, 2009.

Mommsen, Hans. *Die "rote Kapelle" und der deutsche Widerstand gegen Hitler*. Essen: Klartext Verlag, 2012.

Nakagawa, Asayo. "Das Reichsluftfahrtministerium — Bauliche Modifikationen und politische Systeme." Master's thesis, Humboldt University of Berlin, 2009.

Otto, Regine, and Bernd Witte, eds. *Goethe Handbuch.* Vol. 1. Stuttgart: J. B. Metzler, 2004.

Paul, Elfriede. *Ein Sprechzimmer der Roten Kapelle.* Berlin: 1987.

Perrault, Gilles. *Auf den Spuren der Roten Kapelle.* Reinbek: Rowohlt, 1969.

Poelchau, Harald. *Die letzten Stunden, Erinnerungen eines Gefängnispfarrers, aufgezeichnet von Graf Alexander Stenbock-Fermor.* Berlin: Volk und Welt, 1949.

———. "Die Lichter erloschen — Weihnachtserinnerungen 1941–1944." *Unser Appell* 2. 1948.

Roloff, Stefan, with Mario Vigl. *Die Rote Kapelle: Die Widerstandsgruppe im Dritten Reich und die Geschichte Helmut Roloffs.* Berlin: Ullstein, 2002.

Salomon, Ernst von. *Der Fragebogen.* Reinbek: Rowohlt, 1961.

Schattenfroh, Reinhold, and Johannes Tuchel. *Zentrale des Terrors — Prinz-Albrecht-Strasse 8: Hauptquartier der Gestapo.* Berlin: 1987.

Scheel, Heinrich. *Vor den Schranken des Reichskriegsgerichts: Mein Weg in den Widerstand.* Berlin: Edition Q, 1993.

Schmidt, Helmut, ed. *John Sieg, einer von Millionen spricht. Skizzen, Erzählungen, Reportagen, Flugschriften.* Berlin: 1989.

Schulze-Boysen, Elsa. *Harro Schulze-Boysen — Das Bild eines Freiheitskämpfers.* Koblenz: Fölbach, 1992.

Schulze-Boysen, Harro. "Gegner von heute — Kampfgenossen von morgen." *Die Schriften der Gegner.* Berlin: Gegner, 1932. Reprint; Koblenz: Fölbach, 1994.

Silone, Ignazio. In: *Gratulatio für Joseph Caspar Witsch zum 60. Geburstag am 17. Juli 1966.* Cologne: Kiepenheuer & Witsch, 1966.

Später, Jörg. *Vansittart: britische Debatten über Deutsche und Nazis 1902–1945.* Göttingen: Wallstein Verlag, 2003.

Trepper, Leopold. *Die Wahrheit — Autobiographie des "Grand Chef" der Roten Kapelle.* Munich: Ahriman, 1975.

Turel, Adrien. *Bilanz eines erfolglosen Lebens.* Zürich: Edition Nautilus, 1989.

Urwand, Ben. *The Collaboration: Hollywood's Pact with Hitler.* Cambridge: Belknap Press, 2013.

"Walter Habecker, German. A Gestapo Officer in Berlin." British National Archives. KV 2/2752.

Website of the Invalids' Cemetery Association. http://www.foerderverein-invalidenfriedhof.de.

Wegner, Wenke. *Libertas Schulze-Boysen: Filmpublizistin.* Munich: Edition Text + Kritik, 2008.

Weisenborn, Günther. *Memorial.* Berlin: Reclam, 1961.

———. Private diaries. Christian Weisenborn Private Archive, Munich.

"Wir wollen gar keine Tschechen." NS-Archive. Dokumente zum Nationalsozialismus. Https://www.ns-archiv.de/krieg/1938/tschechoslowakei/wollen-keine-tschechen.php.

Wizisla, Erdmut. *Benjamin und Brecht — Die Geschichte einer Freundschaft.* Frankfurt am Main: Suhrkamp Verlag, 2004.

"WW2: Schweiz: 1941: Schweizer- gegen Hakenkreuz: Die Schweiz besiegt Deutschland 2 : 1" Video posted by ww2schweiz. https://www.youtube.com/watch?v+2_u8iwRlRes.

# Additional Reading

Blank, Aleksandr. *Rote Kapelle gegen Hitler.* Berlin, Verlag der Nation, 1979.

Conrad, Robert, Uwe Neumärker, and Cord Woywodt. *Wolfsschanze — Hitlers Machtzentrale im Zweiten Weltkrieg.* Berlin, 2012.

Coppi, Hans, and Jürgen Danyel. *Der Gegner-Kreis im Jahre 1932/33 — ein Kapitel aus der Vorgeschichte des Widerstands.* Berlin, 1990.

Demps, Laurenz, ed. *Luftangriffe auf Berlin: die Berichte der Hauptluftschutzstelle; 1940–1945.* Berlin: Ch. Links, 2012.

"Der Polizeipräsident in Berlin" (zu Gisela von Poellnitz). April 6, 1937. R/30171. Archive number 5574. Bundesarchiv, Koblenz.

ED 335/1–2. Institut für Zeitgeschichte, Munich.

Kettelhake, Silke. *Erzähl allen, allen von mir! Das schöne kurze Leben der Libertas Schulze-Boysen 1913–1942.* Munich: Droemer Knaur, 2008.

Krauss, Werner. *PLN.* Berlin, 1980.

Larson, Erik. *In the Garden of Beasts — Love, Terror, and an American Family in Hitler's Berlin.* New York: Crown, 2011.

Mommsen, Hans. *Alternative zu Hitler — Studien zur Geschichte des deutschen Widerstandes.* Munich: C.H. Beck, 2000.

Moorhouse, Roger. *Berlin at War: Life and Death in Hitler's Capital; 1939–45.* London: Bodley Head, 2010.

Nauseda, Gitanas, and Vilija Gerulaitiene, eds. *Chronik der Schule Nidden.* Vilnius, 2013.

Nelson, Anne. *Die Rote Kapelle: die Geschichte der legendären Widerstandsgruppe.* Munich: C. Bertelsmann Verlag, 2010. Originally published as *The Red Orchestra: The Story of the Berlin Underground and the Group of Friends Who Resisted Hitler* (New York: Random House, 2009).

Neville, Peter. *Appeasing Hitler: The Diplomacy of Sir Nevile Henderson.* London: Palgrave Macmillan, 2000.

Orbach, Danny. *The Plots against Hitler.* London: Head of Zeus, 2017.

Ohler, Norman. *Der totale Rausch.* Cologne: Kiepenheuer & Witsch, 2015.

Ohler, Norman. *Blitzed: Drugs in the Third Reich.* Trans. Shaun Whiteside. New York: Houghton Mifflin Harcourt, 2017.

Paul, Elfriede, and Walter Küchenmeister. Undated correspondence. NY 4229/21. Bundesarchiv, Koblenz.

Pynchon, Thomas. *Gravity's Rainbow.* New York: Viking, 1973.

Roewer, Helmut. *Die Rote Kapelle und andere Geheimdienstmythen: Spionage zwischen Deutschland und Russland im Zweiten Weltkrieg 1941–1945.* Graz: Ares Verlag, 2010.

"Röhm-Putsch." Wikipedia. https://de.wikipedia.org/wiki/Röhm-Putsch.

Sabrow, Martin, ed. *Skandal und Diktatur — Öffentliche Empörung im NS-Staat und in der DDR.* Göttingen: Wallstein Verlag, 2004.

Sälter, Gerhard. *Phantome des Kalten Krieges. Die Organisation Gehlen und die Wiederbelebung des Gestapo-Feindbildes "Rote Kapelle."* Berlin: Ch. Links Verlag, 2016.

Sammlung Rote Kapelle. German Resistance Memorial Center, Berlin.

Sudoplatov, Pavel, and Anatoli Sudoplatov. *Special Tasks: The Memoirs of an Unwanted Witness, a Soviet Spymaster.* Boston: Little, Brown, 1994.

Vinke, Hermann. *Cato Bontjes van Beek: Ich habe nicht um mein Leben gebettelt.* Munich, 2007.

Weisenborn, Günther. *Der lautlose Aufstand: Bericht über die Widerstandsbewegung des deutschen Volkes 1933–1945.* Frankfurt, 1974.

Weiss, Peter. *Die Ästhetik des Widerstands.* Frankfurt, 2005.

Würmann, Carsten. "Zwischen Unterhaltung und Propaganda: Das Krimigenre im Drittenreich." Diss., Free University of Berlin, 2013.

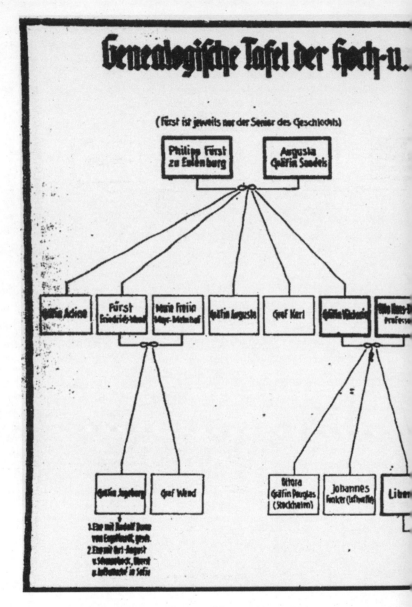

From the Gestapo's closing report: "Genealogical chart of the
*Hoch -und Landesverräter* Schulze-Boysen and Wife."

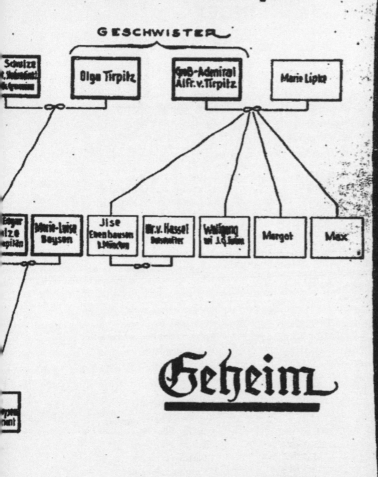

vernüter Schulze-Boysen u. Frau

GESCHWISTER

Schulze
...

Olga Tirpitz

Groß-Admiral
Alfr. v. Tirpitz

Marie Liptz

Edgar
...

Marie-Luise
Boysen

Ilse
Ebenhausen
b. München

Dr. v. Hassel
Botschafter

Wolfgang
mi 16 Iwen

Margot

Max

𝔊𝔢𝔥𝔢𝔦𝔪

# INDEX

292